Ordinary Stalinism

For E. V. A. and Sara Tiersky

Ordinary Stalinism

Democratic Centralism and the Question of Communist Political Development

RONALD TIERSKY

Boston
GEORGE ALLEN & UNWIN
London   Sydney

Allen & Unwin, Inc.,
Fifty Cross Street, Winchester, Mass. 01890, USA

George Allen & Unwin (Publishers) Ltd,
40 Museum Street, London WC1A 1LU, UK

George Allen & Unwin (Publishers) Ltd,
Park Lane, Hemel Hempstead, Herts HP2 4TE, UK

George Allen & Unwin Australia Pty Ltd,
8 Napier Street, North Sydney, NSW 2060, Australia

First published in 1985

Library of Congress Cataloging in Publication Data

Tiersky, Ronald, 1944–
   Ordinary Stalinism.
Bibliography: p.
Includes index.
1. Democratic centralism. I. Title.
HX77.T54   1985   320.5′32   84-21692
ISBN 0-04-320168-7 (alk. paper)

British Library Cataloguing in Publication Data

Tiersky, Ronald
   Ordinary Stalinism: ''democratic centralism''
   and the question of communist political
   development.
1. Communism – Political aspects
I. Title
320.5′32′09047   HX44
ISBN 0-04-32016-7

Set in 10 on 11½ point Palatino by Computape (Pickering) Ltd, North
Yorkshire
and printed in Great Britain by
Billing and Sons Ltd, London and Worcester

Contents

Preface

This essay on communist political development began as a chapter in Heinz Timmermann, *Die kommunistischen Parteien Südeuropas* (1979), which compared the ideology and practice of internal party organization—"democratic centralism"—in various Latin American communist parties. The subject deserving deeper consideration, I then set to investigate more thoroughly to what extent democratic centralism, an old ideological warhorse once again a focus of controversy because of "Eurocommunism," was really the main issue of communist party internal politics, at least in West European communism.

The respective fortunes of French and Italian communism over the past decade have failed to trick only the most clairvoyant observers. The stronger Italian Communist Party (PCI) has been kept out of the Italian government yet has prospered electorally, while the weaker French Communist Party (PCF) first entered then quickly exited the government, in the process losing a considerable part of both its organizational base and political influence. These French and Italian surprises confirm that luck in politics remains full of ironies, and that even virtue requires skill and persistence in order to prevail.

Overall, Eurocommunism's relegation to the famous dustbin of history should not dispense scholars from further serious thinking about communism in Western Europe. In fact the 1980s are already more decisive for West European communism than were the 1970s: trends are finally coming to unmistakable fruition and the force of circumstance is more compelling than ever. *Survival*, *decline*, and the potential for *development* are today as much achieved conclusions as they were processes ten years ago.

To study democratic centralism is a powerful focus for the complex issues of West European communism's political development. Furthermore, as my initial paper had shown, the crucial and most durable problem of democratic centralism is the question of *factions*—meaning communism's historically morbid fear of the consequences of internal party factionalism for communist identity and purpose. In following up the evident connection between communism's formal prohibition of factions and generic communist monolithism, I was drawn gradually to consider communism in general, communism "as such." A new and broader premise emerged in my thinking, and this essay was reconceptualized so as to ultimately interpret democratic centralism as a reading of the general dilemma of communist political development, East and West. John Dewey's maxim—"In any experiment of thinking, premises emerge only as conclusions become manifest"—was once again validated.

One particular influence in working out my argument deserves comment in this preface. As I began to see the possibility of using a study of democratic centralism to speak about communism in general, I encountered the French edition of Alexander Zinoviev's essay *Le Communisme comme réalité* (1981). *The Reality of Communism* (English translation, 1984) is a sociological account by the author of earlier brilliant, rambling satires of orthodox communist politics and cultural life. The originality of Zinoviev's satires—*The Yawning Heights* (1979), *The Radiant Future* (1980), and *Homo Sovieticus* (1982)—had already deeply impressed and perplexed the academic students of communism. Whatever confusion Zinoviev sowed, it was clear that, if Arthur Koestler's *Darkness at Noon* epitomized the tragedy of "high Stalinist" totalitarianism, then Zinoviev's books dissected the absurd farce of contemporary "ordinary Stalinist" communism.

None the less, Zinoviev's marvelous insight into what I call "ordinary Stalinism" remained largely inaccessible for scholarly purposes until *The Reality of Communism* appeared. Abounding in paradoxes and problematic assertions, Zinoviev's analysis beyond all its defects was for me powerful reinforcement of several lines of my own argument: (1) the continuing importance of ideology, rightly understood, in communist politics; (2) the centrality of the theme of "unity" and the struggle against "faction" in orthodox communism (compare Zinoviev's study of the "communitarian reflex" in communist society); and (3) the hypothesis that, barring some unforeseeable (and hence unanalyzable) cataclysm, Soviet-type regimes will either decay or can develop, not through some unwilling embrace of an alien model, but "on the basis of Communism itself" (Zinoviev, 1984, p. 259).

This radical conclusion, though contrary to much received wisdom (and hope), seems to me a profound realism; at the same time my own views, unlike Zinoviev's, cannot be mistaken for any sort of apology for Soviet communism. Zinoviev sees communist development resulting from "the struggle for the blessings of civilization" (ibid.). By this he means, it seems, an eventual fracturing of political regimentation as a secondary consequence of society's desire for a higher standard of living and convenience. My study, which focuses on the communist *party*, reaches a conclusion which may seem comparable, yet it implies fundamental differences of premise and approach. Most important, I find—in democratic centralism—evidence for *autonomous political developmental potentialities* on the basis of communism itself. How my understanding differs from Zinoviev's, as well as from the so-called "interest group theory of communist politics," will be a recurring theme. In any case, this book ends in no flat or simplistic forecast of a liberalization of communist politics; the realm of wishful thinking is not my territory.

I want to thank Heinz Timmermann for suggesting my original paper, and I want also to acknowledge a large intellectual debt to Pierre Hassner in the present matters over many years. I would like to thank Eusebio Mujal-Leon, Kevin Devlin and Piotr Sztompka for discussions and other help in this work, and also to thank Jack Hayward, George Kateb, Howard Machin, Angelo Panebianco and William Taubman for valuable comments on the manuscript. I have also a special debt to acknowledge during two years at The Bologna Center to my friend Stefano Zamagni. Readers should assume, as always, that an author is solely responsible for his book.

For various forms of institutional and financial support, my thanks go to Amherst College, the American Philosophical Society, and The Johns Hopkins School of Advanced International Studies Bologna Center. Lurleen Dowell, Sara Upton and Midge Bowser have my gratitude for producing the final manuscript, and Andrew Nelson for doing the index. Let me conclude by expressing my genuine appreciation to Allen & Unwin Ltd., in the persons of two editors—Mr. Michael Holdsworth and Mr. John Whitehead—for perpetuating the most honorable traditions of publishing, especially patience.

May 1984
Amherst, Massachusetts

A *faction* . . . is as it were a city in a city . . . Forasmuch therefore as it is true, that the state of cities among themselves is natural and hostile, those princes who permit factions, do as much as if they received an enemy within their walls: which is contrary to the subjects' safety, and therefore also against the law of nature.

(Thomas Hobbes, *De Cive*, XIII-13)

we cannot fully understand the acts of other people, until we know what they think they know. . .

(Walter Lippmann, *Public Opinion*, 1922, p. 85)

PART ONE

The History and Theory of Ordinary Stalinism

1

Introduction: On Communist Political Development

The Historical Deadlock of Communist Political Development

Let us begin by revising a cliché. Marx was correct—but prematurely, and not in the sense he intended—to describe communism in his 1848 manifesto as "a specter haunting Europe."

Communist revolutions occurred much later than Marx originally had expected. (Bell quotes Marx writing to Dr. Kugelmann at the end of 1857, "I am working like mad all through the nights at putting my economic studies together so that I may at least have the outlines clear before the deluge comes": Bell, 1976; p. 371.) The communist revolutions also took place elsewhere than Marx had predicted, and their results, as one well imagines, were not what he calculated and desired.

None the less, communism indeed has been a specter haunting Europe. It now rules in Eastern Europe and, after long menacing Western Europe from within, threatens the rest of Europe today, from the East, with finlandization, destruction, or both.

Yet at the same time communism today, ruling not only in the Soviet Union and half of Europe, but also in China, Indochina, and Cuba, is doubly haunted in its turn: first, by a profound disillusionment worldwide of communism's original hopes; and secondly, by an internal "constitution" whose incapacity for self-reform prevents changes necessary to the adaptation and even the survival of communist states. In consequence, communism today is just as much the prey of its own reformers and revolutionaries as old Europe in 1848 was of its liberals and communists.

In communist party-states nearly all the post-Stalin regimes, despite certain signs of flexibility, remain essentially machines of

3

political repression. Such regimes are widely despised by populations whose discontent is manifested, as the situations permit, either in spontaneous enthusiasm for unexpected revolutionary surges (Hungary in 1956, Czechoslovakia in 1968, Poland in 1980—and even, albeit in a paradoxical or perverse sense, the 1960s Cultural Revolution in China) or else in a generalized apathy whose quietism and submission is often interpreted as a form of political legitimacy. The equivocalness of this legitimacy is continuously attested by a stream of emigrations and political defections— which can suddenly become torrents, as was demonstrated again a few years ago by the mass flight from communist Cuba or the recent sharp increase in emigration from East to West Germany.

It would surely be mistaken to assert that communist regimes have failed to satisfy all groups, classes, and strata in their societies. But even given communism's visible successes—to begin with, the assured provision of basic decencies to the mass of society—the closed borders of communist states imply a unique message of political and human despair. In this sense communism is a historic failure against whose continuing developmental deadlock one must read the significance of such internal challenges as the "Polish August" and Eurocommunism.

Poland: The Meaning of *Solidarity*

Solidarity was a free trade union. In both theory and practice it was revolutionary in that simple fact. For one thing, communism has always meant, going back to Lenin's *What Is To Be Done?*, the idea that trade unions are an adjunct to the communist party's political action. Left to themselves, trade unions would always, Lenin said, be contented with "bread and butter." Party control of the trade unions was thus a requirement of organizing the struggle for revolution. It was, so to speak, merely a matter of getting the division of labor straight, and of holding the unions to what otherwise they would fail to accomplish: instilling a revolutionary, anti-capitalist consciousness in the workers they represented.

For another thing, Solidarity's political wildfire constituted a flat rejection not simply of communist ideology, but also of the gap between communist ideology and the humiliating reality of communist societies. In short, the "Polish August" organized by Solidarity *had to be revolutionary* because, in itself, it was *intrinsically* so.

Fervid expectations were generated in the Polish August that the

4

historical deadlock of communist political development had finally been broken, at least in one country. International opinion in early 1981 agreed with Polish optimism: it was believed generally that, despite the Soviet Union's major interest in prolonging Poland's conformism and foreign policy subservience, the price of Soviet military intervention—in Russian blood and Russian treasure, as well as in political costs to pay elsewhere—had simply risen too high. The Polish people's resistance appeared indomitable. What is more, the Polish Communist Party (that is, the Polish United Workers' party, or PUWP) itself had badly disintegrated. For a time, as party insiders admitted here and there to foreign leaders and journalists, the PUWP simply lost its cohesion as an organization. Solidarity, on the other hand, in only a few months' time enrolled almost the entire Polish workforce in its ranks. Tens of thousands of deserting Communist Party members also joined the free union, some certainly simply to turn their coats, but others in an act of true freedom whose goal was to help overthrow the communist regime.

To the extent that any mass organization ever actually "embodies" individuals in a collective identity and ever actually expresses the will of its membership, Solidarity was true to its name. For months Solidarity in effect *was* Polish society, whose strongest political wishes it enunciated.

Few observers thus foresaw or even believed possible Solidarity's sudden, crushing defeat—not by Soviet troops either, but by a local military-secret police counterrevolutionary action—and the relative lack of resistance against the Polish December coup in 1981. Whatever the mechanisms of Solidarity's internal collapse—political naiveté and a lack of proper contingency planning, a lack of courage at the top in the face of extreme danger, or rather the effects of a finally inescapable set of geopolitical and strategic facts of life that have decimated Polish dreams more than once in history—the Jaruzelski counterrevolutionary coup amounted to a *de jure* restoration of the Polish Communist Party's authority. The PUWP's subsequent retraction of most of what had been conceded in the Gdańsk Protocol and on other occasions bitterly disappointed the hopes that Poland had fought its way off the dead-end path of Soviet-controlled political development.

Solidarity had seemed an irresistible force, a massive structure thrown up on a social base of tremendous enthusiasm and courage. At its zenith it was in fact a free, self-governing organization. Moreover, it had unique external support in its struggle against the communist hierarchy: the influence of the Polish Catholic Church, traditionally semi-autonomous in a communist society where a majority are believers; the mutual reinforcement of political liberty and religious liberty in Solidarity's program; and, finally, the historical connection between Catholicism and national independence in Polish history.[1] In short, a free trade union and a powerful Catholic Church constituted a formidable combination of anti-Sovietism and anti-communism

The Polish counterrevolution, with its successful dissolution of Solidarity and political containment of the church, has gone far to reestablish a grim judgment within the international community concerning the nature of orthodox, Soviet-modeled communism and its possibilities of development. First, the judgment was reaffirmed that communist orthodoxy not only seeks but requires isolation. "Iron curtain" politics, in other words, are a necessity rather than an option in communist political systems. And one could even say that hermetically sealed borders are a *defining* characteristic of communist states—Yugoslavia, from this point of view, is rightfully considered no longer a communist state properly speaking—just as a tightly closed organizational network is a defining characteristic of orthodox nonruling communist parties.

In May 1984 the Polish leader General Jaruzelski signed a fifteen-year economic agreement binding Poland more tightly into the Soviet political orbit in exchange for Soviet economic assistance. Beyond the facts of the matter, the deeper significance of the agreement was to reaffirm the connection between isolation and orthodox communist identity. The Soviet leader Chernenko reasserted Moscow's argument that the broadening of Polish economic ties with the West in the 1970s had contributed to the rise of the Solidarity movement and its challenge to communist rule. Thus the new agreement was not limited to economic benefits, but would constitute "dependable protection against the attempts of imperialism to use trade and economic levers for subversive political purposes" (*New York Times*, 5 May 1984, p. 1).

The lesson of the "Polish August" from this perspective seems to be that communist orthodoxy is intrinsically threatened by external contact. External contact, in other words, is one possible path to the development or significant reform of communist orthodoxy. In the Polish case, as Solidarity's experience shows, the result (or in another sense the alternative) is revolution. Thus to the extent isolation can be maintained or reimposed, and if revolutions can be prevented or overturned, the future of communist politics can consist only in secondary refinements of a monolithic regime whose

6

intrinsic tendency, however much it is weakened with the passage of time, remains the totalitarian control of society. Communist political structures, from this point of view, cannot significantly develop or be genuinely reformed from within. Communist regimes can only be contained on the exterior, overthrown from within, or left to degenerate over the Keynesian long run, in which case the issue of communist development does not much concern the rest of the world other than as a frustration or a danger. The argument I offer in this study—even though it may be unpopular to search out the case for communism's political development—is to show from historical studies that such conclusions are either unjustifiably exaggerated or, on a reading of initially disparate forms of evidence I put together, simply wrong.

The Importance of Democratic Centralism

The main contention of this book is that the *internal organization* of communism, correctly understood, can be read as the problem of its political development generally speaking. The focus of my study is "democratic centralism," the internal organizational or "constitutional" doctrine of what I later will call "ordinary Stalinism."

Democratic centralism is, of course, a time-worn communist ideological dogma. Too often it has been taken to be no more than an ideological *slogan*, a sort of doctrinal figleaf manipulated by orthodox ideological high priests to hide (poorly) a political regime of ubiquitous coercion. The persistent tendency, even among scholars, to underestimate or to misread the significance of democratic centralism in communist politics historically is all the more remarkable in that communists themselves, and even their adversaries, have always said that what distinguishes communism from all other types of politics is a unique *organizational* ideology and practice. In explaining, for example, how communism differs from other versions of socialist aspiration (social democracy or "direct action"), and how communism differs from other forms of totalitarian politics (nazism), this is of particular relevance.

In the last decade, however, a good deal of newsprint and some serious books have once again taken up the issue of democratic centralism. This rediscussion of an old problem was provoked initially by the rise and fall of Eurocommunism—in which the reform of democratic centralism was a key issue—but its larger context is the continuing general disintegration of communism as a coherent international ideological and organizational power. An initial contribution of this study will thus be to explain what appears at first as a paradox: that democratic centralism should become once again a central issue of communist development as communism's international appeal struggles to survive.

This issue, however, is but a part of a larger initial paradox which derives from what some writers on political development choose to call the "effectiveness" of communist politics (Huntington, 1968), meaning the enhanced capacity of communist governments to survive and to govern, compared to other types of regime. The paradox here is that *it is precisely the anomalous "effectiveness" of communist government which has brought its development to a historical deadlock.*

"A particular type of society," Alexander Zinoviev writes, "contains in itself internal restrictions on that society's potential" (1984, p. 41). Differences in the very capacity for development from within, it is safe to say, result in considerable measure from the way societies are constituted and structured. And this means ultimately that differences in the capacity for self-generated development are intrinsic in the values upon which societies govern themselves or are governed by self-coopting elites. Zinoviev's books have demonstrated, in this regard, the anomalous effectiveness of communist politics. He depicts a system deadlocked and frustrated as a natural consequence of what it is, a system in which few care any longer about the ideology's grand promises, but in which nearly all none the less think and behave "orthodox," that is, according to the ideology's "practical rules." As he says: "The practical ideology of a society is an aggregate of special rules and behavioral skills which people apply in situations which are intrinsically important" (Zinoviev, 1984, p. 231).

Zinoviev's method, whether in his satires or even in his more recent straightforward sociology, is basically to present us with a *characterization* of communist society. What needs to be further studied and elaborated are the answers to the questions *why* and *how*: what logic or principles underlie the political habits of ordinary Stalinism? Why are they what they are? How did they come to be?

I will try to argue compellingly that democratic centralism—understood as it really has worked in communist politics rather than as a merely hypocritical ideological slogan—*is* the "practical ideology" of orthodox communist behavior. The prodigious effect of democratic centralism in producing generic, that is, "typical," communist thinking and behavior can be shown, it seems to me, to be a major explanation of the anomalous effectiveness of communist politics. Thus the "problem" of democratic centralism, stated in its fullest form, can be read as communism's self-imposed developmental limits and a key to the general historical deadlock of communist political development. In essence we will have found a new way to analyze, within communism's own terms, the internal struggle between orthodoxy and reform for communism's political and moral soul.

Michels's Law and Kirchheimer's Rule

It is worth specifying immediately that, up to a certain point, the oppressive character of communist organizational life created by democratic centralism is no more than the classic dilemma of internal party oligarchy analyzed in such rich detail by Robert Michels already before World War I (see Michels, 1962). As Michels first formulated his famous "iron law of oligarchy";

> It is organization which gives birth to the domination of the elected over the electors, of the mandatories over the mandators, of the delegates over the delegators. Who says organizaation says oligarchy.

All parties internally are oligarchical in nature, in other words. And if the "problem" of democratic centralism were no more than some extreme or even eccentric form of Michels's law, I would be writing another book. The point, however, is precisely that democratic centralism, as it really is, is a unique form of organization, whose political consequences extend far beyond the realm of oligarchy into the deepest recesses of politics' capacity to repress and to oppress. Indeed, not even an early participant with remarkable powers of insight could have predicted what democratic centralism would come to be, and how it would be used: Antonio Gramsci wrote that the history of a political party involves "a whole series of problems, much less simple ones than Robert Michels dealt with." This is certainly true, but Gramsci had in mind not the difference between the routine of oligarchy and the horrors of totalitarianism, but rather the need for a larger context:

> The history of a party, in other words, must be the history of a particular social group. But this group is not isolated; it has

friends, allies, opponents and enemies. Only from the complex picture of social and State life (often even with international ramifications) will emerge the history of a certain party. It can therefore be said that to write the history of a party means in fact to write the general history of a country from a monographic point of view, in order to bring out a characteristic aspect. (Gramsci, 1957, pp. 148–9)

I can only endorse Gramsci's further inference, "That is why one's conception of what a party is and ought to be results from the way in which one writes the history of a party."

Gramsci, in prison from 1926 on, cannot be criticized for his inability to witness the devastating apotheosis of democratic centralism (although Kautsky, already in 1918, had some inkling of what was coming in the Soviet experiment: "The absolute rule of the bureaucracy has its foundation in the hypothesis of rule without end," quoted in Salvadori, 1979, p. 262). Yet whereas Gramsci did understand the significance of different possible forms of party internal organization—that is, that there was more to say than to repeat Michels's law—others more recently, as I mentioned above, have tended to deemphasize or else ignore completely the significance of a certain ideology and practice of organization. This is the "policy" point of view, which tends to see only the factors of power, interest, and technology in decision-making, and to isolate these from their political cultural context. Particularly in the explanation of foreign policy such analysis will often rest on the conceptual and methodological shortcut of assuming complete cynicism (the contrary error—complete fanaticism—used to be dominant) as the outlook of communist decision-makers.

In sum, neither Michels's "iron law of oligarchy" nor the assumption of absolute cynicism can be the main postulate of a study of what Alexander Zinoviev implies in the phrase "the reality of communism." At the same time, however, one must avoid the homologous fallacy of assuming that communism's uniqueness or originality as a form of politics means that it is totally untainted, totally untouched by the outside world. Throughout the study we will trace out this issue in detail; but here we need to establish the point of view from which the analysis can be conducted, a point of view based in what I am going to call "Kirchheimer's rule."

The late Otto Kirchheimer, one of the prescient scholars of modern party politics, concluded the following rule concerning the relation between parties and party systems: "[the] forms of competition dominate the structure and the organizational principles of parties" (Kirchheimer, 1969, p. 246). Already in 1954 Kirchheimer emphasized the influence of television on American political party structure and functioning, and he seemed to believe that the future would see an increasing homogenization of parties, in Western Europe also, as a consequence of "universal suffrage and the related necessity to reach as many voters as possible by means of the latest technological developments." Yet he still made a tripartite distinction among party types at that moment, and parties and party systems even today resist any simplistic theory of some homogenization of types. Systems of liberal parliamentary electoral politics, for example, elicit regularized, open competition over *internal* party policy and leadership positions. Similarly, the major alternative electoral systems—single-member constituency and proportional representation—favor either a candidate-centered or a program-centered party electoral machine.

In short, internal party structures and principles are deeply conditioned by the forms of competition in a liberal regime; there is also obviously a functionally reciprocal (although, in Kirchheimer's estimate, less strong) influence in the opposite direction. The West European communist parties, on the other hand, have long been the exception which, as one wrongly says, has proved Kirchheimer's rule. To be more precise, the West European communist parties have marked the limits within which Kirchheimer's rule applies.

As a general principle of *established* political systems Kirchheimer's rule, in some highly abstract sense, can no doubt subsume communist systems as well. That is, in established communist regimes the form of political competition might be said to dominate the structure and the organizational principles of the ruling communist party. However, if we think of the *origins* of communist systems, it is evident that Kirchheimer's rule is accurate only if we stand it on its head: *in communist regimes the structure and the organizational principles of the communist party first create and then dominate the forms of political competition.* The single exception, as we will see in Chapter 2, is the origin of the Soviet regime itself, where Kirchheimer's *original* formulation applies, albeit in an extreme situation. The importance of this for questions of political development will come clear later on.

Democratic centralism *is* the "structure and organizational principles" of the orthodox, paradigmatic communist party—that is, democratic centralism understood, to reemphasize the point, as it really works. To raise the issue of democratic centralism in the

11

context of Kirchheimer's rule generates immediately a whole series of questions which frame the problem of communist political development as a function of communism's *internal* political–organizational logic. Why have communist parties been impelled irresistibly *from within* to try to dominate not only the *results*, but also the *forms*, of political competition (that is, not only to "win," but to set all the rules and to monopolize the game as a whole)? How are the internal structures of communist parties responsible for the relative "effectiveness" of monolithic regime politics? And finally, since *political* monopoly implies a monopoly of *economy* and *culture* as well, how does internal party structure and principle work to diffuse and co-opt any *autonomous* social energy? How does the communist party's internal structure, to put it differently, reproduce constant pressure for party domination not only of the state, but of society as a whole?

Then, in conclusion, having formulated the problem of communist political development as the problem of democratic centralism, we can ask what sorts of not inconceivable, or perhaps already gestating, modifications in internal party structure and organizational principles might substantially alter the party–state–society relationship in communist politics—in effect, to stand Kirchheimer's rule right side up again, turning orthodox communism back to its original choices, but in new circumstances.

Communism's Deadlock: The Lesson of Eurocommunism

As mentioned in the Preface, my general line of inquiry began in a chapter-length study (Timmermann, 1979) of democratic centralism in the West and South European communist parties. Waller's small monograph on democratic centralism, which appeared not long after (1981), was useful. It confirmed the broader relevance of the subject without, however, providing more than a rapid and in certain respects disputable sketch of what the appropriate analysis might look like. My book certainly makes no claim to provide a full historical and political account either. Indeed, my "case-study" chapters are essentially pointed illustrations rather than exhaustive documentation of my general theoretical interpretation. Yet because the argument, as I frame it, is localized within *party* organizational principles and structure, my studies of the Soviet experience and of two West European communist parties—initially disparate as they may seem—are finally adequate to set the problem. On the level of a theoretical conception of communist development, to consider ruling and nonruling parties together is precisely a way of focussing on what, at least historically, was essential or generic in communism. From such a perspective contemporary similarities and differences among parties, national situations, and geopolitical factors (to name only a few elements) stand out the more clearly, their significance perceived more precisely.

In the end we are led to formulate the issue of decommunization itself—not as wishful thinking, but as a series of pertinent, real problems of political development. We are able to begin to discuss its thresholds and turning-points as matters of history, not theory. Specialists of the West European communist parties, for example, followed precisely these sorts of development, perhaps not always or entirely aware during the 1970s; and the double lesson of Eurocommunism for the present study derived, one can say, from its failure. First, there turned out to be no such thing as Eurocommunism. It was rather a theoretical or preconceived idea of what a general reform tendency in world communism would be if it successfully developed. But Eurocommunism as a general tendency did not develop, and this marked out the second lesson: development sometimes succeeds and sometimes (probably more often) fails.

2

Logic of the Fear of Faction: Democratic Centralism from Lenin to Stalin

Organization as *Deus ex machina* of Revolutionary Politics

At the core of communist political thinking historically resides Lenin's belief in the potency of organization as a sort of *deus ex machina*. For Lenin, organization itself, as such, was a fantastic new power in mass politics which could transform the stalled, obstructed play of political development in pre World War I Europe. Organization—he believed with his considerable passion—would be able to achieve what otherwise might not be done: a proletarian socialist revolution throughout Old Europe, backward Russia included.

In *What Is To Be Done?* (1902) Lenin said simply that "Our fighting method is organization . . . We must organize everything." In "One step forward, two steps back" (1904) he began from the same premise: "In its struggle for power the proletariat has no other weapon but organization."

In short, what distinguished both Bolshevism and, later, Soviet communism from European social democracy was, first of all, the intensity of the Leninist belief that organization had become an extraordinary, quasi-magical power with the creation of mass politics. But one should not forget that the European social democrats themselves had already made a fetish of organization. The German Social Democratic Party (SPD), for example, propounded the doctrine of "prefiguration," meaning that the social democratic movement develops, in its midst, the structures of socialism. The party and its flanking organizations—above all, the trade unions, but also a gamut of mutualist, cultural, and leisure fraternal bodies—constitute a sort of "countersociety," a socialist society in

14

gestation which "takes power" organically in society by growing gradually to replace the disintegrating structures of bourgeois capitalism. Progress in building this socialist counterculture was assumed, generally without even remarking it, to be equivalent to constructing socialism (Abendroth, 1980; Guttsman, 1981).

Lenin always was uncomfortable with this "spontaneist," waiting-game strategy of achieving socialism. In his judgment the evident "economism" of even Marxist trade unions and the *attentisme* of socialist parliamentary parties like the SPD were deeply mistaken in assuming that the growth of "socialist" organizations had, in itself, revolutionary significance. In the case of Russia he had concluded already by the time of *What Is To Be Done?* that trade unions were intrinsically reformist rather than revolutionary. In the next decade, bitterly disappointed with the Second International's failure either to prevent World War I or thereafter to take revolutionary advantage of its destructiveness, Lenin concluded that his view applied generally to the European situation: social democracy had become a series of giant working-class-based bureaucracies, in which the power of organization had been misunderstood and misused. It is worth noticing here that Lenin's judgment that social democracy had degenerated into a self-serving, self-reproducing bureaucracy was shared often by liberal and conservative critics as well. One thinks obviously of Robert Michels's prescient study of pre World War I European social democratic parties (1962). Taking a different vantage point, Michels stressed the danger that the socialist mythology of organization could pose for democracy, inside and, ultimately, outside the party should it come to power:

> the contention being that democracy is only a form of organization and that where it ceases to be possible to harmonize democracy with organization, it is better to abandon the former than the latter. Organization, since it is the only means of attaining the ends of socialism, is considered to comprise within itself the revolutionary content of the party, and this essential content must never be sacrificed for the sake of form. (ibid., p. 35, quoting Hans Block)

Given the general tendency in pre World War I European social democracy to mythologize the significance of organization, Leninism up to a certain point appears no longer to be quite such an aberration. Rather it appears as a plausible ideological and strategic outlook, reachable by taking established premises of social democratic thinking to an extreme. This is not to propose that Leninism is Second International thinking taken to a logical conclusion (indeed a radical discontinuity is evident), but rather to make the important point that both Leninism and orthodox social democracy were built on a scientistic understanding of the potential of organization. One can say that this tendency in socialist thought continued, even among social democrats, long after its defects appeared in the Soviet Union. For example, in criticizing the radical programs of British Labour and other West European socialist parties looking toward the end of World War II, Friedrich Hayek was simply reformulating a permanent criticism of socialist and communist scientism: "Organization is . . . to all socialists who derive their socialism from a crude application of scientific ideals to the problems of society, the essence of socialism" (Hayek, 1944, p. 71).

Yet as I have just said, beyond the common passion for organization among Leninists and social democrats a radical disagreement is formed. The Leninist conception of the revolutionary party, though successful in making revolutions, has historically been unacceptable to socialists, as have been the results of those revolutions. On the other hand, the European socialist parties have themselves never achieved their revolutionary goals, appearing naive and incompetent so long as they maintain a socialist ideology, and disillusioned reformers or "traitors" if they abandon it. Neil McInnes, looking back at the entire history of communist-socialist relations in Western Europe, took the issue back to its root:

> It is in reaction against . . . the pathetic incompetence of social-
> ists . . . to agree, to organize and to persist . . . that communism
> has made its way within the Left. Organization and structure
> were its *raison d'être*, and though Togliatti denied that they
> were its *only* superiority over socialism, whenever communists
> have objected . . . as Garaudy, Ernest Fischer, and others did,
> the answer has been sharp: "The whole history of our party is
> marked by the resolute struggle against social-democrat hang-
> overs in the matter of organization." (McInnes, 1975a, p. 96)

It is possible to interpret the history of communist political development from this point of view, which is my purpose in this and the following chapters. What I am asserting is that communism's specific originality as a form of politics—here we find agreement among communists, their political adversaries, and scholars— is found in its organization and structure. And I want to demon-

16

strate that in this context the importance of democratic centralism needs to be reevaluated drastically. Far from being merely an ideological slogan and a brief set of essentially hypocritical rules of order, democratic centralism in the Stalinist period became the real political culture and practical ideology of communist orthodoxy, as it still is today wherever communism remains essentially Stalinist.

The Circumstantial Origins of Democratic Centralism

"The Leninist principle of democratic centralism" was in fact *not* one of Lenin's contributions to the theory or ideology of revolutionary socialism. Lenin and the Bolsheviks picked up the term in late 1906—the Russian Social Democratic Workers' Party (RSDWP) held its First Congress in 1898; Lenin wrote *What Is To Be Done?* in 1902—to take advantage of a situation. It must be said that democratic centralism's significance between 1905 and the Russian Revolution in 1917 was totally secondary. Its original adoption as the "principle" of party organization was not, as we shall see presently, the occasion of either great enthusiasm or controversy. Rather it was an ambiguous slogan whose very ambiguity—the combination of democracy and centralism—was the main point. Until the Russian Revolution became a single-party dictatorship dominated by an internally monolithic communist Party in the decade of 1917–28 the idea of democratic centralism implied a small set of vague and self-contradictory notions of party life, which could as circumstances demanded, as well justify more democracy or more centralism. Democratic centralism, in other words, was a "principle" primarily of convenience. It was more a weapon in an ongoing political struggle than an autonomous rule of the game, worthy in itself.

To be sure, democratic centralism implied a certain claim to be a "new"conception of social democratic organization. But this meant a new method of internal party organization among revolutionary social democrats rather than some principle for constructing a political regime. This it would become only later when the Stalinized Soviet political system, and the international communist movement, required a constitutional doctrine which expressed—and would serve to legitimize and sustain—a Stalinist international political order.

In sum, had the Russian Revolution turned out differently we would not today be much concerned with democratic centralism.

Burke wrote that "Circumstances give in reality to every political principle its distinguishing color and discriminating effect. The circumstances are what render every civil and political scheme beneficial or noxious to mankind" (see Burke, 1960, p. 345). This aphorism is a radically inadequate account of intrinsically substantive principles such as democracy, autocracy, and totalitarianism. But it is, on the other hand, an apt point of view regarding such an intrinsically ambiguous "scheme" as democratic centralism. Lenin, given his own experience, would surely not have disagreed, perhaps adding only that circumstances determined whether "the Leninist principle of democratic centralism" would survive at all. Thus if as one political historian recently asserted, democratic centralism "must be reckoned one of the major political concepts to emerge in the twentieth century" (Waller, 1981, p. 5), this cannot refer to its intrinsic interest as political theory. Democratic centralism is indeed one of the century's major political concepts, but rather because of the way it was manipulated in constructing orthodox communism, and because of the fact that it came to embody the logic of Stalinism as a political culture.

Any study of Leninism or the origins of communism must take full account of one key circumstance: from the beginning of his political struggle for a revolution in Russia the young Lenin was confronted with the ineluctable (because apparently "scientific") Marxist deduction that Russia was not yet on the agenda of socialism. This conclusion was inescapable because in Marx's theory proletarian socialist political revolution becomes possible only in the final state of a full bourgeois, capitalist-industrial process of economic and social development of society's productive forces. As a consequence of being good Marxists, therefore, Lenin and nearly all the other Russian revolutionaries (Bolsheviks and Mensheviks alike, Trotsky being significantly an odd man out on this vital subject) continued to accept the frustrating political premise that the coming revolution could be only bourgeois and capitalist rather than proletarian and socialist. In other words, the Russian social democrats—like it or not—were obliged to help build bourgeois capitalism in order to force the most rapid maturation of its inner contradictions so as to create the preconditions of socialism.

However, during the revolution itself, at a certain moment in summer 1917, an older but not less radical Lenin perceived that his own small Bolshevik Party could probably seize power from the provisional government of Mensheviks, Constitutional Democrats and Social Revolutionaries. Thereby Lenin and the Bolsheviks could take control of the policy of the revolutionary government. In this circumstance it would have been a fantastic irony—Lenin today might be known as the godfather not of Russian communism, but of Russian capitalism!—had he kept to an orthodox, "scientific" Marxist judgment of the revolutionary potential of Russian society.

The choice Lenin made is one of the epochal decisions of modern times. Presented with an opportunity irresistible to a man of his temperament and intentions, Lenin made of theory a sacrifice to action. He in truth had no stronger argument in convincing the other Bolshevik leaders to stage a coup (the October Revolution) than Machiavelli's *fortuna*: "History," he said, "would not forgive" the Bolsheviks if they failed to take power.[1] But, of course, a new ideological and "theoretical" justification was necessary for what the party would attempt. Trotsky's erstwhile heretical idea of "combined development"—the notion of a "permanent revolution" in backward societies—suited the circumstances perfectly (as Trotsky had argued in vain to this point). Lenin did not hesitate to embrace the Trotskyite godsend. Trotsky himself, long hostile to Lenin and in particular to Leninist ideas of how a revolutionary party should work internally, joined the Bolsheviks in July 1917.

Together the two leading Bolsheviks—not only theorists of strategy, but also (it was now clear) strategists of theory—changed the party's purpose. From the regrettable but apparently necessary task of completing Russia's capitalist development the Bolsheviks made ready to announce the "world-historical" task of building socialism in Russia in a process of "permanent and combined development."

In retrospect the party's ideology had, quite simply, triumphed over its theory. Given the circumstances, this was easily enough explained, even if the corruption of theory was evident to all who cared about such matters and was rejected or criticized by "orthodox" Marxists of the left and right everywhere in the Second International. For one thing, the *raison d'être* of Bolshevism had always been socialism, not capitalism; it makes sense to say that the Bolsheviks had been committed *ideologically* to socialism, and *theoretically* to the necessity of a capitalist stage of development for Russia. For another thing, Lenin's rejection of the Second International in 1914–16, now to be of radical significance, had resulted from his deeply revolutionary temperament, from his overwhelming and even compulsive desire for the revolutionary act itself. Not for nothing had Lenin demanded from the Second International a policy of "revolutionary defeatism" at the outbreak of World War I or had he totally rejected its acceptance of the war, its "social patriotism." In sum, in the Bolshevik decisions to seize power and to declare a "proletarian dictatorship" socialism as an ideology—a passionate desire and the interpretation of reality to suit a purpose—won out over socialism understood as a theory of the scientifically demonstrated stages of historical development.

Events had presented the Bolsheviks with irresistible temptations, and their willingness to take advantage of circumstances soon had the effect of upping the stakes immeasurably in the revolution as a whole. In a context of rapidly rising pressures previously unrefined notions of democratic centralism as a principle of organization and of discipline became of increasing interest to leaders such as Lenin and Trotsky. Indeed, it began to appear that Lenin's embracing of Trotsky's idea for the revolution's policy implied that Trotsky needed "Leninist" organizational ideas—which he long had rejected—to serve the cause of "permanent and combined development." The mix of Lenin and Trotsky, obviously, was powerful and dangerous. With respect to democratic centralism, the necessity of dealing with practical problems in given conditions—in fact critical problems in desperate circumstances—provoked what would be democratic centralism's "distinguishing color and discriminating effect" as a principle of rule. That is to say, a history of democractic centralism can only be simultaneously the analysis of its substance as a political principle.

When "democratic centralism" first entered the ideological jargon of Russian Marxism in 1905, it curiously enough was suddenly adopted by both the Menshevik and Bolshevik factions of the RSDWP, meeting in separate party conferences in November and December. The Mensheviks, while stressing democratic rules of election, accountability, and recall, also adopted language to the effect that the decisions of higher party levels were binding on those below, and that local autonomy was subordinate to the party center. This "centralism" was a change of emphasis for the Mensheviks.

The first clause of the Bolsheviks' resolution at Tammerfors in December began by proclaiming that "the principle of democratic centralism is beyond dispute" (in fact it was being invented!), going on to say that "the conference regards it as essential to establish a broad electoral principle while allowing to the elected central bodies full power in ideological and practical leadership, together with their revocability, and with the widest publicity and strictest accountability of their actions" (quoted in Waller, 1981, p. 22). This stress on elections and publicity was, of course, a change of Bolshevik emphasis.

Like much of Russian Marxist thinking at this time, the idea of democratic centralism and its practical connotations was borrowed from the German Social Democratic Party, whose leader Karl Kautsky—known with either respect or irony as the pope of the Second International—may himself have coined the phrase. Barrington Moore has established that the term does not appear at all in Lenin's own voluminous writings on party organization until 1906 (Moore, 1950, p. 64). This fact, and the circumstance that the Mensheviks adopted democratic centralism a month before the Bolsheviks, indicates that it was not a matter of contention between the RSDWP factions and, on the contrary, united rather than divided them. Given that the Bolsheviks and Mensheviks were opposed most bitterly precisely on questions of organization and internal party life, the adoption of such an ambiguous constitutional rule as democratic centralism—in which the Mensheviks could make ambiguous concessions to centralism, while the Bolsheviks could pay lip-service to the ideas of a "broad electoral principle" and "the widest publicity and strictest accountability"—demonstrated, above all, a desire for reunification, which in fact occurred in 1906. One could say that Nicholas II, by allowing constitutional reforms and a Parliament following Russia's defeat by Japan and the Petrograd Soviet episode, had unwittingly facilitated the reunification (albeit short-lived) of Russian social democracy. The Menshevik–Bolshevik reunification congress adopted a statute which stated "all organizations of the party are constructed on the basis of democratic centralism," and Lenin himself said that, concomitant with the emphasis on executive powers, democratic centralism meant "guarantees for the rights of minorities and of all loyal opposition" (Waller, 1981, p. 23). Out of a desire to take advantage of circumstances the main questions dividing Bolshevism from Menshevism, *petitio principii*, were successfully begged.

Thus in the temporarily liberalized circumstances of 1905–6 Lenin's interest in Parliament as a propaganda platform and in legal politics as an arena for mass organizing led him to use the introduction of democratic centralism in Russian social democracy to accept much of what he had previously opposed in the Menshevik program: enlarging the party's membership significantly (for a short time he advocated "thousands more" members), creating more official and legal forms of party action (as opposed to clandestine operations alone), and open internal party elections. None the less,

Lenin's endorsement of a more liberal conception of democracy at this moment, just as his usual opinion that open politics and constitutional procedures were "a dangerous plaything" for a revolutionary party, fundamentally was a reflection of circumstances as they affected the primary thing for him, which was always the struggle for revolution and political power.[2]

Anyhow, in most circumstances during the years 1906–17 *both* centralism and democracy were problematic. The Bolsheviks were in no position to impose *any* set of strict rules in an organization whose leadership and membership was constantly underground or in exile. The problem, to put it another way, was not so much whether to impose discipline or to vote democractically as it was simply to keep local organizations in contact with the party center, wherever it happened to be inside Russia or abroad, at a given moment. The Bolshevik Party leadership, furthermore, really was Lenin's creature for the most part. As the historian Knei-Paz says, "Bolshevism still appeared to be not so much an independent force as the heresy of a single man" (Knei-Paz, 1978, p. 193), and the other Bolsheviks followed Lenin's lead even though inner-party debates often were remarkable for their vigor.

The chief element of democratic centralism for Lenin in this early period, and what he really prized in Kautsky's ideology of party organization, was the possibility of neatly separating democracy and centralism, summarized in the notion of "unity of action"—that is, the distinction between an openly debated decision and its full implementation by all: "The principle of democratic centralism and of the autonomy of local Party organizations implies universal and full *freedom to criticize*, so long as this does not disturb the unity of a definite action—it rules out *all* criticism which disrupts or makes difficult the unity of an action decided on by the Party" (quoted in Waller, 1981, p. 27, from Lenin, *Collected Works*, vol. 10, p. 443). Alfred Meyer, one of the few scholars to have given democratic centralism serious attention in the original sources of this early period, says that all the rest was insignificant compared to this one central point: "Apart from certain details concerning party discipline and centralization, [the] formula of 'free criticism plus unity of action' is almost the whole meaning of 'democratic centralism'." For example, Lenin's conviction that the trade unions had to be subordinated to the revolutionary will of party leadership (the main policy point, it is worth recalling, of *What Is To Be Done?*) was not yet connected to democratic centralism. Nor did democratic centralism yet have anything to do with the principle that parliamentary deputies were strictly party representatives, instructed in their voting by the party. Nor did democratic centralism yet encompass the requirement of periodic purges. Yet all of these were established organizational principles of Bolshevism.

"Free criticism plus unity of action" meant, first, that party decisions and policies were to be arrived at in open debate. Decisions, once taken, were to be accepted by all and carried out by all with absolute loyalty, discipline, and enthusiasm. Criticism of a decision once reached was impermissible, although—in a paradoxical attempt to separate strategy and tactics—there could be criticism of the *manner* of its application. Furthermore, to the extent possible, decisions were to be based on wide consensus or even unanimity— in addition to being unanimously applied. For one thing, the potential for unanimity on important issues was considered to be implicit in the fundamental agreement of party members on the goals of revolution and socialism. For another, the fact that Bolshevism was politically ostracized in Russia clarified choices and made "correct" decisions often obvious. Finally, and most important in practical terms, Lenin argued that in any case unanimity should not result from the *coercion* of minorities, but should rather be the product of persuasion, compromise, and "correct synthesis." Particularly on those occasions when inner-party disagreement was deep, consensus or unanimity was to mean compromise, based on the political wisdom that it would not be advisable—even if possible—to force the majority will on large minorities (Meyer, 1957, pp. 93–4).[3]

Historians tend to divide into two opinions when comparing the actual record with these laudable aspirations. Some stress Lenin's own influence and overweening personality, and take the fact that his own opinion generally won out in leadership conflicts to mean that the combination of democracy and centralism was, as Meyer says (ibid., p. 95), "no more than a verbal solution of the problem of combining free discussion with discipline." In this view democracy lost out to centralism continuously in the most important location of Bolshevik decision-making—inside Lenin's own mind. To quote Ulam (1965, p. 621), "The words 'Party unity' were forever on Lenin's lips ... But his maneuvers and chicaneries were to have an ominous influence."

As is well known, Lenin's ideas and mode of operating during the prerevolutionary period often were violently attacked by other revolutionaries. Trotsky, for example, compared Lenin to Robespierre, arguing that Lenin's attempt to create a "Jacobin Social

Democracy" was a blending of chalk and cheese, that is, generically impossible.[4] In Trotsky's explanation Lenin believed that socialist revolutionaries could use the despotic and terrorist tactics of "bourgeois" revolutionaries because he thought that while the *social* content of revolutions shows a historical progressiveness, the *methods* of revolution remain the same. On the contrary, Trotsky argued that goals and methods could not be separated in such a way. The goals of a bourgeois revolution are related to their means of realization, and the same is true for socialist revolution. Jacobinism would always win out over social democracy in a mixture, and a choice therefore could not be avoided: "Jacobin *or* social Democrat . . . two worlds, two doctrines, two tactics, two mentalities, separated by an abyss" (Knei-Paz, 1978, p. 200).

Rosa Luxemburg considered Lenin to have an elitist conspiratorial, Blanquist attitude, whereas she believed that socialist revolution would be an essentially leaderless, spontaneous mass uprising of the proletariat (in this she agreed with the Mensheviks, though she despised the Mensheviks' reformism and waiting-game mentality). She also opposed Lenin's policy of bringing the "struggle against reformism" inside the party, meaning Lenin's desire for ideological–political homogenization of the leadership based on the idea of "correct synthesis." Lenin's doctrines were rejected even by Plekhanov, Lenin's original teacher and now the grand old man of Russian Marxism, who defected to the Mensheviks and attacked Lenin in a pamphlet infused with ironic condescension: "What is not to be done? A New Attempt to bring to their sense the Frogs who asked for a King" (see Carew Hunt, 1963, p. 186). Trotsky, until he joined the Bolsheviks in 1917, maintained that Lenin's view of revolutionary democracy would not last even if it could be imposed on society. Following in his comparison of Lenin and Robespierre he wrote that Lenin's unwitting political "substitutionism"—replacing the working class with the party, the party with the leadership, and the leadership with a single dictator— would collapse inevitably because of "too little bread and too many executions" (Knei-Paz, 1978, p. 185). To be sure, Trotsky also advocated centralism. But he said, "I am talking about a 'European' centralism and not about an autocratic 'Asian' centralism" (ibid., p. 192). As Trotsky's own behavior later demonstrated, this distinction was but another verbal solution to a real problem.

Another group of historians tends to accept Lenin's explanation that circumstances ruled out regular democratic procedures in prerevolutionary Bolshevism for the most part. Such writers usually cite the continuous conflict and factionalism in the party's leadership as evidence that not even legitimate anxieties about party security were used as a pretext for abolishing substantive discussion of policy. From this perspective the absence of open elections for leadership positions is of less significance than the permanence of open, vigorous debate once the leadership met. And the fact that Lenin's point of view most often won out is taken as evidence less of dictatorship than of the force of his own personality, his skill at maneuvering and—whether one likes it or not—the substance of what he said. Even such a violent critic as Ulam (1965, p. 621) says that "Lenin's talent as a parliamentarian has never been properly appreciated" (adding "and perhaps it was largely wasted: he was dealing with people who were ready to follow him anyway").

A more recent account considers the maintenance of certain constitutional procedures after the revolution at least up to 1921 as conclusive evidence that neither Lenin nor the other Bolshevik leaders had the goal of crushing internal party democracy, and that democratic centralism was not conceived or developed with this end in mind:

> One has only to read the records of their conferences and congresses in that period [1905–21] to appreciate the scrupulous attention to constitutional procedures and the care with which delegates' credentials were scrutinized. Even between the Bolshevik accession to power and the tenth congress of 1921 debate was open and vigorous at meetings and in the party's press. The major decisions of the period were taken on the basis of a free vote after full discussion: the timing of the revolution itself, the question of whether or not to share power with other socialist groupings, the signing of the Treaty of Brest-Litovsk. Indeed, a debate on the military question at the height of the Civil War was decided by a vote of seventy-five to seventy-four. (Waller, 1981, p. 29)

An immense library of testimonies by participants and close observers of this period exists to correct the credulous or unnecessarily unilateral interpretation in such a judgment. But enough of the argument remains for one to say that while the Bolshevik hierarchy in the prerevolutionary period was hardly a democratic apparatus, party life at the top was a continuous, vigorous debate in which any "terrorism" was more likely than not the intimidating effect of Lenin's political intelligence and force of personality. As far as democratic centralism is concerned, until 1917 it remained still a vague and elastic formula accepted by Leninist Bolsheviks, Bogdanovite Bolsheviks, and Mensheviks alike (see ibid., p. 30). The need for greater centralism was on everyone's lips, but it had a great deal to do with the fact that the main organizational problem of Russian social democracy was, as Trotsky put it, the perpetual "isolation and dispersal of its branches and local committees" (Knei-Paz, 1978, p. 187).

The Obsession with Factionalism Emerges during the Revolution

Upon taking power in 1917 the Bolsheviks were faced not simply with the problem of governing, but with the "world-historical" task of creating some new form of government, once it was decided that a socialist strategy of "combined development" would be attempted. And the central fact about the Leninist or Bolshevik political theory of government at this moment was that the party itself was its only distinctive, tangible institution. Lenin's Marxism had distinguished itself in 1902 through its conception of the party. The party had made the revolution and now the party had to create government institutions, despite the fact that it arrived in power with essentially no definite plans or projects.

Two improvised results turned out to be critical: (1) within a few years' time the regime became a monopoly of political life for the Communist Party; and (2) within the party itself, over a slightly longer period, politics became a monopoly of power wielded by a monolithic, unanimous leadership. One distinguished historian of political theory offers a perspicaciously practical explanation of the connection between what actually occurred and prior conceptions and slogans:

> The [original] theory of communist government, therefore, was essentially the theory of the party. In a sense, also, the answers evolved were not new but were explications of two terms that had been in the Leninist vocabulary from the start: the party as vanguard of the proletariat and democratic centralism as the organizational principle of the party itself ... When these terms became names for actual procedures, they got a precision of meaning that they had lacked earlier. (Sabine, 1963, p. 857)

26

The years after 1917, to put it another way, forced Bolshevism, now "Soviet communism," to define itself as a political regime. The process of initial formation, stabilization, and codification took a decade; and rather than seeing at work, as does Alexander Zinoviev, some immanent process of development—which is to commit the fallacy of assuming that what occurs is inevitable—I find more fruitful, and faithful to the facts, a harder stress on the contingent and the circumstantial. Lenin died in 1924, for example, and he had at that moment been seriously incapacitated by a stroke and grave continuing illness for two years. To be sure, many fateful decisions already had been made by 1922. Yet all possibilities to avoid a permanently monolithic and totalitarian outcome had not been shut off. Stalin was a top leader by 1923–4, but it is difficult to believe that at that point he had formed a grand design of totalitarian autocracy. He attained dictatorial powers only over a period of several years, during which his own "project" was clarified often through the elimination of rivals and the force of circumstance. Stalin could have been stopped—he might even have died or been assassinated—and the Soviet organization of party, state, and society surely would have been substantially different even if a regime of liberal citizenship was in any case precluded by a whole series of factors. None the less, having said all this, it is also beyond question, as countless writers have argued, that the supposedly temporary dictatorial politics of the 1917–22 period were logical transitions from certain previous political cultural, political, and institutional dispositions to Stalinist orthodox communism.

First, the unavoidably crisis-strewn path of the revolution—international war, civil war, economic disintegration, political, cultural, and moral confusion—created massive pressures on the Communist Party to resolve inter-party policy disagreements by simply eliminating other parties and concentrating the government and political system within the confines of the Communist Party itself. The Bolsheviks had started neither the Great War nor the Great Revolution. Yet they bore the primary responsibility for having, in the course of the revolution, raised the stakes to an even more unsustainable level by introducing the goal of a "transition to socialism." In a situation in which political life was lived constantly at the extremes, as a struggle for existence itself against a combination of Russian and foreign adversaries, the Bolsheviks proclaimed a "dictatorship of the proletariat." Meyer succinctly describes this grim struggle for simultaneous survival and utopia, "Fighting desperately for its very existence and at the same time attempting to

reach a utopian goal, the party governed by sheer violence, impos-
ing the emergency rule of a besieged fortress on the entire country"
(Meyer, 1965, p. 37):

> Food supplies and raw materials needed for the war effort were
> taken from whoever had them in his possession, usually the
> peasants, direct producers of these commodities. Everyone
> possessing any skill or knowledge or simply muscle power was
> pressed into service, willing or not. The workers, in whose
> name the regime claimed to govern, were forced to work under
> unbelievably hard conditions. Control over many economic
> enterprises, which they had seized in the early months of the
> revolution, was wrested from their hands, and their unions
> were subjected to the command of the party. Police terror
> deliberately sought physically to destroy all remnants of poli-
> tical opposition. Military force was applied to recapture the
> areas that had belonged to the Russian empire but had set up
> their own non-Bolshevik governments. (loc. cit.)

The Bolsheviks created a "monocolor" all-Bolshevik government
in 1918 when they ousted the left Social Revolutionaries. The
middle-class or "bourgeois" parties had already been outlawed as
"counterrevolutionary," and not long after the various socialist
parties—including the Marxist Mensheviks—were silenced and
then banned outright. All this is well known and has little to do with
democratic centralism directly. In these matters we are essentially
witnessing the working out of the party's "vanguard role" in the
definition of a "proletarian dictatorship" as a single-party regime.
On the other hand, what is less well known is the role that
democratic centralist notions played in subverting the soviets. With
the Paris Commune as a vague model, the soviets were initially
designed to embody a politics of complete and direct democracy, in
effect an absence of any division of powers. The soviets were to be
the instrument of direct rule by the masses—on all levels "the
fountainheads of legislation and administration, as well as adjudi-
cation. In the hands of this one and only directly representative
body all political functions were to be concentrated" (ibid., p. 268).
The soviets were a utopian enterprise even without the dire circumstances in which they were attempted. In any case they could not
have lasted as the basis for a national political system, and in the
desperate circumstances at hand the Communist Party had either to
change its plan to combine centralism and local autonomy or else

abandon the revolution to an even more utopian faith in the soviets, which were either weak and inefficient or oppositionist. Again Alfred Meyer is worth quoting directly on the result:

> Inherently weak, the *soviets* were deprived of their initial autonomy by the rules of "democratic centralism," which allowed the small caucus of the Communist party within any *soviet* organization to establish its leadership. The same rules of democratic centralism, as well as mere arguments of efficiency and expediency, were used to establish the preponderance of executive over legislative agencies, of central over territorial and local chambers. In short, the party succeeded in a very short time in taming the *soviets* into service organizations for carrying out the party's politics". (ibid., pp. 268–9)

In fact the requirement of centralism was explicit already in the 5 January 1918 decree on the Organization of Local Self-Government which created the soviets:

> All previous orders of local self-governments ... must be replaced by ... regional, provincial, and county Soviets of Workers', Peasants' and Soldiers' Deputies. The whole country must be covered with a network of Soviet organizations, which must be in close relation to one another. *Each one of these organizations, including the smallest, is absolutely autonomous* in questions of local character, but their decrees must be of a character corresponding with the decrees and laws of the larger Soviet organizations and the decrees of the Central power, of which they are a part. Thus is being organized a united uniform state—the Republic of Soviets. Under such circumstances the regional, provincial and county Soviets ... have a tremendous responsibility in solving the organization problem. (Meisel and Kozera, 1953, pp. 52–3)

The democratic centralist subordination of lower to higher institutions as a matter of binding authority here was extended in practice, seemingly for the first time, from a rule of internal party organization into a constitutional principle of the regime at large. More than this, as Meyer suggests, "mere arguments of efficiency and expediency" were used to the same end, in addition to the rule itself. As we shall demonstrate in detail as the story of democratic centralism's imperialist political career goes along, these arguments of expediency—in particular, the orthodox communist fetish of party "unity and effectiveness"—became the *unwritten* rules of democratic centralism, generally speaking the most crushing, most totalitarian-prone elements of the Soviet political culture of "revolutionary" discipline. It is in this context that Lenin's well-known description of early Soviet government (in *"Left-Wing" Communism, an Infantile Disorder*, 1920) conveys the full measure of its portentous meaning: "Not a single important political or organizational question is decided by any state institution in our republic without the guiding instructions of the Central Committee of the Party." Richard Lowenthal, paraphrasing a famous Lenin aphorism, is quoted as once remarking that "Stalinism ... equals Ivan the Terrible plus electrification of the whole country" (see White, 1984, p. 356). Similarly, one could say that as we are beginning to see, Stalinist monolithism equals Russian centralism plus democratic centralism. The crucial elements in the story, however, are still to come.

While the Communist Party was defining (that is, improvising) the nature of Soviet government after 1917, the nature of the party itself was much affected both by the evolution of the Soviet regime and by the CPSU's intimate intense relations with the new foreign communist parties in the Comintern (created in 1919). The *vieille maison* socialist parties of the Second International rejected the Russian Soviet experiment as a dictatorship *over* the proletariat rather than *of* the proletariat. (Kautsky's polemic *The Dictatorship of the Proletariat*—written in 1918—was to be the enduring, classic expression of European social democracy's schism in reaction to the claims of Bolshevism.) With respect to democratic centralism, it is significant that the 1919 CPSU Party statutes contain a first formal specification of the evolving principle (Reshetar, 1971, p. 152) but that the standardized "four clauses" of democratic centralism (see p. 44 below) appear only in 1934, that is to say, as part of the Stalinist codification of Soviet "constitutionalism" (Waller, 1981, p. 62). None the less, already in June 1920 Soviet communism was defined as a model for other revolutionary experiments, in the so-called "Twenty-one conditions for admission" to the Comintern, or Third International, which had been set up helter-skelter in 1919. The "Twenty-one conditions" were written with the express purpose of forcing the genuine radicals among European social democrats, whom Lenin characteristically (and rightly) assumed to be a minority, to choose for or against the Soviet revolutionary regime. (That the choice was taken seriously is attested to by the facts that the Italian and Norwegian socialist parties, which had joined in 1919, now seceded; and the Czech party split deeply, while in France Léon Blum's historic speech in praise of "la vieille maison" at the Tours Congress could not prevent a starry-eyed majority of the SFIO's delegates from voting to join the Comintern.)

The Bolsheviks' plan (or hope) was to galvanize a European-wide revolution which they continued, as Marxists, to believe necessary to their own survival. The means was to create a "determined vanguard party" in each European country. As its chairman Grigorii Zinoviev said, the Comintern was a single, worldwide communist party, consisting of "national detachments" which conceived all local action as part of a world-scale calculation.

Article 12 of the "Twenty-one conditions" imposed democratic centralism as the organizational principle of member parties, and specified three basic rules: (1) that higher party bodies shall be elected by the lower; (2) that all instructions of higher bodies are categorically binding on the lower; and (3) that "there shall be a strong party center whose authority is universally and unquestionably recognized for all leading party comrades in the period between congresses" (Daniels, 1960b, Vol. 2, pp. 95–9). Beyond this, as implied above, a series of unwritten rules or derivative norms of democratic centralism had begun to develop, based on arguments of "efficiency and expediency" (to use Meyer's formulation again) or rather party "unity and effectiveness" (to quote the emerging orthodox communist formula). Another one of these is to be found in a March 1919 resolution of the Eighth Party Congress. This resolution on "Centralization of the Communist Party" first extended party discipline to the non-Russian communist parties (meaning at that point the party organizations in the Ukraine, Latvia, Lithuania and Belorussia). The existence of "special Soviet republics" organized on the principle of nationality "does not at all mean that the Russian Communist Party in its turn should be organized on the basis of a federation of independent Communist parties ... All decisions of the Russian Communist Party and its leading institutions are unconditionally binding on all parts of the party, regardless of their nationality composition." This was democratic centralism in a by now familiar mode. A *new* norm of "centralism and discipline," however, was the following:

> The party finds itself in a position where the strictest centralism and the most rigorous discipline are absolute necessities. All decisions of a higher jurisdiction are absolutely binding for

lower ones. *Each decision must above all be fulfilled, and only after this is an appeal to the respective party organ permissible.* (Quoted in Daniels, 1960b, Vol. 1, p. 173)

The notion of "unity of action," so pliant in the prerevolutionary period, was in the revolutionary period, when "outright military discipline is essential for the party" (loc. cit.), acquiring more and more its "distinguishing color and discriminating effect." It is not surprising that these rules and norms were also quickly enough introduced into the Comintern, whose policy began with the premise not to say hope of a general revolutionary civil war throughout Europe. In "the present epoch of sharpened civil war," as the "Twenty-one conditions" put it, the logic of development was for the internal history of the Communist International to become a *Doppelgänger* of the Soviet party's own history, and so for the most part it did.

Lenin thought the Second International's lack of binding authority on member parties to be partly responsible for their "opportunist patriotism" at the outbreak of World War I. This was true only to the extent the Second International's "center" would have adopted a policy of "revolutionary defeatism"—not likely given that its main leaders were orthodox Marxist establishment parliamentary social democrats such as Kautsky, Jules Guesde (Jean Jaurès was assassinated just before war was declared), and even old Plekhanov, who had told one exponent of revolutionary defeatism: "So far as I am concerned, if I were not old and sick I would join the army. To bayonet your German comrades would give me great pleasure" (see Ulam, 1965, pp. 395–6). The real issue thus rather quickly emerged: it was the same issue as the problem in *What Is To Be Done?*, that of instilling revolutionary will and discipline from an outside source into recalcitrants and backsliders. As the Soviet trade unions had been regimented, so now the Comintern parties were regimented—more or less rapidly, more or less thoroughly from party to party.[5] The institutional mechanism was the democratic centralist rule of making Comintern Executive Committee resolutions binding on member parties. The growing political culture of unwritten rules and norms of democratic centralism gradually was absorbed throughout the international communist movement as well. During Lenin's few remaining years of activity after 1919 relatively open discussion with foreign communists continued. But in Stalin's first decade as leader the Soviet leadership's goal became clearly to make the Comintern Executive Committee a rubber stamp for Soviet decisions, and a mechanism for transmitting instructions from the center to the periphery—the famous "orders from Moscow."

The Critical Moment

The critical moment came when in 1920–1 the central leadership group in the young Soviet government faced the so-called "two deviations," the "Democratic Centralism" group and the "Workers' Opposition."

The Democratic Centralists, or *decists*, had developed out of the "left communist" movement of early 1918. Their main concern was to speak against the trends toward radically increasing centralism and hierarchy in the party, the government, the army, and the economy. They argued all this was leading not toward democratic centralism—which contrary to its real history, they took to be a major new principle of democratic theory and the necessary basis of socialist democracy—but rather toward "bureaucratic centralism." (In one sense this can be seen as an echo of the classic opposition between a "Western" and an "Eastern" centralism, a very familiar issue in prerevolutionary Russian Marxism, as we saw above in Trotsky's early attacks on Leninist ideas.) The *decists* said that democratic centralism had to emphasize the autonomy rather than the subordination of local party and state organs not only in carrying out Central Committee directives, but also in the sense of giving them control of certain kinds of party work as a whole. In addition to this inversion of the going relation between centralism and localism, they wanted a collectively run elected board—a "collegium"—to make decisions, meaning a return to the collective leadership principle well established (if hardly ever well practiced) throughout European socialist doctrine. They particularly thought the revolution should not give in to practical pressures for "one-man management," in whatever sphere, given that this contradicted the whole idea that the Soviet "dictatorship of the proletariat" would found a new and qualitatively superior form of democracy. A typical example of *decist* rhetoric was Osinskii's speech at the Ninth Party Congress (March 1920), which reproached Lenin and Trotsky for governing with an oligarchical expediency, and in particular spoke against Trotsky's scheme to militarize the organization of society as a violation of basic revolutionary principles. Osinskii portrayed the issue as a "clash of several cultures" in the young Soviet society—"a military–Soviet culture, a civil–Soviet culture, and, finally, the

33

trade-union movement has created its own sphere of culture."
Osinskii concluded that

> Comrade Lenin has revealed here today a very original under-
> standing of democratic centralism . . . Comrade Lenin says that
> all democratic centralism consists of is that the congress elects
> the Central Committee, and the Central Committee governs
> . . . With such an original definition we cannot agree. We
> consider that democratic centralism—a very old concept, a
> concept clear to every Bolshevik and fixed in our rules
> [*sic*!]—consists of carrying out the directives of the Central
> Committee through local organizations; the autonomy of the
> latter; and their responsibility for individual spheres of party
> work . . . this is democratic centralism, i.e., the execution of the
> decisions of the center through local organs which are respon-
> sible for all the particular spheres of work in the provinces . . . If
> you reduce the collegial principle to nothing in our institutions,
> bear in mind that this signifies the downfall of the whole
> system of democratic centralism. I advise careful thought about
> this although the speakers following me may try to "smear"
> the argument . . . In the unpublished part of his [speech]
> Comrade Trotsky raised the question, what to do with demo-
> cratic centralism in the area of the party, and the answer
> was—replace the party organizations with political depart-
> ments, not only on the railroads, but in all the basic branches of
> industry. Comrade Stalin (*sic*; it is useful to remark that this is
> March 1920], whom I deeply respect, but with whom I do not
> go along on this question, has already surpassed Comrade
> Trotsky's idea, and has established a political department for
> coal in the Donets coal industry. In general we need to take all
> this into account as a manifestation of familiar tendencies. We
> will also recall how Comrade Lenin, speaking of democratic
> centralism the first day of the congress, called everyone who
> spoke of democratic centralism an idiot, and called democratic
> centralism itself antediluvian and obsolete, etc. If the separate
> facts are connected, the tendency . . . is clear. (Daniels, 1960b,
> Vol. 1, pp. 187–8)

As, indeed, it was. The *decists* were quixotic figures of a classic
populist revolutionary type, whose views are based in abstractions
and whose generous practical intentions are persistently set aside
by the force of circumstance working in the minds of the real leaders

of any modern revolution, those who marry radical intentions with an equally radical commitment to action, realizing that in the process they will depart from their original ideals and are likely to cover their hands in blood.

Thus the Democratic Centralist group's challenge to the leadership group headed by Lenin and Trotsky was easily foiled, even though it posed, if only for a short time, fundamental questions about the emerging "constitution" of the Soviet regime. On the other hand, the rebellion in 1921 by the sailors of the Kronstadt garrison—whom Lenin not long before had called "the pride and beauty of the Russian revolution"—created a true crisis challenge to the growing dictatorship. This was because the Kronstadt rebellion was supported within the Communist Party by the so-called Workers' Opposition tendency, which counted in its ranks many among the oldest and the most loyal of the Bolsheviks, and also because the rebellion coincided with the Tenth Party Congress, which had to deal with the Workers' Opposition demands to free the trade unions again (Ulam, 1965, p. 618).

The Workers' Opposition program wanted a return to the sort of workers' control regime that Lenin had promised in *The State and Revolution*, that euphoric, uncharacteristically naive or anarchist vision of the future drafted by Lenin in March–August 1917. The Opposition's main practical postulates were an economy run by the labor unions, and equality of pay and status for all. (Lenin now had no use at all for such "anarchosyndicalism.") The Kronstadt program—including the prescient slogan of "Soviets without communists"—reflected above all else the general working-class desperation and popular resistance to the government's policy of forced grain collection from the peasants. However, it also contained a series of demands which amounted to the reestablishment of free politics, at least among the groups which accepted the revolution: (1) reelection of the soviets by secret ballot, with unrestricted electoral campaigning: (2) freedom of speech and association for worker, peasant, anarchist, and left socialist political parties; (3) freedom for the peasants to establish autonomous organizations, which would certainly have been self-defense organizations against government requisition; and (4) of greatest potential significance in terms of the internal political struggle in the regime, freedom for the trade unions. Not only were the trade unions the most important potential source of internally organized countervailing power to the Communist Party and the Soviet state, but their fate was of the greatest symbolic value—after all, the trade unions *were* the proletariat—and they had a tough, influential internal party faction, the Workers' Opposition, fighting for them politically.

However this may have been, Kronstadt was soon taken militarily by "loyalist" forces, and the Workers' Opposition leaders—such as Shliiapnikov and Alexandra Kollontaii—did not last much longer in positions of influence. Kronstadt, it turned out, was the last openly organized challenge to the cementing of all the regime's institutions into the "vanguard role" of the Communist Party, which had become the real meaning of "dictatorship of the proletariat." The long-term significance of the Kronstadt mutineers' defeat, as Barrington Moore puts it, was that thereafter the "process of presenting alternative solutions to the problems facing the country was confined to the ranks of the Communist party itself" (Moore, 1950, p. 123). Yet even more occurred at this moment, within "the ranks of the Communist Party itself." The combination, on the one hand, of Kronstadt and the short-lived apotheosis of Workers' Opposition with, on the other hand, the Tenth Party Congress's furious debate to continue regimentation or to grant autonomy to the trade unions provoked a decisive moment as well in defining the second element of the regime: that is, democratic centralism. For at the Tenth Party Congress the last remaining principle of free politics in the regime— the grudging toleration of internal party "factionalism"—was debated and eliminated in what Waller (1981, pp. 29, 37) not incorrectly terms a temporary "self-denying ordinance." While the actual toleration of all the forms of free internal party politics—differences of opinion, debate, groupings, tendencies, formal factions, and so on—did not immediately disappear, the *principle* of monolithism inside the party (in addition to the party's monopoly externally in the regime) was established. It still remained to be seen how long this supposedly "temporary" ban on factions would persist, and what exactly it would mean. What was clear in any case was that the same combination of external pressures, party ideology, and leadership will-to-power which had eradicated political opposition to the Communist Party itself, was now working inside the party to guarantee not the "Leninist" internal politics of prerevolutionary Bolshevism, but a new internal monolithism which orthodox communism has since carried for six decades as an identification card.

Some 200 of the Tenth Party Congress delegates (almost one-half) actually left the meeting temporarily to take part in the storming of Kronstadt. This gives some sense of the panicked atmosphere in which the debate on the trade unions occurred, and in which the famous resolution "On party unity" was voted, with only twenty-five delegates opposing the clause establishing a self-denying formal ban on internal party factionalism. The congress vote to continue regimentation of the trade unions was 336 for Lenin's position, against 50 for that of Trotsky and Bukharin, and 18 for the Workers' Opposition (ibid., p. 29).

In retrospect it appears not entirely unthinkable that the trade unions could have been granted autonomy, for in March 1921 the Soviet leadership was debating the shift from "war communism" to the "new economic policy," or NEP, announced in April. Confident-sounding slogans hardly concealed the fact that Lenin, Trotsky, and the other leaders were continually improvising the regime's development, and that the "Marxist unity of theory and practice" was evident only *post facto* rather than planned. Lenin, for example, might have said that the policy of subordinating the unions to the party applied only to the revolutionary phase itself. This "clarification" of the historical reach of *What Is To Be Done?* could have been rationalized to the party and it would have met the fierce demands found within the unions themselves, in the Workers' Opposition, in the Kronstadt program, and in large, sympathetic sectors of "the masses," who at this point had they been given the chance, surely would have voted the Bolsheviks out of office. Yet it was not done because a pattern had been established: whenever the central Bolshevik group was faced with a choice between reestablishing free politics (to regain mass support and to return to earlier ideas of socialism as a superior form of democracy) and guaranteeing further their monopoly of power as "vanguard" and guide of the revolution, they chose themselves. Psychologically they entered even deeper into the rationalization that only they— and "they" were becoming ever fewer—were equipped to determine the "correct" policy to survive and build utopia at the same time.

The Double Debate: Unions and Factions

Trotsky ridiculed the Workers' Opposition demands as "syndicalist nonsense." In the Tenth Congress debate he argued violently that in conditions which continuously verged on war the unions should be subordinated to the state. This was not simply to control the unions as such, but also, through the unions, to control the factories, to maintain the nationalized industrial sector as a whole, and to guarantee industrial production in conditions of dangerous "capitalist encirclement." Lenin and Trotsky agreed that the unions should remain regimented, but Lenin—characteristically—preferred subordinating them to the party, not the state. Lenin proposed a full Central Committee debate on the role of unions in a "dictatorship of the proletariat." This implied his usual practice in such situations, of building a "unity" policy through persuasion and maneuver, a "correct synthesis" which avoided outright coercion of significant minorities and did not risk losing an important vote. Trotsky, however, unexpectedly refused to join the commission organized to write a unity resolution; instead he made separate proposals to the Central Committee. The discussion veered out of control and Lenin moved quickly to denounce "factionalism" in any such discussion of basic party policies. For Lenin, faction-based debate on the union issue had become "an excessive luxury . . . really absolutely impermissible" given the critical situation the party faced in the country.

The congress thereupon adopted Lenin's "On party unity" resolution condemning factionalism and prohibiting organized factions in the party. The Central Committee was authorized "to carry out the complete destruction" of all factional groups, whose separate programs and autonomous group disciplines were a threat to the "unity and effectiveness" of the entire party.[6] Paragraph 7 allowed the Central Committee to exclude members from its own ranks (violating the principle of election and recall only by "constituents") and even, by a two-thirds vote, to exclude members from the party as a whole (violating the integrity of the party cell). Because de-democratizing the rules in this way would likely cause an internal party uproar, Lenin successfully made paragraph 7 into a secret clause. He argued it would probably never be used anyway, but within a few months he himself used it against the Workers' Opposition leader Shliiapnikov and several other "old Bolsheviks" associated with that group. Moore's commentary is again to the point: "In this manner a bench mark was established, to which the party was to return" (Moore, 1959, p. 146). Indeed, in 1924 the secret clause was made public by Stalin, and not for the purpose of abolishing it.

Logic of the Construction of External and Internal Monolithism

From the point of view of setting out the logic of communist political development Trotsky later (1937) provided a definitive analysis of the two phases passed through in arriving at a regime of external and internal monolithism:

> The present doctrine that Bolshevism does not tolerate factions is a myth of the epoch of decline [of the party and of the revolution]. In reality the history of Bolshevism is a history of the struggle of factions ... The regime of the Bolshevik party, especially before it came to power, stood thus in complete contradiction to the regime of the present [parties] of the Communist International ... Democracy had been narrowed in proportion as difficulties increased. In the beginning, the party had wished and hoped to preserve freedom of political struggle within the framework of the soviets. The civil war introduced stern amendments into this calculation. The opposition parties were forbidden one after the other. This measure, obviously in conflict with the spirit of Soviet democracy [*sic*], the leaders of bolshevism regarded not as a principle, but as an episodic act of self-defense.
>
> The swift growth of the ruling party, with the novelty and immensity of its tasks, inevitably gave rise to inner disagreements. The underground oppositional currents in the country exerted a pressure through various channels upon the sole legal political organization, increasing the acuteness of the factional strugle. At the moment of completion of the civil war, this struggle took such sharp forms as to threaten to unsettle the state power. In March 1921, in the days of the Kronstadt revolt, which attracted into its ranks no small number of Bolsheviks, the tenth congress of the party thought it necessary to resort to a prohibition of factions—*that is, to transfer the political regime prevailing in the state to the inner life of the ruling party*. This forbidding of factions was again regarded as an exceptional measure, to be abandoned at the first serious improvement in the situation. (From *The Revolution Betrayed*, 1937; quoted in Mills, 1962, pp. 306–7, emphasis added)

In terms of untangling the strands and setting straight the sequences of orthodox communist political development in this formative period, Trotsky's analysis well stands the tests of time and evidence, in spite of his continued stake in preserving his own reputation and minor self-serving slips. In particular, it is of crucial importance to observe that the monolithic conception of *internal* party life and the institutional mechanism of its eventual achievement—the absolute prohibition of faction—arose as a *deriva-tive* of "the political regime prevailing in the state." Just as compe-tition from other political parties came to be seen as an "excessive luxury" in the dire circumstances of 1917–21, so the competition of alternative policies *within* the party, which could be genuine only if opinions could be organized and thus forcefully advocated and adequately defended, was now seen also as too dangerous.[7] What I have called "Kirchheimer's rule" of the relation of the forms of political competition and the structure and organizational principles of parties, although meant to describe only the situation of parlia-mentary regimes, applies also in this case: in a situation of civil war the competition of adversaries is by definition a struggle for exist-ence itself. In a sense it is no longer political. But to the extent war is also the conduct of politics by other means one can say that the regime of permanent regimentation or martial order which the Communists introduced in 1917–21 was finally transferred into the party's internal life, which became itself a regime of permanent regimentation and martial order. A monolithic internal Communist party life was, in short, the practical corollary of a Communist single-party-state regime. (This point was made long ago by Richard Lowenthal, 1964, p. 49: "The monopolistic control of the state by the ruling party, excluding the toleration of other independent parties in opposition or even in coalition, [leads] logically also to a ban on the formation of organized tendencies or 'factions' *within* the ruling party.")

At the same time, it is true that the interdiction of factionalism was in another sense not simply a practical response to circumstance, but also the working out to a logical conclusion of one aspect of Marxist and Leninist doctrines: the imputation of superiority to a class and then a party and then the leadership of that party. The definition of Communist "unity," as monolithism in the organi-zation and unanimity in the leadership, combined Marx's doctrines of "scientific socialism," class consciousness and class destiny with Lenin's ideas of a single genuinely revolutionary working party and the "correct" policies or "correct political syntheses" of its leader-ship. To put it another way, Lenin's views led logically, in the context of a Marxist theory of class struggle, to the politics of a "single correct political line," the only practicable basis for which is organizational monolithism. Yet politics is not intrinsically a matter of logic and "Leninism" could have had a vastly different meaning absent particular circumstances.

Even Trotsky, by nature an intellectual and a man of opposition more than a man of power, could not resist, once he was a top leader in the government, the scientistic notion of "correct decisions." Similarly, he appeared perpetually undecided about whether there was some necessary connection between the freedom to organize contradictory opinions, that is, factionalism, and free discussion as such. In *The New Course* (1924), for example, he endorsed the principle of complete freedom of opinion inside the party yet also defended the ban on factions (Knei-Paz, 1978, p. 377 *passim*). Trotsky's ambivalent commitments (Knei-Paz and even Deutscher's well-known political biographies both demonstrate a curious naiveté in addition to a politician's routine hypocrisy in Trotsky) were later fully tested in the struggle with Stalin for control of the party, and they cost him dearly as is well known. First of all, Trotsky's endorsement of the ban on factions was evidently contradicted by his own behavior. And already in April 1924 Stalin masterminded a resolution against the "Trotskyite opposition" in the party, accused of seeking to replace the "Bolshevik conception of a monolithic party" (which Stalin was now himself consecrating) with "the conception of the party as the sum of all possible tendencies and factions" (Moore, 1950, p. 155). It is of interest to remark Trotsky's justification of his own position against the main leadership group, from which he was increasingly estranged. He knew that willy-nilly his name was now dangerously linked to an endorsement of "faction" and therein, in the emerging orthodox vocabulary, to "anti-party" and, *ipso facto*, anti-working-class and counterrevolutionary politics. Foreshadowing the general critique of Stalinism as a system that he would formulate later in exile, Trotsky now said that leadership "bureaucratism" (shades of the Democratic Centralist group) was itself "anti-proletarian," and intrinsically also a form of faction! In his later books "conservative bureaucratic factionalism" became Trotsky's label for Stalinism.

But what of democratic centralism? At the Tenth Party Congress the ban on factions had not been conceived as a new formal rule of democratic centralism (Waller, 1981, ch. 3); indeed, it was voted by the party congress as a temporary measure altogether. Already by 1924, however, it was clear that the original Leninist pragmatism of "free criticism plus unity of action" could not possibly be reestablished in a party run increasingly as a permanent regime of martial order. The ban on factionalism was originally an effect of the crisis in the Soviet regime. But then it became a cause of making that besieged fortress mentality a permanent condition, above all, in internal party life, which increasingly set the tone for Soviet political life generally speaking. As the Soviet regime stabilized initially, in other words, the rules of competition inside the party now dictated the rules of competition in the regime as a whole. The logic of Kirchheimer's rule was reversed, as it should be in the very distinction between monolithic single-party regimes and pluralist regimes. The ban on factions, given the newly consecrated goal of a permanently monolithic party, became in reality the main rule of party internal life and, therefore, in effect the main rule of democratic centralism.

In conclusion, what are the lessons of tracing the origins of democratic centralism? First of all, we have been able to show democratic centralism's original lack of substance as a "principle" of political theory. At the beginning democratic centralism amounted to little more than a few rules of internal party authority wrapped in a paradoxical formulation which unrealistically separated a "moment" of democracy from a "moment" of action. It is unjustified to see the original idea of democratic centralism as even potentially the theoretical basis of participatory or socialist democracy, or any other allegedly superior mode of democracy. Secondly, democratic centralism's original ambiguity was resolved through the profoundly sectarian choices Bolshevik leaders made in response to the pressures of circumstance. The superiority of leadership to constituency, the superiority of majority to minority, and the exaltation of discipline became democratic centralism's main characteristics; these were then pushed to extremes, first, in the formal prohibition of factionalism, and then in the latter's extension to its logical conclusions—monolithism and totalitarianism—during Stalin's years as leader. Thirdly, we have seen that the monolithism of orthodox communism was neither random nor completely determined, but that it had specific political causes rooted in specific circumstances. Communist monolithism is neither the result of the logic of "Marxism" or of "Leninism," nor of the iron corset of Russian political culture historically, nor of the political requisites of central economic planning, let alone the political psychology of a few historic leaders. Each of the above factors had its influence in what finally occurred. In the end circumstances gave Stalin his opportunity and unforeseen consequences largely made him what he became.

Stalinism as Morbid Anti-Factionalism

Soviet communism under Stalin's autocratic dictatorship was the most thoroughgoing and longest-lasting totalitarian episode in history. The Stalinist "system," moreover, was not limited to the Soviet Union. Stalinist communism was intrinsically imperialistic, both for the typical reasons any new and potentially powerful state seeks to perfect and impose its power internationally and, more important in the case of Comintern-epoch communism, because of a deep, internally propulsive ideological messianism. Within the Comintern the international movement of communist parties was Stalinized in the 1920s and 1930s through the method of "Bolshevization." In effect these radical splinter groups of European social democratic parties were attacked in their indigenous politics and cultural diversities—Stalin thought of this as "ideological confusion" (Stalin, 1932, p. 99)—and were re-created as internally monolithic organizational weapons having the same totalitarian goal, the total absorption of political and social life into the Communist Party, as the Soviet Communists had already achieved. Likewise the communist regimes created in East European nations after World War II were fixed into the Soviet model, even though they never were to become, generally speaking, such pure models of the Stalinist idea as was the Soviet Union itself during its "high Stalinist" epoch.

In any case, the immense, perverse achievement of Stalinism had many faces. In one respect it was the result of absolute dictatorship exercised by a pathological mind, a "cult of personality" regime in which the supreme leader's evil psychology was not simply unrestrained in the license of absolute authority and popular adulation, but rather was stimulated to ever greater excesses. In another respect Stalinist totalitarianism was the absolute triumph of an absolutist ideology, in which the profound credulity of tens of millions of people concerning Stalinist goals and methods led them to join willingly in the construction of a terrorist regime of monolithic "socialist" unity whose most characteristic institution was not a collectivized economy, but rather the gulag. In yet a third sense Stalinist totalitarianism was an enormous achievement of organization, the *deus ex machina* of Leninist revolutionary ideas gone wild. It is this latter aspect which is at issue here. For the ideological–organizational basis of Stalinist totalitarianism was the new democratic centralism, that is, democratic centralism writ large—gone wild—not simply a set of rules, but rather a whole system of written and unwritten codes designed to achieve the Stalinist goal, to embody the Stalinist identity of monolithic unity. Democratic centralism in the Comintern period became another name for Stalinism, although it was far from expressing all of Stalinism's faces. In particular, one can say that democratic centralism, now focussed on the absolute prohibition of faction as the means to achieve monolithic unity and perpetual unanimity, provided the rationale for Stalinist terrorism and the great purges. But democratic centralism itself did not imply either the methods or the monomaniacal ruthlessness and thoroughness of that terrorism. In the period of "high Stalinism," or what one might also call heroic-terrorist Stalinism, the rules and values now stuffed into the concept of democratic centralism became the specific organizational and ideological mechanisms through which totalitarian autocracy functioned as a machine for producing "party spirit" and "communist discipline." The vocabulary of democratic centralist thinking was the language reproduced in Zamyatin's *We* and Koestler's *Darkness at Noon.*

To be sure, all this was little apparent in official party documents. The 1936 Stalin Constitution remains a monument to the abyss which separates communist words and deeds. Likewise the standardized "four clauses" of democratic centralism written into the CPSU's statutes in 1934 were eloquent, above all, in what they did not say:

(1) Election of all leading party bodies, from the lowest to the highest.
(2) Periodic accountability of party organs to their respective party organizations.
(3) Strict party discipline and the subordination of the minority to the majority.
(4) The decisions of higher bodies are absolutely binding on lower bodies and on party members.

By the time the 1934 party statutes were written the first two clauses were, as Waller aptly puts it, "nugatory"; and the third clause was implicitly also, since the ban on factions meant that the terms "majority" and "minority" no longer had substantive meaning in communist practice as it was both illegitimate and practically impossible to organize minority opinions or programs. Stalin's working method was to insist on absolute unanimity, so to speak, not the "consensus" or "correct synthesis" which had been Lenin's *modus operandi.* This was the difference between Stalinism's total unanimity, mechanically produced and hysterically implemented, and the never-flagging political instincts of "Leninist" behavior even when the need for action was urgent (cf. Lenin's behavior at the Tenth Party Congress).

In the Stalinist years communist public discussion became a politically colorless performance acted out on the basis of previously written scripts. And elections became a means of ratifying candidates chosen from on high, whose task was to agree "spontaneously" and unanimously with whatever was presented—uncontested and unaccompanied by any explanation or reservation—as the "correct policy from the point of view of the working class for the next period." Communist meetings became celebrations of unanimity rather than debates. Democratic centralist values of loyalty and discipline maintained a constant façade of party "unity and effectiveness," amid adulation of Stalin's "scientifically correct" leadership. Behind the façade of Stalinism was, of course, hypocrisy, violation of conscience, and the gulag, whose keepers received genuine "dissenters" and those randomly selected for persecution with undifferentiated enthusiasm, since they couldn't know the difference.

The logic of the ban on faction, for two kinds of reason, became the bridge between monolithism and totalitarianism, between enforced political unanimity on the one hand, and the absolute regimentation of economy, social relations, culture, and conscience on the other hand.

The first has to do with the logic of politically forced economic and social development. In making the revolution and reorganizing all important political, economic, and social structures, a communist dictatorship of development, as Richard Lowenthal has observed, produces a paradoxical effect. Obviously communization is revolutionary; but the communist party cannot stop at this single restructuring of society. It is obliged to impose on society repeated revolutions from above because economic development produces social changes which throw into question the supposed "unity" of communist society. This is not simply a matter of forcing the pace of development out of impatience or because of the need to legitimate communist dominance through practical results. More important is the fact that development produces new social stratifications whose more successful elements, to consolidate their own interests, naturally tend to press their particular claims in some way on the political system. This very act of pursuing group interests is intrinsically a form of factionalism from the point of view of communism, a behavior which threatens the communist party's freedom of action *vis-à-vis* society and throws into question both its claim that socialist society is organically "unified" and its vanguardist pretension always to maintain the initiative. Thus, says Lowenthal, the orthodox communist regime is "compelled again and again to intervene forcibly to prevent the consolidation of ideologically undesirable new class structures. It cannot preserve its control of the direction of social development without repeatedly wrenching society from the path it would 'naturally' take, since all natural paths lead away from the utopian goal" (Lowenthal, 1970, pp. 47–8).[8]

The logic of the ban on faction also produces a second type of reason for Stalinism's impulsion to bridge the gap between monolithism and totalitarianism, one that has to do with the communist ideological commitment to a Rousseauist idea of democracy. Claude Lefort is surely correct to write that "Totalitarianism becomes comprehensible . . . only on the condition of understanding the relation it maintains with democracy" (Lefort, 1981, p. 170; also Arendt, 1966). As a Rousseauist conception of democratic community, communism requires the enrollment of all members of society, and not simply in some generally acceptable political "rules of the game," but rather in some form of general will, the correct policy in the interest of all. From this point of departure orthodox communism must insist that all the members of society are necessary to the unity of socialism, and the communist party—in its role of "revolutionary vanguard" of the "dictatorship of the proletariat"—must ensure their participation. The ban on faction thus became the Stalinist embodiment of a Rousseauist conception of democratic unity, worked through a progressive narrowing of Marxist and Leninist ideas in response to the force, and the temptations, of circumstance.

Moreover, this absolute unity must be *voluntary*; it must be *consent*. The false image of a utopian unity of society—absolute unity and absolute consent—thus impelled Stalin to create a dictatorship of *conscience* in order to produce the "correct" motivations for his dictatorship of behavior. With that step communism became the perverse, absurd world of Stalinist orthodoxy portrayed in *Darkness at Noon*. Stalinism became a morbid anti-factionalism because the very existence of "faction" in communist politics, while conceivably not of much practical consequence, had been transformed ideologically and psychologically into a matter of identity, that is of life and death.

3

The Political Theory of Ordinary Stalinism

Communism as the Generalization of Internal Politics

The essence of Stalinist communism is its monolithic internal politics, and Stalinism is the attempt to make *all* politics into internal politics. Communism began as the Leninist conceptions of (1) a radically centralized internal party politics, and (2) a potential structure for the relationship of party and society, as suggested in *What Is To Be Done?*'s demand for subordination of trade unions to the revolutionary party. Communism, once in power, developed by extending the realm of internal politics to encompass all those political relations which could be communized not only domestically in the Soviet Union, but also internationally in the world communist movement. All this presages the hypothesis that communism finds its likeliest future in some development of its internal politics—development founded, that is, on some basis in communism itself.

Marxism has had little to do with the real politics of twentieth-century communism. The Marxist analysis of class conflict, it needs no commentary, has been immensely persuasive to tens, even hundreds of millions of people. But Marxism's essential contribution to communist politics, after all, has been to provide an honorific theory of history and an ideological, quasi-religious inspiration derived from its compelling legend of the implications of class and class conflict. However much the brilliantly written Marxist classics have been responsible for communism's powers of attraction, they do not account for, let alone justify, communism's real political history.

The real politics of communism begin not in Marxism, but in Leninism, that is, in Lenin's own thinking and action, and in the prerevolutionary Bolshevik Party's internal life. Lenin's life as a "professional revolutionary" provided a concrete example of a coherent, effective, and durable form of revolutionary politics: Lenin exemplified a social democratic praxis of a new type. In particular, his heretical view (as contrasted with the Second International's "orthodox" Marxism) of politics as an autonomous field of activity transformed the Marxist inspiration into a profound desire actually to seize power. In a sense, then, Lenin created communism as a theory of political development: whereas Marx posited social classes as the evolving essence of an immanent historical process, Lenin conceived of the revolutionary party as the self-conscious midwife of a forced-pace radical leap in development. The Bolshevik seizure of power put the party permanently at the center of socialist politics, and during Lenin's brief career as leader of the Soviet revolutionary state the Communist Party put politics into ascendancy over class conflict and the "material infrastructure of society" generally speaking. The result, as I have already said, was to create a state which denied autonomy to all other structures of politics, a regime in which all politics were transformed into internal politics and the very vocabulary necessary to posit political autonomy from the state was expunged from the official political culture.

Thus Soviet communism in its first decade developed into a single-party regime ruled by an internally monolithic party. One historian has said that "What happened between 1917 and 1927 was simply the logical development of the so-called democratic centralism" (Salvadori, 1952, p. 44). This, as I have shown in Chapter 2, is to mistake effect for cause, although such a retrospective confusion does suggest implicitly the fundamental importance democratic centralism was to assume. Stalin's policies, after he became the key Soviet leader, completed the total obliteration of the distinction between party and regime, creating a party-state in which party instances were a *Doppelgänger* for state institutions and the real locations of Soviet government. In the following decade, 1927–36, the realm of internal politics was extended from the regime to society as a whole. The single-party monolithic regime became a monolithic society, justified with the state's ideological or "constitutional" rejection of the very distinction between politics and society. And once communism was defined as meaning that "everything is political," to the extent Stalinist doctrine was true to itself the result had to be totalitarianism. The realm of internal politics therein was extended even to the minds and souls of citizens, who were assigned the task by the state of embracing, even abetting enthusiastically their moral reduction to "good communists."

During the decade 1922–34, roughly speaking, this gestating "high Stalinism" was introduced by the Soviets into the foreign communist parties through the Communist International and a program of international party schools and extended indoctrination "visits." Quite specifically and self-consciously the leaders and bureaucrats of the foreign communist parties were persuaded to conceive of themselves, before any other identity, as the local detachments of a single world revolutionary communist party, which meant in effect a sort of external citizenship in Stalinist political culture and Soviet political life. Then, in the post World War II period, the new communist party-states in Eastern Europe—with the single exception of Yugoslavia (which, it should be remembered, had been well launched on the Soviet path until it "deviated" in 1948)—were established on the Stalinist model. In these two steps Stalinism manifested its character as an intrinsically imperialist politics, and Soviet communism, more than any earlier empire in history, became, so to speak, a system of international internal politics. "Orders from Moscow," during those decades when they were more or less daily facts of life for local communist bosses, embodied the primacy of the international internal politics of Stalinist orthodoxy over any local party integrity and interests.

Today the deadlock of communist political development, wherever orthodoxy continues to reign, results from a double inertia: (1) the general inertia of ongoing systems; and (2) the particularly crunching inertia of bureaucratic monopoly as a form of politics, or rather as a substitute for politics.[1] In this chapter the purpose is to construct a theoretical account of communism as internal politics, the political theory not so much of "high Stalinism" as of the more durable "ordinary Stalinism," the routinized orthodox communist politics of the post-Stalin epoch.[2]

Political Belief, Political Ideology, and Political Culture

Do communists any longer believe in the ideology of communism? The question seems intuitively to be of considerable importance in understanding contemporary communist development. Surely large numbers of professors, students, ordinary citizens, and—hopefully—political leaders and government officials cannot avoid a genuine curiosity when the question is put as to whether the communist governments and communized peoples are really mostly like the rest of the world, or whether there is not an extra ingredient, "ideology," which determines the character of communism domestically as well as its dealings in international politics. The Soviets consider the credibility of their claim to be ideologically motivated of some significance, as one can attest with innumerable quotations such as the following from a widely circulated volume which carries the pious title *Scientific Communism*:

> The thesis advanced by bourgeois ideologists about the alleged erosion of communist ideology is in fact nothing more than the attempt to take one's desires for reality ... [part of a] never-ending search for new methods to undermine the working class movement from inside and to "integrate" it into the capitalist system. (Fédoséev *et al.*, 1974, p. 731)

It is hardly contestable, despite Soviet protests, that the fate of communist ideology in its grandiose formulation more and more embodies Herbert Spencer's "tragedy of the Murder of a Beautiful Theory by a Gang of a Brutal Facts"; we need not make long counterquotations here.

Yet from a historical point of view, at least, it is nevertheless evident that communist beliefs and communist ideology must be taken seriously. The problem, first, is how; and then how to connect this understanding to the analysis of communist political development.

Any study of communist politics, it seems to me, must take account of the fact that historically communism has been a system of immensely strong beliefs, and a coherent ideological worldview, as well as a system of the most brutal power structures and a dictatorship of economic and social development. In a certain sense the political systems of communist orthodoxy remain still today based on ideological belief as well as on structures of power and ambitions for development. For despite the unquestionable withering away of belief in communism's millennial grand symbols and slogans, now underway for three decades (cf. Lowenthal, 1964), the political culture of routinized, ordinary Stalinism—the quotidian communist orthodoxy—can be shown to exist still to some extent in every communist party and state whose history stretches back into the Stalin period. The case of Italian communism (Chapter 4) and those of certain communist party-states (Yugoslavia and China) demonstrate that political cultural transformation from within is not impossible, and that the serious study of communist development must now accept as a real issue the whole problem of thresholds of decommunization. At the same time, the analysis of French communism (Chapter 5) and the remaining Soviet-linked or controlled party-states demonstrates the durability, greater or lesser from country to country and party to party, of orthodox communism as a historical political culture.

Since social science in the West often conceives of political culture as a national or ethnic phenomenon, it may seem eccentric to speak of communism itself as a political culture. Of course, communists have always insisted that workers have no fatherland and that "proletarian internationalism" was an immanent and superior patriotism. What is most remarkable on this score is surely that "proletarian internationalist" loyalty indeed developed among tens of millions of workers and peasants around the world—that the Marxist theory of internationalist solidarity was specious is irrelevant here. "Proletarian internationalism" was lodged within communism's international structure as a movement: the Comintern, the Cominform, and then the series of informal networks, formal conferences, and continuous party schools and "visits" among the communist parties after the Cominform's dissolution by Khrushchev in 1956 (cf. Marcou, 1979). The fact that the international communist network had the Soviet Union at its center created a useful ambiguity: the symbolic myth of "proletarian internationalism" permitted communist militants worldwide simultaneously to feel a genuine internationalism *and* a genuine nationalism (albeit for a distant and foreign state); as well as a necessarily ambivalent patriotism regarding their own country, whose "ultimate" and "superior" interests they thought were being served in a local communism's dual and ambiguous political creed (Kriegel, 1972a, 1974; Blackmer and Kriegel, 1975; Tiersky, 1974). Thus to understand the durability of orthodox communism, that is, ordinary Stalinism, we need to consider communism in its period of empire as a kind of nationality or at least its functional equivalent, an "international nationalism" with its specific political culture. This definition has two considerable advantages. First, it is empirically reasonable: the communists actually reasoned in this manner. Secondly, it establishes a vantage point from which we can well perceive the decline of communist *ideology*, understood as a coherent, messianic worldview organized around certain great symbolic myths such as "proletarian internationalism," without losing the ability to recognize the persistence of a routinized communist *political culture*.

We are led back again, as I have already demonstrated in the previous section, to a conception of orthodox communism—even at the international level—as essentially a form of internal politics. This conclusion has an immediate, important methodological consequence: an epistemological priority given to *internal* analysis, that is, to the study of communism *sui generis*, as opposed to *comparative* analysis, that is, the attempt to understand communism by discovering similarities and differences in relation to other types of politics. Alfred Meyer rightly pointed out the advantage of comparative thinking in his own approach to the Soviet political system: "comparison is a useful didactic device, because we understand the unfamiliar much more easily when it is presented in terms of the familiar" (Meyer, 1965, p. 10). The great danger of comparative analysis is that of false reasoning by analogy—in other words, the attempt to find, in a given foreign political system, analogs of the structures or functions of a familiar system, *ceteris paribus*, and leaving out of consideration the *general* character of the foreign system, which may nullify the essential element of the analogy, the "comparable" characteristic. Zinoviev's *The Reality of Communism* stresses this primary rule of method: "We must observe the properties of Communist society independently of the question as to whether or not they exist in societies of another type. I do not deny the usefulness of comparisons in general. But in this case comparisons should not play a decisive role" (Zinoviev, 1984, p. 44).[3] In thinking about communist political *development*, in particular, we stand to gain more from conceptualizing the problem as one of internal movement than we do from reasoning by analogy with the development problems of other forms of regime.

At the same time, we must remember that the abstract conception is not the reality, that theory is not history. This means, as I say above, that not even the Soviet Union (or the neo-Stalinist French Communist Party, studied below) "is" orthodox communism in some pristine incarnation. Rather there are a multitude of communist parties, societies, and states, with their particular histories, cultures, ecological influences, and governing agendas. To put the matter another way, it is intrinsically problematic to observe behavior in a communist party, state, or society and then to decide what is communist and what is not—as one Sovietologist puts it, to solve "the complicated problem of the national versus the system, the 'Russian' versus the 'Communist' elements in the political culture" (White, 1984, p. 357). Zinoviev is eloquently prosaic on this point:

It is naïve to think that the specific features and laws of the Communist order can be observed constantly in the streets and in the villages, in the corridors of institutions and the shop-floors of factories. One can observe directly only millions of people, billions of actions and some buildings and events. (Zinoviev, 1984, p. 42)

Yet for Zinoviev, *The Reality of Communism* is the study of communism "as such, in itself" (ibid., p. 58), that which is the object of satire in *The Yawning Heights* and *The Radiant Future*. To pose serious questions of method, in other words, need not end in one's tying oneself in self-defeating methodological knots.

Thus the conception of ordinary Stalinism as a political culture is a way to take the measure of beliefs, in addition to power, interest, and intention, in our theoretical understanding of communist politics. It is worth stressing again that we are speaking of beliefs in a particular sense: the historical residue of an original experience of millennarian passion and terror, maintained by a long mental conditioning of communist parties and societies in the politics of everyday life. There is an analogy between this argument and that made by many studies of American politics which indicate that democratic behavior and beliefs persist often by inertia, if for no more worthy reasons. Even when a democratic political culture has suffered general demoralization—many observers compare the intensity of contemporary American democratic commitments unfavorably with that of the Jacksonian period, for example—the beliefs and formal behaviors of liberal democracy may well persist if only because they are not seriously challenged (cf. Huntington, 1983; Dahl, 1961). Likewise in a communist system the people, not to mention the leaders and officials, may no longer believe in the "radiant future" promised by the ideology, but they very well may continue to act as, and to hold the beliefs of, "ordinary Stalinists." In this sense Zinoviev's satires are, I think, the functional equivalents of all the behavioral and social-psychological studies which document the political apathy of most citizens in contemporary Western political systems. Just as in American politics the habit of democratic beliefs will favor democratic behavior, even among the disillusioned, so the ordinary Stalinist Soviet citizen who sardonically ridicules the claims of "real, existing socialism" may none the less endorse the Soviet government's "right" to jail individuals for not having a job ("parasitism"), will agree that Ukranian coalminers have no right or need to form a free trade union, and will, at a sort of

53

absurd limit, think it more or less self-evident that whistling in public elevators be the object of a legal prohibition, since it is "anti-social."

To sum up, and also to answer a question often posed as to how Stalinist political culture was able to survive the death of the egocrat: surely some *combination* of power structures, interests, and beliefs was required for the transition to ordinary Stalinism. Neither the compulsion of vested privileges nor the desire to remain in power, alone or together, would have been sufficient to elude the decisive challenge to Stalinist hierarchies which, at the time, was widely expected. Nor could orthodox beliefs and habits alone, for that matter, have perpetuated the Stalinist order, without an adequate organization as a network of power structures, rewards, and sanctions. In order to endure, to govern from one day to the next, a party or a regime requires both beliefs and organization, a rule of permanence as true of orthodox communism as of any other form of politics. The class content of Lenin's original insight; "The proletariat can become ... an invincible force only when its ideological unity around the principles of Marxism is consolidated by the material unity of an organization," turned out to be historically irrelevant, but its machiavellian political logic was sound.

A Holy Trinity: The Three Orthodox Doctrines of Organization

Communism in its period as an empire of internal politics was organized and disciplined at three levels: *party, society,* and at the *international* level. To these three levels of organization corresponded appropriate doctrines of the orthodox ideology: *democratic centralism, dictatorship of the proletariat,* and *proletarian internationalism* (Figure 3.1).

Party/Democratic centralism

Society/Dictatorship of the proletariat

International/Proletarian internationalism

Figure 3.1 The three orthodox doctrines of communist organization.

As a matter of doctrine, in Stalinist orthodoxy these were not all vague or honorific notions; each had a precise organizational meaning.[4] The dictatorship of the proletariat meant an initial transition stage toward "mature socialism," a doctrinal theme upon which the "people's democracy" label used in Eastern Europe was a variation. In practical terms to establish a dictatorship of the proletariat meant a revolutionary seizure of power by a local communist party, and a reconstruction of politics and society built as closely as possible on the model of the Soviet Union. These foreign copies of the Soviet model were never complete, nor did the Soviets want them to be completely successful replicas. For one thing, local conditions (Poland's strong Catholic Church and its geographical and cultural proximity to Western Europe; China's unquenchably peasant society and its "inscrutable" language, ethnic, and cultural characteristics; and so on) nearly always precluded total Sovietization and vicarious Russification (Bulgaria is perhaps a unique exception). Moreover, Soviet prestige and authority inside the international movement required that the Soviet leaders be able to demonstrate the Soviet advance over newer "fraternal" regimes: this was the myth of the Soviet Union as the "most battle-hardened and experienced" socialist state.

Proletarian internationalism, on the other hand, was the myth of a single world revolutionary communist party, which in practical terms meant a willing subordination of local communist party interests to an international "revolutionary" (that is, strategic) calculation in which the Soviet interest was paramount. Whence came the principle that the "touchstone" of proletarian internationalism, orthodox communist *bona fides* in the international game, was "unconditional loyalty" to the Soviet national interest, and unconditional acceptance of Soviet guidelines (unspoken norms as well as "orders from Moscow") in the making of policy. Endorsing (1) the Nazi–Soviet pact of 1939; (2) the Cold War and creation of the Cominform in 1947; (3) the repression of revolution in Hungary in 1956; (4) the Soviet argument in the Sino-Soviet split; (5) the Warsaw Pact's invasion of Czechoslovakia in 1968 (justified with the so-called Brezhnev Doctrine, itself merely a reworded version of proletarian internationalist internal politics); and (6) the military coup against Solidarity in Poland in 1981 are the extreme "touchstone" tests of proletarian internationalist fealty, historically speaking. But proletarian internationalism in Stalinist orthodoxy was also a rigorous political culture of daily life whose influence for decades in the international communist movement would be hard to underestimate.

Finally, in Stalinist orthodoxy democratic centralism as well acquired a precise meaning as a principle and a practice of organizational life. Certainly, as I have shown in Chapter 2, democratic centralism was *not* the mold into which the new Soviet institutions were poured. Rather the reverse is the case: democratic centralism was built as a mold around a set of institutions and a political culture whose origins were the encounter of a particular worldview with a particular set of circumstances. However this might be, during the high Stalinist period and in the transition to ordinary Stalinism democratic centralism became an integral and absolutely characteristic element of the orthodox communist identity.

This explains why, whatever else may change, so long as a communist party is organized on the orthodox rules and political culture of democratic centralism, it remains intrinsically committed or impelled toward the destruction of free politics.

The explanation, to put it another way, is simply that, at each level of the historical organization of communism as an empire—party, society, internationally—any one of the "holy trinity" doctrines of organization constituted a functional translation of the other two. The "dictatorship of the proletariat," "proletarian internationalism," and "democratic centralism," all were but different versions of the founding idea of Stalinist political and social life: "unity," in the characteristically Stalinist sense of unanimity and monolithism, the intrinsic tendency of which had to be totalitarian. Stalinist politics, one could say, was an absolutist struggle against "faction," which meant in practice a total war on differences implying, ultimately, the extinction or death itself of politics.

The "unity in diversity" of the orthodox communist holy doctrinal trinity is caught in a passage in which Kriegel attempts to define correctly the "place" or location of communist ideology: "The ideology," she says, "is not found in the substance of the network of Leninist ideas with their precise definitions. The location of ideology is rather in the conviction that the system must remain closed within itself, so that no external element penetrates inside without having been duly selected, tested and 'naturalized'" (Kreigel, 1977, p. 120). This is yet another way to formulate the idea that orthodox communism is a system in which all politics are internal politics— meaning all *legitimate* politics are internal politics. The rest is punishable "dissent," exactly as the much-overworked but not at all irrelevant analogy of communism and the church would have it.

The great doctrinal anxiety, as Kriegel says, is "that which threatens to destroy the circularity of the ideology." Spinoza's system of thought had nothing at all in common with orthodox communism except this characteristic of circularity: "One has to travel round the whole circle once," Stuart Hampshire has written of Spinoza's thought, "before one can begin to understand any segment of it" (Hampshire, 1951, p. 55). Once one has, so to speak, been around the whole circle of orthodox communist doctrines and seen the connections and functional equivalencies, the decline of communist ideology's main symbols assumes its real significance in the analysis of communist political development. In particular, the repudiation and discredit of "proletarian internationalism" and "the dictatorship of the proletariat" among the communist hierarchies themselves puts more emphasis than ever on democratic centralism. It is the last of the three organizational doctrines which used to constitute the three pillars of the temple, propping up the myth that communist parties are the "vanguard" of political development.

The Last Universal Communist Doctrine

All the Marxist–Leninist parties have recognized democratic centralism as the guideline of their organizational structure. Theory and practice in the world communist movement confirm the efficacy and expediency of this principle ... The Central Committee of the CPSU has time and again emphasized that democratic centralism is an indispensable condition for the activity of the Party as a political organization. (Titarenko, 1971, p. 182)

This passage from a typical Soviet publication, for all its hack quality—the lines are extracted from an article entitled "Modern times and Lenin's teaching of the party"—was completely indisputable at the time of its writing. Such is no longer the case.

Under Stalin the movement toward a political and logical extreme of orthodoxy came to fruition. The specific organizational characteristics of Soviet politics, in a monstrous provincialism, were elevated to so-called scientifically demonstrable general laws of revolution and socialist development. (Stalin's *Foundations of Leninism*, 1924, is an early example, still somewhat hesitant in certain respects; Fédoséev's *Scientific Communism*, 1974, is one among innumerable examples of routinized Stalinism's codification of charismatic dogma.) Among these general laws of revolution and socialist development—the necessity of violent revolution, of a vanguard communist party, of a single-party regime— was that which proclaimed democratic centralism in its Soviet orthodox form to be the *only conceivable* principle of organization for a truly communist party.

Democratic centralism, in the period of communism's grand ideological withering away, has thus assumed a particular importance in the struggle of communist orthodoxy to survive and in the struggle of reformist communists for development. In the Soviet Union itself the symbol of democratic centralism's importance is article 3 of the 1977 Soviet Constitution, in which democratic centralism is announced no longer as merely the principle of internal communist party organization, but as the constitutional doctrine of the Soviet state itself:

> *Art. 3*—The organization and activity of the Soviet state is constructed in accordance with the principle of democratic centralism, namely the electiveness of all bodies of state authority from the lowest to the highest, their accountability to the people, and the obligation of lower bodies to observe the decisions of higher ones. Democratic centralism combines central leadership with local initiative and creative activity and with the responsibility of each state body and official for the work entrusted to them.

The 1936 Stalin Constitution did not mention democratic centralism at all.[5] The simple fact of its appearance in the 1977 Brezhnev Constitution is in itself of some significance. Moreover, since as S. E. Finer (1979, p. 30) observes, "constitutional draftsmen seem to place items in order of importance," its appearance as the third article of the current Constitution indicates not only a "promotion," but an evident constitutionalist intention at least to state what and where the real rules and institutions of government are. Even were the new and privileged status of democratic centralism essentially a gloss, such glosses, again to quote Finer's expert view, "are not simply juridical. Often they incorporate the working practice, and the theory behind this, of political institutions and processes. Instead of amending the Constitution piecemeal over time to incorporate these changes, the Soviet authorities have—first in 1936 and now again in 1977—swept them all up together into a new coherent document" (ibid., p. 29). Finer's conclusions about the new Soviet Constitution and contemporary Soviet "constitutionalism" are quite suggestive: "Even the Soviet Constitution," he says,

58

is less fictive than usually alleged, while the recent efforts at revising the Civil and Criminal Codes, culminating in the new Brezhnev Constitution itself, are attempts to give the fundamentally illiberal and despotic behavior of that state's authorities the veneer of "socialist legality." In practice such "socialist legality" is often a sophisticated and perverse legalism, but it vindicates the view I have put about the behavioral foundation of public law. If, as alleged, Soviet legislative legalism is hypocritical it is as well to remember the aphorism that "hypocrisy is the tribute that vice pays to virtue." (loc. cit.)

This first evaluation would be of some relevance to our study, but Finer draws a yet stronger conclusion about the 1977 Constitution which really makes our point: whatever the changes from one Soviet Constitution to the next historically,

> the central preoccupation of the Soviet authorities remains identical with what it was sixty years ago. The Soviet constitutions, all four of them, have existed to maximize the legal authority of a revolutionary government and the unbounded exercise thereof. To this end all Soviet constitutions have concentrated the "three powers" of government, not separated them; and they have likewise operated on the principle of the "subordination of lower bodies to higher ones," i.e. the principle of hierarchy. Thus whoever controls the Supreme Soviet legislates, executes and adjudicates without any institutional check or balance on its authority and controls every inferior echelon of government throughout the Union. That which controls the Supreme Soviet is the Communist Party of the Soviet Union. This was stated implicitly in Article 126 of the Stalin Constitution. But in the Brezhnev Constitution it is stated openly and grandly in Article 6, along with the two operational principles: the concentration of powers (Article 108) and "democratic centralism" (Article 3). *These three elements—party, concentration of powers and democratic centralism—comprise the mainsprings of the Soviet polity.* All the rest of the Constitution is machinery or decoration. (ibid., p. 29; emphasis added)

In a regime in which the "three powers" of government are *concentrated* rather than *separated* the justifications of each main element must also be concentrated, so to speak. That is, just as the "holy trinity" doctrines are all rooted in the Stalinist idea of unity, so the three elements here are all based on the orthodox conception of a monolithic unification of powers. In this sense the Brezhnev Constitution is, literally, a routinized (Max Weber would have said "disenchanted") rewriting of the Stalin Constitution. It is an incipient constitutionalization of the Soviet regime, in which democratic centralism has both a literal (it is article 3) and a legal–symbolic pride of place.[6]

The tendency is thus for both the party's vanguard role and the idea of a constitutional concentration of powers to be expressed in terms of democratic centralism, which becomes ever more the constitutional doctrine of routinized Stalinism. There seems to be a slow but unmistakable general tendency toward legal routine and constitutionalism in Soviet political life, with, as the moving force, the emergence of democratic centralism as a constitutional doctrine of the "concentration of powers" in the sense that liberalism is the constitutional doctrine of the "separation of powers."

Of course, since the Soviet "regime" is not simply the state institutions, but also a collectivized economy, the party-controlled soviets and mass organizations, and so on—in short, a regime of concentrated powers and authority at the level of society as a whole—one would expect to find democratic centralism there also. And this is precisely the case, as Waller's recent study demonstrates.

Waller (1981, pp. 62–70) went through the Soviet writing on democratic centralism, reporting on several representative works which demonstrate the wide scope it is given in contemporary Soviet self-descriptions. One is a historical account by Fédoséev, published in 1962 (all references are combined below in n. 7). This is a broad analysis of Soviet history which turns out to be, above all, "an exercise in public relations in favour of Khrushchev's politics," arguing that democratic centralism must emphasize now centralism, now democracy, according to the correctly understood requirements of circumstances. The evident goal here was to justify Khrushchev's decentralization policies. A book by Lavrichev on international communist relations, published in 1971, argues that disagreements within the international communist movement are contradictory to the "Leninist principle of democratic centralism." This emphasis, not surprising to find in the period after 1968, sets up the Soviet system and party life as a model, and then attacks deviations. The "Prague Spring" reformers get the brunt of abuse, followed by well-known West European communists critical of the

Soviet Union (Fischer, Marek, Garaudy, Rossanda, and Magri). The Yugoslav Praxis group and the Chinese party as a whole are also attacked. Waller points out the interesting fact that a separate section is accorded the little-known Petkoff of the Venezuelan party, because he had been not simply critical of democratic centralism, but had argued it had become hopelessly tainted and therefore ought to be dropped. In a third text, a joint book by the CPSU's Institute of Marxism–Leninism and the East German Higher Party School (1973), the issue is an explanation of orthodox habits of political participation: "mass meetings, letters concerning the plan and the new GDR constitution, personal plans, high turn-out at elections, and developing the initiative of the masses," as Waller sums it up.

In a book by Vasilev (1973) democratic centralism is shown, in an extensive study, to be the working principle of the entire system of soviets (Soviet commentary has apparently finally caught up with Meyer's observation that the soviets were taken over by democratic centralism already in 1918–19!). The Soviet economy too is said to run according to democratic centralism—"the Basic Principle of Soviet Economic Management," according to a book by Moiseenko and Popov (1975). Finally, V. G. Afanasev's work (1971) on "The scientific management of society" is shown to present the entire Soviet system, in all its parts, as the expression of democratic centralism. It seems clear enough that democratic centralism is a kind of constitutional doctrine in these works. But the issue is blurred, in that Afanasev (the editor of *Pravda*, and before that the editor of *Kommunist*, the CPSU's theoretical journal), and also Vasilev and Moiseenko and Popov, discuss democratic centralism not only as a principle of government, but in the language of systems theory as well. Thus Vasilev says the soviets require different mixes of centralization and decentralization according to circumstances, arguing that the key elements in proper soviet functioning are information flows, adequate resources (because scarcity leads to the danger of too much centralism), and the cultural level of cadres. It is interesting in itself that the language of systems theory has become a doctrinal gloss on the old Soviet fascination with "businesslike" modes of operation. It is more interesting for our discussion that in the vocabulary of systems theory factionalism is defined as a *dysfunction of the system*. Thus we have here a very modern justification for the prohibition of faction, so to speak a pseudo-scientific rationalization of a new type![7]

In short, Waller concludes, "Soviet theorists describe all the essential workings of the Soviet political system in terms of democratic centralism . . . Democratic centralism has become, in a sense, the hallmark or symbol of Soviet political relationships in all their ramifications. It is the 'honorific term' which Soviet theorists apply to particular political institutions or policies, and to the Soviet system overall" (Waller, 1981, p. 86). But as we have already seen, democratic centralism is a great deal more than simply a symbol or an honorific term. In orthodox communist politics, of which the Soviet system is the archetype, democratic centralism has a profoundly substantive meaning. In fact the issue here is really whether the observer chooses to define the Soviet practice as a "deviation," an unfortunate perversion of an originally good idea (this is Waller's position) or whether one chooses to consider democratic centralism's original meaning as insubstantial, in which case the analysis of democratic centralism's history is, as I said above, also its analysis as a political principle.

What is true is that democratic centralism has become, as Waller says, a "contested" concept. In West European communism, as I will demonstrate in Chapters 4 and 5, the issue of democratic centralism increasingly has become the growing edge of communist political development, generally speaking. Democratic centralism has also become a central subject of discussion and political conflict in several communist party-states. Waller finds that the East European regimes, however, have elaborated democratic centralism as a constitutional doctrine much less than the Soviets.[8] They are also less interested or able than the West European parties to raise directly the issue of democratic centralism as a basis of reform efforts. Thus, as I said in Chapter 1, Solidarity's struggle, for example, had to be fought as a revolutionary attempt to impose a plural order by decisively changing the "correlation of forces" in Polish politics. During the "Polish August" period reforms of orthodox democratic centralism's written and unwritten rules—the right of "horizontal communication," for example (for more on the practical rules, see below)—were not unknown. But in the nature of the struggle they were reformist particulars of a genuinely revolutionary attempt. The "Prague Spring" reforms (cf. Leonhard, 1974, ch. 6) added up more to an attempt to radically change the regime than to develop its internal mechanisms gradually toward what might ultimately have been a similar result. Perhaps because the "Prague Spring" and the "Polish August" were indeed genuinely revolutionary attempts rather than reforms, the Soviets, in a calculation that united Machiavelli (the Soviet Union had the power to achieve its end) with Lenin ("history would never forgive" this group of Soviet leaders if it "lost" Eastern Europe), had to wage counterrevolution even though they well realized the Soviet Union's revolutionary credentials would in the doing become irrevocably tainted.

There remain the non-European communist regimes, about which I will only make a few comments. Cuba and the communist regimes in Indochina remain, according to the common wisdom, essentially orthodox Stalinist states. I see no reason to challenge the common wisdom on this score. China, on the other hand, seems to me launched on a profound internal transformation which cannot yet speak its true name. There are many journalistic and contemporary-history accounts to support such a view, but only time will tell and the process, however it turns, is still in an early stage.

Finally, there is Yugoslavia. A recent monograph (Burg, 1983, pp. 308–18) shows that a serious debate continues in Yugoslavia over the meaning of democratic centralism (cf. especially Kardelj, 1977) in conjunction with the extremely complex issues of the Yugoslav self-management system in industry, and in territorial government administration, as well as ethnic regionalism. I will have a few occasions later on to refer to the Yugoslav case but will here only reiterate my earlier assertion that Yugoslavia is no longer a communist state, even though it still carries the name. One invariable characteristic of "communism" (understood as a substantive phenomenon and not simply as a name) is missing: the Yugoslav borders are open, not closed. Methodically sealed-off borders are an emblem of what we generally understand to be a "communist" regime. As I show later in this chapter, sealed borders are not simply gratuitous repression, but are organically connected to the communist idea of unity, part of the orthodox political culture of democratic centralism. The intrinsic *tendency* or temptation of communist rule is always totalitarianism, though the degree of its actual realization varies widely. Closed borders are the emblem of a totalitarian intention and one of the first means of its realization. As is shown by the (all things considered) limited nature of political repression in Yugoslavia, it has become some original combination of "right-wing" authoritarianism and residual communist structures and ideology.

Democratic Centralism as Praxis

The Written and Unwritten Rules
Strictly speaking, the written rules of orthodox democratic centralism are the "four clauses" of party internal life (see p. 44) and, for communist party-states, the Soviet constitutional model as given in articles 3, 6, and 108 of the 1977 Constitution (see pp. 58–60). There is a certain range of insignificant variation to be found in the constitutional documents of orthodox parties and states; and in the nonruling orthodox parties fighting over internal reform there may be, here and there, a significant variation or two, or perhaps even a stray organizational commission minority report of remarkable heresy (cf. a 1980 British Communist minority report on democratic centralism).

The rest of democratic centralism's rules are unwritten. By this I mean either literally unwritten, in the sense of being a set of well-established, coherent, and binding set of norms which every orthodox communist has learned, or else written but not connected explicitly to democratic centralism. Democratic centralism, as I have argued throughout, has to be "written large" to be comprehended by the outsider. According to the written rules, for example, the uninitiated might think clause 1 is simply a guarantee of elections to all party and state offices: it is not said anywhere formally that there will be only one candidate per office, that candidates are nominated from above (allegedly to get the best and most experienced candidates, and to prevent nomination to office from degenerating into a process based on "accident"—this term, of course, echoes the whole history of communism's struggle for "consciousness" against "spontaneity"); nor that, in consequence, communist "elections" are a confirmation process rather than a matter of choice. Clause 2—the principle of leadership accountability—is a matter of such evident monumental hypocrisy that an entire chapter could not exhaust even the narrow bases upon which accountability is avoided. Suffice it to say that, except at lower party and state levels—the party cell and the local or district administrative committees—the principle of accountabililty means leaders reading long "reports" in the orthodox *langue de bois* which are accepted unanimously, or nearly so. Nowhere is it explained why the *process* itself of accountability is predicated on a complete lack of free questioning and genuine scrutiny of leaders. Nor is it explained how the orthodox conception itself of the vote implies unanimity. What is offered is clause 3, which subordinates the minority to the majority as a principle of *action*, but does not formally require the minority to abandon its positions in votes so as to make results unanimous. In any case, as we have seen above briefly and will detail below in this chapter, true minorities cannot form in communist organizations because the ban on factions prohibits the very organization they would need. The principle of majority and minority opinion simply has no meaning in the political culture of orthodox democratic centralism. (Perhaps significantly, the 1977 Soviet state Constitution elides clause 2.) Clause 4, finally, tells the truth about centralism: that the decisions of higher bodies are absolutely binding on lower bodies. And although such a principle is foreign to liberal politics, in which political struggle continues in the implementation of a policy, and even in the interpretation of what the results have been, without the rest of the democratic centralist apparatus clause 4 would not be devastating to freedom. Its centralism would be a mixed bag, as it is in right-wing authoritarian parties which have such rules.

It remains to comment upon the Soviet state Constitution's addendum: "Democratic centralism combines central leadership with local initiative and creative activity and with the responsibility of each state body and official for the work entrusted to them." The possible interpretations of the effective connations here are numerous. For one thing, this expresses a genuinely pious admonition to local levels to be creative in political mobilization and policy implementation. For another, this phrase gives an ideological hostage to fortune, by appearing to solicit genuine participation and "input" rather than instructed activity and "output." But so long as the apparatus and the rank-and-file know their respective places, rules and norms, such risks are minor and well worth taking. Finally, "the responsibility of each state body and official for the work entrusted to them" has a double-edged connotation: first, the very notion is the object of absolute cynicism in the orthodox communist politics of widespread lying and corruption; a second implication is a sort of "kiss of death" for those officials who, for whatever reasons, find themselves apprehended and punished for dereliction of duty,. (One thinks both of political purges and criminal prosecutions for "economic" and other crimes; as opposed to "high Stalinist" times, communist party-state officials today are sometimes executed for the latter offenses, but hardly ever for the former.)

The Rule of Rules
The crucial unwritten rule of democratic centralism is that its entire structure is erected on the prohibition of faction and factional

behavior. Democratic centralism's "four clauses" are written and the ban on faction is written; but the formal connection is not made. The ban on faction, one could say, is the implicit working principle of each of the four clauses, the master rule of the rules of the game. The ban on faction is the orthodox communist categorical imperative, a principle which has always been evident to every high and ordinary Stalinist communist alike.

In a new *Critical Dictionary of Marxism* a "critical" (that is, left-wing) French Communist observes that "In the history of the communist parties the question of the *droit de tendances* has crystallized ... the essential elements of the debate on organizational forms." Furthermore, the author goes on, "rejection of the *droit de tendances* is the foundation stone [of the] monolithic party conception" (Balibar, 1982, p. 92). This is substantially the same argument I am making, although in this study Balibar's "debate on organizational forms" is nothing so modest as the phrase implies. It is in fact the problem itself of Stalinist communism.

It is interesting to detail one element of Balibar's left-wing communist critique. Hostile to Stalinism, yet exiting from it on the Marxist-Leninist left rather than the reformist right, Balibar (and other well-known left-wing communist thinkers, such as Balibar's teacher Louis Althusser) condemn the Stalinist absolute ban on faction for its "mechanistic" and "juridical" (*sic*) approach. In other words, the goal of "unity" is correct, but the rules of the Stalinist ban on faction are a "mechanistic" and "juridical" false solution to the old Leninist problem of achieving a correct synthesis of political differences. To Balibar any "juridical" approach is a form of "bourgeois" thinking, and the "mechanistic" imprisonment of factional behavior is a "negative" way of conceiving the problem of free debate (ibid., pp. 95–6). The conclusion of this line of argument, stated baldly by two younger and less cautious left-wing French "critical" Communists, is no less than the assertion that "Stalinism is in fact a bourgeois political practice within the working-class movement!" (Bouillot and Devesa, 1979, p. 25).

I wish to draw two implications from the above: both the orthodox communists and their internal and external left-wing critics understand that the ban on factions is the central element of "the debate on organizational forms" in communism historically; my purpose is to demonstrate that the rest of us should begin from the same premise. Secondly, the massive intellectual and political confusion evident in asserting that Stalinism is "bourgeois" is a first glimpse, if only through a mirror as it were, into the radically eccentric political culture of orthodox democratic centralism.

Given my argument thus far, much might be thought to depend on the manner in which "faction" and "factionalism" are defined. As we shall see, however, the issue of disagreement about definitions will not shadow the rest of the study.

Balibar and also Althusser (1977, pp. 59–68) distinguish between "tendencies" and "factions." The distinction is based on the degree and permanence of their organizational crystallization. A "tendency," on the one hand, is relatively weakly organized and is basically a temporary congealing of sympathetic views and interests. A faction, on the other hand, is a more or less fully crystallized "party within the party," having its own identifiable program, structure, and characteristic leaders, who fight to dominate the party.

This is a straightforward usage which is unobjectionable. It is a traditional distinction, empirically based in the sense that it marks out easily observable differences, and is fuzzy, as are all fruitful distinctions, only at the margins.

Yet we want to refine this simple difference, in order to account for the finer organizational gradations between the individual member and the whole party, which history has evolved and made important, above all, in the West European party systems. Particularly among the communist and socialist parties in Western Europe the making of these distinctions is often a means itself to *fare politica*, as the Italian Communists say.

Let us, then, say that there are not two but three increasingly comprehensive forms of internal party political pluralism (Hayward, 1981, pp. 1–2; Cayrol, 1978, p. 165 ff.; Belloni and Beller, 1978). There are *opinion currents*, *tendencies*, and *factions*. The first is an unorganized and noninstitutionalized internal party grouping, which shares a set of identifiable views and may even have its own publications. A yet still more refined conception, as Hayward (1981) says, would distinguish a "sensibilité" from an opinion current, the former meaning a set of shared values which does not necessarily issue in agreed opinions on given policy issues. A tendency then takes pluralism a step further, moving from the clash of ideas to the clash of personalities as well, implying a struggle for control of party policy and even a struggle over the party's program as a whole. Finally, a faction is a fully structured potential "party within the party": it holds its own meetings and, most important, holds first priority in members' loyalty. In a deeply factionalized party the threat of party disintegration is continuous. Party life becomes, first of all, the struggle of its internal factions for influence. The party's clarity of external purpose and force of external influence are confounded.

Why do fully crystallized factions often remain within the same party? One must here ask why its members joined one party rather than another in the first place, a perspective derived from a question about party *development* rather than party *fragmentation*. Harold Lasswell's essay on "faction" in the 1931 *Encyclopedia of the Social Sciences*, recalls the basic point:

> The term faction is commonly used to designate any constituent group of a larger unit which works for the advancement of particular persons or policies. The faction arises in the struggle for power and represents a division on details of application and not on principles. The position of the faction is that of the qualified dissenter who embraces collective goals subject to reservations upon the tactics appropriate for their realization. Thus a faction presupposes some measure of unity in fundamentals. The term itself drops out of usage when certain lines of cleavage have become rather permanent features of the political life of a group; these divisions are accepted as parties. (Lasswell, 1931, vol. 6, p. 49)

And Lasswell adds: "Divisions within the group are profoundly affected by the external relations of the group" (ibid., p. 50). In times of success, especially the exercise of governmental power, factionalism "subsides spontaneously." On the other hand, in periods of crisis and failure, factionalism may indeed split a party. In other words, the result of even full-fledged factionalism depends on the force, and the temptations, of circumstance.

All this notwithstanding, the problem of Stalinism is a different one because the goals of monolithic unity of the membership and a unanimous hierarchy are an attempt to eradicate *all* gradations of party internal pluralism or fragmentation. In Stalinist communism the expression of political differences is supposed to be entirely personal, to protect against the coalescence of factional groupings. The apparent permission of conflict of opinion on the one hand, with the absolute interdiction of faction on the other hand, is however a Catch-22 mechanism. This was becoming apparent in the Soviet experience already by 1924. In his lectures on the *Foundations of Leninism* Stalin said:

Achievement and maintenance of the dictatorship of the proletariat are impossible without a party strong in its cohesion and
iron discipline. But iron discipline in the Party is impossible
without unity of will and without absolute and complete
unity of action on the part of all members of the Party. This
does not mean of course that there will never be any conflict of
opinion within the Party. On the contrary, iron discipline does
not preclude but presupposes criticism and conflicts of opinion
within the Party. Least of all does it mean that this discipline
must be 'blind' discipline. On the contrary, iron discipline does
not preclude but presupposes conscious and voluntary discipline, for only conscious discipline can be truly iron discipline
... It follows that the existence of factions is incompatible with
Party unity and with its iron discipline ... The same thing
applies, but to a greater degree, to discipline in the Party after
the establishment of the dictatorship. (Stalin, 1932,
pp. 116–17)

In *The New Course* Trotsky first drew out the tendency of internal
party life in Stalin's argument:

What follows from this? If factions are not wanted, there must
not be any permanent groupings; if permanent groupings are
not wanted, temporary groupings must be avoided; finally, in
order that there be no temporary groupings, there must be no
differences of opinion, for wherever there are two opinions,
people inevitably group together. But how, on the other hand,
to avoid differences of opinion in a party of half a million men
which is leading the country in exceptionally complicated and
painful conditions? That is the essential contradiction residing
in the very situation of the party of the proletarian dictatorship,
a contradiction that cannot be escaped solely by purely formal
measures. (Trotsky, 1943, pp. 27–8)

What was Trotsky's suggestion? "It is in contradictions and differences of opinion," he said, "that the working out of the party's
public opinion inevitably takes place. To localize this process *only*
within the apparatus which is then charged to furnish the party with
the fruit of its labors in the form of slogans, orders, etc. is to sterilize
the party ideologically and politically." Yet none the less Trotsky, as
noted before, again endorsed the prohibition of factions; he only
pleaded that "the leading organs of the party must lend an ear to the

voice of the broad party mass," must find "a correct course adapted to the real situation," and must find an "intermediate line between the regime of 'calm' and that of crumbling into factions" (ibid., pp. 29–30). In short, Trotsky hoped to save the idea of the "correct synthesis." He wanted to convince Stalin to make politics rather than bureaucracy, to make unity on a basis of *fare politica* rather than "administrative measures." But why should Stalin have given away his growing advantage? Only Trotsky's single-minded or naive dedication to the revolution could have prevented him from admitting the desperation of his struggle.

What Trotsky said but did not work through to its conclusion was that, as a matter both of principle and of action, "opinion currents" and "tendencies"—and, ultimately, the individual's right to speak and to his own opinion—cannot exist unless the right to "factions" exists. The principles and structural requisites of factionalism are necessary to freedom of opinion and speech if these are to signify anything more than a lapse of ideological vigilance or the inevitable gap between a totalitarian theory and even the most brutal attempt to put it into practice. The absolute prohibition of faction is thus the rule of rules in democratic centralism, just as democratic centralism is the theory and practice of monolithic unity.

The Mechanisms

With no pretense at being complete or exhaustive in the following discussion, let us detail the main mechanisms through which the ban on faction, and orthodox democratic centralism as a whole, work as a praxis of monolithic unity, unanimity in decision-making, and absolute discipline.[9]

Inside the orthodox communist party democratic centralism works through six basic mechanisms: (1) vertical compartmentalization of discussion, that is, a ban on "horizontal communication" between party structures; (2) voluntary unanimous votes, that is, accepting leadership policies secretly debated, decided, and presented as "correct"; (3) interdiction in the party's press and media network of nonconformist, that is, anti-leadership, opinions and discussions; (4) interdiction to discuss internal communist politics outside the party in order to present a "block of steel" façade of unity and discipline to the exterior; (5) limitation of public inner-party debates, for example, at national and regional congresses, to discussion of a single policy platform presented by the leadership; this platform may be summarized, supported, and at a limit, amended in minor, generally previously approved ways (amendments are often extremely numerous to provide an impressive statistic), but not challenged; and (6) political homogenization of the ruling group of the party through occasional purges, but more usually through methodic political filtering of candidates for elective and appointive office by the party's candidate commissions and central control commissions. This forces a tacit pact among the party's leaders, including the top bureaucratic levels, not to break the monolithic solidarity of the hierarchy at pain of extreme consequences. After mechanisms 1–5 have cut off the possibility of pluralism emerging from the bottom or the middle of the party, this last mechanism undercuts the possibility of potential minorities being constructed from the top down.

The interdiction of horizontal communication among party cells, sections, or regional committees is of such importance that one is tempted to think it the "efficient secret" of the ban on faction. This is because its transgression by the divergent opinions which must arise as a matter of course in any political or social body would tend to explode *all* the other constraints, including the production of non-conformist leadership in the act itself of transgression. Historically the ban on horizontal communication dates back to Bolshevism's prerevolutionary experience, when the party, a necessarily secret, underground movement, was organized into horizontally and vertically integrated small units—the famous Leninist "cell" which constituted the local level of the revolutionary party's capillary structure. This grassroots organization of party cells had as one purpose to maximize local actions ("agitation") and contact with the population ("propaganda"). But just as much the cell structure was dedicated to party security: the least-experienced party militants, in this structure, were limited in the damage they could cause by making mistakes, allowing outside infiltration, or being captured and subjected to police interrogation. The local militants knew only the members of their own cell, and so on at each higher level. The main contact at each level could, if necessary, rapidly reorganize all the contacts and codes under his responsibility.

Eliminating horizontal communication and maximizing vertical control was reasonable behavior for an underground revolutionary party. In the Stalinist reconstruction of Leninism, on the other hand, what originally maximized offense and defense became, above all else, a means of control of the entire party apparatus from above. Horizontal communication is obviously a necessary basis of minority groupings or opinions in any political organization. Without horizontal understandings—across structural levels or territorial boundaries—there is no possibility of exchanging the information and making the promises necessary to allow even a sizable internal minority to express itself, let alone to organize its position against policy coming from the top. The ruling group becomes invulnerable in policy-making. And given leadership's natural tendency to co-opt its membership when possible, the ruling group becomes vulnerable also in the selection of the party's leading personnel. Historically the massive advantage gained from the interdiction of horizontal communication has led to the corruption and stagnation of communist leadership generally in orthodox parties: orthodox communist ruling groups are, generally speaking, cliques of men growing old together in power.

What must be remarked further is the generally *voluntary* compliance at all party levels with the ban on horizontal communication: the orthodox communist party still presents itself as a "combat party," surrounded by enemies and engaged in a class war which is always ideological even when not physically violent. The "combat party" mentality, and the nostalgic myth on which it rests, trace their roots back to "Lenin's party," the image even worn-out communist bureaucrats sometimes must want to have of themselves. And, of course, this is all the more true of militants in the orthodox nonruling communist parties, where the "combat party" image is part of the political cultural baggage of day-to-day militancy in circumstances often quite discouraging. The problem is that in accepting the justification for the ban on horizontal communication the loyal or simply worn-out party member fails to notice that he has become his own jailer, locking himself up in a prison certainly not of his own making, but now largely of his own keeping. Beyond this, wherever nonconformism might none the less arise, the prevention of unauthorized horizontal communication in party and also in *state* bureaucracies is a further guarantee of the efficiency of vertical control. Within the inner-party intelligence network, in a system in which "party and state discipline" are the same and so specified constitutionally, the top can always know what is going on below it (even if it is not always interested), but the lower levels have no way of knowing either what goes on at the top or what goes on in other parts of the organization.

Similarly, in a communist *social structure* whose "cells" or "units" run on democratic centralist principles a high premium is placed on preventing horizontal communication among the secondary or "public nonstate" organizations—both within themselves and among them. Success in this task precludes the basis for "faction" in society at large. Put differently, preventing the circulation of politically nonconformist opinions in a communist society forestalls the formation of a genuine *public opinion* as such.

In this regard the operation of Solidarity in Poland, and its mutually reinforcing relations with the Polish Catholic Church (whose existence was already a massive "dysfunction" in an ordinary Stalinist system), were pertinent examples of what happens when an orthodox communist state is no longer able to prevent horizontal communication. Solidarity's mode of operation (cf. the Gdańsk Protocol and, in general, Kemp-Welch, 1984) broke all the rules and taboos in democratic centralism in, for example: (1) demanding that the divergence of its own interest from party and state interests be recognized publicly; (2) negotiating in an openly adversarial relation on television; and (3) forcing competitive elections at the Polish Communist Party Congress, which resulted in a massive defeat of the established ruling group, and so on. All of this was symbolized in Lech Walesa's pointed insistence on avoiding the communist habit of the familiar form of address, and calling negotiating adversaries "mister" rather than "comrade." And the subsequent creation of Rural Solidarity was a further indication of the elaborate organized pluralism which would result if orthodox, counterrevolutionary violence was not able to reverse the transgression of Stalinist "constitutionalism."

The ban on horizontal communication works essentially to prevent factionalism from below. But as I have said, the prevention of faction needs to be guaranteed within the leadership as well. The particular character of communist *elections* and the *secrecy* of communist leadership disagreements are the two major elements in producing a publicly monolithic leadership; the political *purge* prevents leadership disagreements—whenever they become irreconcilable or public—from becoming a focal point for factional organization.

As is well known, the orthodox method of election is not a choice among candidates, or among lists with opposing views on important policy questions. "Voters" are simply asked to confirm a list of candidates presented to them from above. It is illegitimate in such a system to seek election on the basis of a policy or program (other than the leadership's program) because to do so is self-evidently factional activity. Thus in an orthodox communist election no matter whether there is more than one nomination per position or not, candidates are completely interchangeable regarding policy (at least publicly). Their characteristic attribute as a group is that they are being co-opted, through the appropriate candidates' commissions and through informal relations, as useful to the top leadership's own purpose. This is justified as "conscious" or "scientific" planning of leadership. In reality a previously decided specific combination of personalities, skills, experience, social origins, age, and gender is fulfilled, in order that the hierarchy be able to give the image—largely working class, nonsexist, and so on—that it wants of itself. Elections are thus a political ritual of approval or passivity rather than of choice and accountability of leaders. Communist electors are thus deprived of choice of policy and choice of leaders alike. Their only hope is that leaders for other reasons will do what voters want (or perhaps what is good for them). In any case, the elected public leadership in an orthodox communist regime is generally irrelevant in running a system in which important decisions are taken in secret by a small ruling group, which the rest of society has no institutional means to hold accountable.

The secrecy of top leadership debate, finally, is an integral aspect of ordinary Stalinist democratic centralism. This is, however, not simply because of the general consideration that publicity is always the first remedy against despotic government, but also because any substantial publicity of disagreement within a Stalinized leadership provides a potential basis for factional division of even a communized public opinion. Leaders in an orthodox communist hierarchy are thus held to the strictest possible definition of collective responsibility. Whatever their private beliefs or policies, in public they must speak and act the party line. The fetish of unanimity takes this rule to its logical conclusion in two ways: (1) by making political *resignation* from office an unspoken taboo; because political resignation means disagreement with or rejection of leadership, it is stigmatized as politically equivalent to treason; and (2) by requiring that the party line be spoken and defined in the same terms, literally more or less the same words, everywhere. Thus arises the incomparable monotony of communist language, a mind-boggling litany of ritual slogans and orthodox analyses which is the poor historical residue of "scientific socialism." What all this adds up to is summarized in Figure 3.2.

The Vocabulary of the Ideology as a Totalitarian Temptation

A former communist, the son of one of Western Europe's long-time communist party bosses, makes this astute distinction between Khrushchev and Brezhnev:[10]

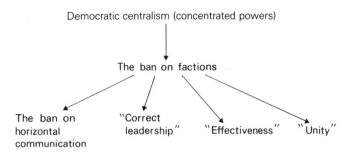

Figure 3.2   Ordinary Stalinist "constitutionalism."

As ridiculous as Brezhnev seem[ed] to us—senile, stuttering, laboriously putting on his glasses to mumble a text written by the Central Committee Secretariat—he serv[ed] the cause. Khrushchev, a crowd pleaser in Copenhagen and Los Angeles, was a mortal threat inside the system. His glibness reduced to nothing the system's keystone, its very essence: the vocabulary of the ideology. (Thorez, 1982, p. 57)

Any analysis of communism predicated on the importance of ideology leads ineluctably to a close focus on communist language, what Paul Thorez calls the "very essence: the vocabulary of the ideology." The definition of political terms creates the perception and definition of political reality. The significance of beliefs implies the significance of the language in which belief is formulated and expressed. Vocabulary is in one sense coextensive with what men, in Walter Lippmann's phrase, "think they know." And to analyze the commonly held definitions in a political belief system is to comprehend how its partisans, citizens, and officials conceive political life. Thus it is that the capacity to *control* a society's political vocabulary is to exercise a power that must be always tendentially totalitarian.

The vocabulary of orthodox communism is a totalitarian temptation because the use of its basic terms justifies, and literally "produces," the party's control of political life and conscience. Close attention to the meaning of words provides the outside observer with a deeper perception of the meaning of ordinary Stalinist behavior than explanations which derive from shortcut assumptions of cynicism or fanaticism. It is, therefore, of great interest to analyze democratic centralism as an ideological vocabulary—that is, as a series of universe-and-mind-forging symbolic concepts whose very ambiguity establishes a set of practical dilemmas the solutions of which create the everyday politics of ordinary Stalinism.[11] I will discuss three of these key terms: (1) the notion of "correct" leadership, decisions, and policies; (2) the concept of organizational "effectiveness," with its corollary distinction between "making" and "implementing" a decision; and (3) the Stalinist idea of "unity," with its implicitly Hobbesian understanding of faction.

The Ambiguity of "Correct" Leadership

The notion of "correct" leadership in politics, to almost any but the communist mentality, is inherently bizarre or misplaced, a misreading of the nature and possibilities of political life and political leadership. Politics is normally conceived as *ipso facto* a realm of indeterminacy, in which choices must be made among competing values and principles (even among one's own) and in which secondary or unintended consequences will often prove more significant than the original intent of a decision or policy.

When an orthodox communist speaks of correct leadership, he is claiming that policy is made and society is managed scientifically, that decisions are correct in the sense of being in a special meaning literally "true," in accord with objective working-class interests derived from a scientific understanding of social forces. The task of party leadership, in a time-worn piety, is "to determine, in any situation, the correct policy from the point of view of the working class." The communist true believer resonates instinctively with this credo, and communist regimes almost everywhere (no matter what their leaders admit privately) still claim that communist policy is scientific—which, since the bureaucrats must either believe it or act as if they believe it, has a chilling effect on what would otherwise be the normal indeterminateness and variety of even communist opinion. This obviously is one factor in producing the deadlocks of communist political development: the dogmas of "correct" leadership and "correct" policies remain an iron corset on the capacity to perceive and deal with real problems.

At its adoption by the Bolsheviks a major effect of democratic centralism was to justify centralism, the leitmotif of Leninist organization from the first outline of it in *What Is To Be Done?* In one sense centralism is equivalent to leadership, and the idea of "correct" leadership naturally became a key aspect of the code's legitimacy. The purpose of democracy in democratic centralism at the beginning was, first of all, to provide for the discussion and persuasion necessary to maintain party unity, whereas the purpose of centralism was to maximize party effectiveness in action. The *justification* of centralism—as distinguished from its purpose—was the idea that leadership's policies were "correct." The problem is that the meaning of "correct" in the early period was very different from what it became later, and a major difference between Leninist and Stalinist types of communism.

In an early text Lenin said the party's task as a decision-making body was a combination of three rules (see Meyer, 1957, pp. 92–3):

(1)   Decisions should be correct.
(2)   Decisions should be made in an acceptable, that is, a democratic manner.
(3)   Decisions should be arrived at efficiently, meaning speedily and without unnecessary conflict.

Generally speaking, the evidence is that, as a matter of his genuine aspirations, Lenin never abandoned (or went beyond) this commonsensical set of rules. Actually to achieve a set goal, beyond its intrinsic importance, was significant in the Leninist conception for two different reasons. First, it demonstrated the political and intellectual superiority of the party's ruling group. Secondly, it justified the clause of democratic centralism according to which the minority submits completely to the majority—applying fully, enthusiastically, and without second thoughts a decision with which it disagrees, on the premise that the decision will most often be proven "correct." Success, in other words, made decisions "correct" and therein it created the leadership's continuing political legitimacy in the absence of some regular procedural legitimation.

We must, therefore, amend Meyer's assertion, quoted earlier, to say that "free criticism plus unity of action" was not quite the whole meaning of democratic centralism in the revolutionary period: a third term is required, "correct leadership," which formed the link between free discussion and total discipline in action. Trotsky, for example, decades later continued to defend the party leadership's mode of operation during the revolutionary period in precisely such terms: "The obvious correctness of the leadership at all critical stages gave it that high authority which is the priceless moral capital of centralism" (see *The Revolution Betrayed*, 1945; quoted in Mills,

1962, p. 306). As one well-known contemporary West European Leninist put it similarly not long ago: in the Leninist view the "problem of internal democracy . . . is not primarily an institutional question, but one of political line and ideological consensus. The degree of democracy within a party is a function of the consensus it achieves" (Magri, 1970, p. 123). This is an excellent standard, but it is hard to apply beyond small groups, for example, the ruling group of the kind of small party in which Lucio Magri has been a leading Italian leftist. Outside a small circle the need for institutional guarantees of minority and individual rights becomes larger as the relevant population (or distance, or lack of face-to-face of meetings) increases. What Magri's aphorism points up is the fact that Leninism is least dangerous as a form of leadership ingroup politics. In a well-known text, Trotsky rightly says that the 1924 "Lenin levy"—which implemented Stalin's decision to open party ranks wide—was crucial in the destruction of Leninist politics:[12]

> The gates of the party, always carefully guarded, were now thrown wide open. Workers, clerks, petty officials, flocked through in crowds. The political aim of this maneuver was to dissolve the revolutionary vanguard in raw human material, without experience, without independence, and yet with the old habit of submitting to the authorities. The scheme was successful. By freeing the bureaucracy from the control of the proletarian vanguard, the "Leninist levy" dealt a death blow to the party of Lenin . . . Democratic centralism gave place to bureaucratic centralism. (From *The Revolution Betrayed*; quoted in Mills, 1962, p. 308)

With the "revolutionary vanguard dissolved" and the influence of Stalin's rivals more and more reduced, the "correctness" of leadership decisions and policies became increasingly declarative. The idea of "correct decisions" was thus transformed—Trotsky's language here is right on the mark—from a *political* to a *bureaucratic* category. Rapidly enough, communist ruling groups everywhere began to economize on political discussions and to act rather on the authority of their positions and on the myth of scientific socialist decision-making.

Here we observe power in the very moment of corrupting those who wield it. The authority to declare one's own policy "correct" is surely an invitation to absolute dictatorship. And the totalitarian potential in the Stalinist, as opposed to the Leninist, idea of

78

"correct" decisions was realized in the expectation—shared throughout the Comintern as the "show trial" confessions as well as books such as Koestler's *Darkness at Noon* testify—that "good" communists will not only accept and enthusiastically implement policies to which they are opposed, but *will work "politically" within their own consciences* to convince themselves that the party is correct and they are wrong.[13] Trotsky's famous confession that "one can never be right against the party" is the apotheosis of this perverse idea of loyalty.

The totalitarian potential in the ambiguous idea of "correct" leadership is thus a combination of two elements. The first is the belief that there exists a permanent, unitary working-class interest which if analyzed with scientific socialist theoretical premises in relation to a given situation leads to a "right answer," *a single possible right answer*, in policy terms. This amounts in effect to a permanent delegitimation of disagreement and/or opposition to any incumbent leadership. Secondly, tactical and strategic success, by obliging dissenters to admit the "correctness" of policies which they originally opposed, reinforces the orthodox communist assumption that the party's general goals never change and that there is never any point (indeed there is only the danger of disunity) in discussing them. Whenever such discussions do occur, therefore, they are initiated by the leadership itself. The party is forced into a sudden debate launched from above (for instance, Khrushchev's unexpected denunciation of Stalin at the Twentieth Soviet Party Congress, or Mao's surprise initiation of the Cultural Revolution) for the leadership's own purpose—whether that be revolution from above or the widening of an internal struggle.

The permanent assumption is that the party is unanimous concerning its basic goals, the Rousseauist "fundamental, voluntary agreement" advertised in orthodox communist texts. The problem is that the basic goals of communist parties—socialism, democracy, the party's leading role, and so on—are all capable of various meanings which can even contradict one another. The inescapably indeterminate character of political life implies the rediscussion of goals within any—even a communist—party: "Not only the method of execution, but the entire program of the party must be redefined again and again" (Meyer, 1957, p. 95). Obviously this does not mean, as communists frequently object in reply, that the party is led either to abandon its principles or constantly to change them, let alone to become a nonstop "discussion club" incapable of prompt action. (The source of this orthodoxy is again Karl Kautsky: "To

79

discuss," Kautsky wrote in 1903, "is a wonderful thing, but a fighting party is not a discussion club.")

This notion of "correct policies" and the presumed intellectual and political superiority of communist leaderships at "scientific socialist analysis" justify the mechanisms of Stalinist democratic centralism which we have already examined in detail: for instance, the ban on faction and the rule of a single proposal for the party's program. In addition, if a policy has been correctly based on working-class interests, then any alternative policy, in addition to being "incorrect," is also *anti*-working class. Thus loyal disagreements are not expressed because they will be labeled anti-working class, therefore, anti-party, anti-socialist, and counterrevolutionary. Nonconformism means treason. The idea of "correct" leadership is thus also the idea of monolithic leadership, the "block of steel" whose first historical reference is the homogeneous Bolshevik government of 1917–18, and whose doctrinal justification is a special notion of class purity and party security. Massimo Salvadori has formulated the full logic of this linkage of political monolithism and class purity:[14]

> The constitutive principle of that type of democratic centralism which rejects factions is the presupposition that in a revolutionary party, that is to say in a party which is to have a proletarian base and which seeks to give the proletariat command of the state and society, factions are not admissible because factions, and the struggle through factions for leadership of the party, are the instrument which is used by social classes and groups different from the proletariat in order to promote degeneration of the party. In other words, given that the communist party is the party of a single class, which struggles to carry that class to power, the homogeneity of the social base must express itself in homogeneity of the political leadership, because the organization of factions is the masked form in which the class struggle penetrates into the interior of the party. (Quoted in Mieli, 1978, p. 8)

In some communist parties (for example, the French Communist Party) this "workerism" has been implemented mechanically: top leaders have always been chosen among workers, that is, most of the upper-level bureaucrats, including the general secretary himself, are former workers who spent a few years on the job and then became full-time apparatchiks and survived in the struggle to get to the top of the party's hierarchy. "Workerism" is a dogmatic proletarian prejudice which assumes that workers, and *only* workers, can possibly implement a consistent revolutionary working-class line. From this point of view the Bolshevik leadership itself is an anomaly, as have been the leaderships of the *majority* of ruling and nonruling communist parties historically.

Whatever the alleged basis of leadership monolithism—common working-class social origins or common political commitment—the dogma of "correct" leadership reinforces conformism. A communist leadership becomes monolithic not only to safeguard its own privileges in an extremely effective way (as I said before, realpolitik alone could never have produced the extraordinary thoroughness and durability of communist power), but also because the vocabulary which makes the communist party organizational culture a recipe for totalitarianism leaves no alternative.

This also indicates why communist parties historically have been unable to develop a mechanism for the routine change of either political leadership or policies. Other than when a leader dies in office, the bases on which succession could occur legitimately— namely, a convincing criticism of previous policy, combined with the organization of a successful electoral/political challenge to incumbent leadership—are precisely precluded in principle itself by the notion of "correct" leadership and by the ban on faction.

The Paradox of "Effectiveness": On the Distinction Between "Making" and "Implementing" a Decision

The ambiguity of the mutual Bolshevik and Menshevik adoption of democratic centralism in 1905–6, as we have said already, lay in the combination of local autonomy with "ultimate" binding authority for the party's center. In the reunified RSDWP the enduring Bolshevik–Menshevik disagreement concerning the proper balance between centralism and localism was simply wrapped temporarily in the camouflage of the "unity in action" notion. The latter in turn was attached to the seemingly innocuous distinction between "making" and "implementing" a decision—the rule which forbade any criticism of a decision once taken, but permitted criticism of the manner or tactics of its application.

There is an evident logical and political plausibility in the attempt to combine democracy and centralism by separating discussion from action. "Unity in action," the rule that defeated minorities accept and unreservedly implement the majority's policies, is a distinctive characteristic of communist organization, supposedly a guarantee of supreme dedication and discipline which ensures that the party will act with maximum effectiveness and that party policy will not be internally sabotaged by factional conflict. However, the apparent plausibility of the distinction between making and implementing a decision disintegrates substantially on a closer inspection. It is "insufficient," as Alfred Meyer points out, because "the function of carrying out decisions cannot be separated entirely from that of making decisions" (Meyer, 1957, pp. 98, 95). This is another way of saying that the lines of separation between strategy and tactics, between strategy and basic goals, and even between bureaucracy and democracy, are really gray areas rather than sharp boundaries. To a certain extent the means are always the ends themselves, and in any case means are inseparable from ends. (One thinks immediately, in this regard, of Bernstein's argument that the final aim of socialism is "immaterial," that the nature of socialism is to be found in the movement for socialism.) Whatever is first "decided," practically speaking—as all politicians and bureaucrats know instinctively or learn—the implementation of a decision *is* in effect the decision. Stalin surely had this in mind when he said that "To govern is not to write resolutions and distribute directives; to govern is to control the implementation of the directives" (quoted in McInnes, 1975a, p. 98). This distinction between word and intention can hypocritically serve one of two kinds of ruse: the leadership can present a vague program whose real meaning, contained later in directives, is intentionally hidden from debate; or (as was the case in the "Paris affair" of 1978–80, studied in Chapter 5) a leadership can launch the party on a policy which it later, for its own, hidden reasons, repudiates in the implementation, insisting that the change is simply a U-turn in tactics rather than an abandonment of the policy's goal. In both cases Stalinist leadership is shown to be a "black box": its internal processes are opaque, hidden from public debate or scrutiny.

Given the leadership's monopoly of the decision-making process, the only possibility of expressing criticism is relegated to the permission to discuss tactics or implementation. However, as Meyer observes so correctly:[15]

Given the demand that every member must loyally adhere to formally accepted decisions, given further the conception of the party as a perfectly co-ordinated machine for action, given, finally, the party's custom of carrying out every decision by a total effort in which all available resources are marshalled— given these characteristic traits of communist thought and behavior, any criticism of the manner of execution is likely to be condemned, because it might jeopardize the total pursuit of the goal that had been established and thus endanger the party's policy. For this reason it was unrealistic of Lenin to allow criticism of the manner of execution while simultaneously demanding absolute loyalty to all decisions. (Meyer, 1957, p. 98)

Individuals may continue to hold nonconformist opinions and may even be resolved to press them. But since all horizontal communication is prohibited as "factional activity," individuals and potentially oppositionist local party organizations have no reliable way of ascertaining if an oppositionist point of view is eccentric or widely shared.

And finally, Stalinist ruling groups can even turn the permission to criticize the manner of executing decisions into another mechanism to control and politically homogenize the party's ranks: by using it *themselves* to criticize lower-level organizations, thus diverting attention and hiding their own responsibility in a difficult situation. An alleged failure to implement policies "correctly" can even become a basis for purge—as is stated in the April 1933 Soviet Central Committee resolution on the necessity and justifications of purge (and as was seen recently in the "Paris affair").

Party setbacks thus never indicate defects of the top leadership. Instead the cadres and membership are launched by the ruling group into exercises of mutual and self-criticism. All this reduces the communist ranks ever more into a politics of leadership infallibility. A communist party's external militancy may be awesome, but inside the party orthodox militants are generally a political soft touch—a voluntary docility of the most selfless and dedicated members. The Stalinist reduction of revolutionary militants into external fighters and internal true believers results from the fact that democratic centralism is like a deck of cards completely stacked in favor of leadership. The internal emasculation of the communist rank-and-file, one might even say, is an extreme result of the "incurable incompetence" of the "mass as mass" in any large political organization, as Robert Michels (1962, p. 367) first called it. Stalinism takes to an extreme all elements of Michels's "iron law of oligarchy."

In sum, the misleading democratic centralist distinction between "making" and "implementing" a decision works as the justification of the ban on faction. It convinces the Stalinist optimist that the party has both centralism and democracy, the best of two worlds. Without this distinction— the "moment" of discussion and the "moment" of action—the dogma of "party unity and effectiveness" would probably seem unreasonable even to communists. And ultimately the Stalinist obsession with "effectiveness," centralism in action, ends in a totally paradoxical result: *"unity" and "effectiveness" come to mean the same thing.* To achieve unity is for the party to be effective; to be effective is to achieve unity. The outside world is lost. The problems of reality are all redefined as problems of unity and organization among the communists themselves. This self-absorption is what Neil McInnes referred to, in observing that historically communist parties have demonstrated "an organizational obsession that constitutes as great a barrier to political effectiveness as socialist indiscipline" (McInnes, 1975a, p. 97).

On "Unity": Stalin and Hobbes

The Rousseauist elements in communist political theory and practice have often been emphasized. Alexander Solzhenitsyn, however, suggests that the more important forerunner of Stalinist communism was Hobbes rather than Rousseau:

> the idea of the totalitarian state was first proposed by Hobbes in his *Leviathan* (the head of the state is there said to have dominion not only over the citizens' lives and property, but also over their *conscience*). Rousseau, too, had leanings in this direction when he declared the democratic state to be an "unlimited sovereign" not only over the possessions of its citizens, but over their person as well. (Solzhenitsyn, 1980, p. 802)

Philosophically speaking, surely *Leviathan* rather than *The Social Contract* constitutes the intellectual–political adumbration of Stalinism, in Hobbes's understanding of the two symbolic concepts of monism and pluralism: that is, "unity" and "faction." Through his delineation of the need for absolutist government Hobbes manifested a monumental pessimism about human nature and the conceivable bases for secure and just government.

An absolutist government, he said, was a logical requirement of government as such because no other regime, given the underlying tendency to a "state of nature" of viciously hostile anarchy, could fulfill the fundamental purpose of government: to guarantee security. Since life itself is at all times potentially at stake, only an absolute sovereign can prevent civil society from lapsing into the state of nature.

Hobbes greatly preferred that the "sovereign" be monarchical because this simplified and strengthened the exercise of absolute sovereignty. In *De Cive* Hobbes argued further that absolute sovereignty must be the character of government within all "corporations" in society as well as in the regime as a whole. The distinction between these secondary corporations and the primary corporation—the state—is merely that the state has no superior and the lesser corporations exist by its permission. In Hobbes's philosophical system, the real existence of the separate elements of society is found only in their relation to the sovereign power. And the sovereign's power must be absolute because the logic of political life is only a choice between absolute power and desperate anarchy.

Hobbes contended that individuals must submit their natural liberty to the sovereign's will in order to safeguard the essential thing: existence itself. The danger of disorder is potentially so great, however, that Hobbes concluded, as Solzhenitsyn points out, that not simply monolithic unity, but dominion over conscience, must be in the sovereign's power. Citizens must believe, as well as act, in monolithic unity.

Thus it is not at all surprising that Hobbes rejected the premise of autonomy from the sovereign power, and it is remarkable that he used a concept of faction now so familiar to us in another context:

> if it be the duty of princes to restrain the factions, much more does it concern them to dissolve and dissipate the factions themselves. Now I call a *faction*, a multitude of subjects gathered together either by mutual *contracts* among themselves, or by the power of some one, without his or their authority who bear the supreme rule. A *faction*, therefore, is as it were a city in a city: for as by an union of men in the state of nature a city receives its being, so by a new union of subjects there ariseth a *faction*

Hobbes's conclusion, given the premises we have just seen, is simple and devastating:

Forasmuch therefore as it is true, that the state of cities among themselves is natural and hostile, those princes who permit factions do as much as if they received an enemy within their walls: which is contrary to the subjects' safety, and therefore also against the law of nature. (Hobbes, *De Cive*, XIII–13)

Orthodox communist ideology, clearly, is more profoundly Hobbesian than could possibly be indicated in Solzhenitsyn's remark in passing. The equivalence between the Hobbesian "state of nature" and the Stalinist notion of a permanent "class struggle" whose intensity does not decrease, but rather increases, is intuitively obvious. The definition of faction as well as the justification and consequence of the struggle against faction are practically identical. Indeed, it seems not far-fetched to interpret the regime of high Stalinism as a concrete example of Hobbes's reasoning that truly absolute, totalitarian sovereignty can inhere only in an individual person, the Great Leader or Egocrat. Trotsky, in the very last lines of his biography of Stalin made precisely this interpretation:

L'Etat c'est moi is almost a liberal formula by comparison with the actualities of Stalin's totalitarian regime. Louis XIV identified himself only with the State. The Popes of Rome identified themselves with both the State and Church, but only during the epoch of temporal power. The totalitarian state goes much beyond Caesaro-Papism, for it has encompassed the entire economy of the country as well. Stalin can justly say, unlike the Sun King, *La Société c'est moi*. (Trotsky, 1941, p. 421; cf. also Lefort, 1981, p. 88 ff.)

Following out this line of interpretation, one can say that the regime of *ordinary* Stalinism is a lesser form of Hobbesian polity. Hobbes's system, as many commentators have said, is in principle compatible with *any* regime—not only absolute monarchy—that can assure security: a party dictatorship, for example. And one would expect that in the transition from totalitarian autocracy to a collectively led party dictatorship certain legal forms or elements of "constitutionalism" would appear and solidify, if only because it is materially more difficult for a group to exercise absolute power than for an individual. At minimum a ruling group in such a regime must first come to agreement within itself, thus limiting the *scope* of power if not necessarily diluting its essentially arbitrary nature. It is precisely in this sense that democratic centralism became the constitutional theory of routinized Stalinism: democratic centralism—the ban on faction writ large—turns out to be the constitutional principle of the communist Leviathan.

From this point of view we also understand more clearly the Stalinist conception of "dissent" and the individual "dissident." (Hobbes gave a priority to suppression of "factions" but he also made it a "duty" of princes to restrain the "factious.") First, *every dissident is a potential faction*. Logically, in the Stalinist mentality, it must be considered that a dissident will in fact become one unless he is persuaded to conform or is controlled and isolated. That is to say, logically in the terms of the ideology, the communist order itself is threatened by the mere *existence* of nonconformists. Secondly, non-conformists are thus inevitably portrayed by the state as a threat to the communist state and to society as a whole, the supposedly homogeneous "mature socialist" community. Moreover, since no individual in his right mind should want to return society to a less perfected condition, it makes "sense" in the terms of the ideology to believe, or at least to say, that nonconformists are either criminals ("traitors" or "wreckers" according to the severity of the case) or are mentally deranged. Thus when it is inconvenient to the ruling group to imprison or to "liquidate" dissidents, they are exiled (either externally as in the case of Solzhenitsyn, or internally as in the case of Sakharov) or interned in mental institutions of a special category: "reformism," as the Soviet psychiatric organization has told the world, is an officially recognized type of mental illness in officially so-called "real, existing" socialist society.

It only remains to add that, in order to maintain the tension necessary to the residual ideological vigilance that even ordinary Stalinism requires to survive, orthodox communism *cannot do without* nonconformism; if necessary, it will fabricate the dissident—*un homme de trop* as Claude Lefort (1981) says. In the high Stalinist period the "show trials," with their knowingly false accusations and confessions, provided the classic example of this mechanism, exploiting the totalitarian vocabulary shared by the victims themselves. The accused often confessed willingly to absurd charges, aware that the truth or falsity of the accusations against them was irrelevant to the real issue, which was the affirmation of absolute, totalitarian power (Kriegel, 1972). Such complicit victims, unlike Solzhenitsyn or Sakharov or other contemporary Soviet resisters, no longer possessed the mental concepts necessary to distinguish truth from unity.

It is the premise that politics is lived tendentially always at the extremes, as a struggle for existence itself, which makes Stalinism a

Hobbesian system. And in this sense terrorist Stalinism and routinized Stalinism are fundamentally the same system. "The sense of crisis in Soviet politics has never been allowed to subside," Robert Daniels wrote in 1962 (p. 97). This is surely no longer true, and the decline of the "combat" and "campaign" mentalities in Soviet political life constitutes a significant difference between high Stalinism and routinized Stalinism. But fundamentally the system is unchanged. In Hobbesian terms one could say that the difference between them is in the *degree* of liberty subjects must cede to the absolute power in order to obtain security; this is not a difference in quality.

Already in 1882 Karl Kautsky, strongly affected by a superficial understanding of Darwinism and evolutionary biology, and in particular by the apparent connection between capitalism and the "survival of the fittest" struggle in nature, had deduced that socialism meant supercession of the social Darwinist state of nature. "The cessation of the struggle for existence," Kautsky wrote, "this is precisely socialism" (see Salvadori, 1979, p. 24). Stalin, in his paradoxical pronouncement that class struggle would become *more* rather than less violent as Soviet socialist development progressed, quite cold-bloodedly rejected a policy of diluting either the struggle for existence that Soviet politics had become, or the Hobbesian mode of assumption which was both cause and result. Today, on the contrary, the doctrines of "peaceful coexistence for a long period" and "peaceful transition to socialism" prevail among communist parties subservient to the Soviet lead. But the ultimate stake, existence itself, has not yet been officially abandoned. Yet even if Communist leaders still see international politics as a struggle for existence itself, they must be less and less certain that this is in their own interest.

The real goal of orthodox communism as a twentieth-century revolutionary principle, in sum, has been not equality, but rather the achievement of a particular organization of polity. The "unity" which Stalinism embodied and made into a principle of imperialism manifested a root desire—its origin can only be a matter of speculation[16]—to remake world domestic politics in the image of organization inside the communist party.

The Political Culture of Absurd Truths

Marx's *18th Brumaire* begins with the famous rhetorical flourish: "Hegel remarks somewhere that all facts and personages of great importance in world history occur, as it were, twice. He forgot to add: the first time as tragedy, the second as farce." High Stalinism is the tragic act of communism, and ordinary Stalinism the farce. The third act, when it finally opens, will be that of political modernity, the act of *Aufhebung*. Of the tragedy, Solzhenitsyn is the historian of its violence, Koestler, the dramatist of its lies, and Stalin himself the theoretician of its self-serving rationalizations. Of the farce we already have, as the humorist would put it, histories and theoretical fragments galore. But the truest studies of contemporary ordinary Stalinism, it seems to me, are the satires and the jokes. The last element of the political theory of ordinary Stalinism is thus a homage to studies on the ridiculously incongruous. As Milan Kundera says in another context: "That's the paradox. When . . . culture is reduced to politics [as in a communist country], interpretation [of it] is concentrated completely on the political, and in the end no one understands politics because purely political thought can never comprehend political reality" (Kundera, 1984, p. 46).

One of the best books on the political development of high Stalinism was published in 1954, just a year after the Egocrat's death on 5 March 1953. It begins by quoting "Georgii Maksimilionovich Malenkov, Chairman of the Council of Ministers, on August 8, 1953": "Never before," said Malenkov, "has the unity of Soviet society been so monolithic . . . as at the present time." Barrington Moore remarks archly of this encomium that, "Only a few weeks earlier the newspapers had briefly informed the Soviet public that Malenkov had brought about the arrest of Beriya" (Moore, 1954, p. 1).

A more recent history and commentary on major documents of the international communist movement (Leonhard, 1974, p. 172) stresses the absurdity of Khrushchev's 1961 CPSU New Soviet Party Program, which ended with the affirmation that the Soviet Union would enter the phase of communism by 1980: "The Party solemnly proclaims: the present generation of Soviet people shall live in Communism!" What did this mean? The answer was necessarily scientific in approach, and technical in character: to establish the "material and technical foundations" of communism in the decade 1961–70 the Soviet Union would overtake the USA in per capita production; all working people would have "good" living standards and "comfortable" homes; collective and state farms would be "transformed into highly productive enterprises with high incomes"; heavy physical work would disappear and the USSR would have the shortest working-day in the world. The decade

1970–80 would be marked by an abundance of material and cultural goods, which would end in the transition to the rule of distribution according to need. With the creation of one universal people's property, "the Communist society will have been established in its principal features."

Konstantin Chernenko, wanly succeeding Yuri Andropov at the top of the Soviet hierarchy in 1984, emphasized that Leonid Brezhnev's announcement at the 1981 Party Congress of a new party program to supplant the 1961 program was one promise which would be kept. The new program is to be approved at the Twenty-seventh Party Congress in 1986. It must be realistic, abandoning the 1961 program's simplistic ideas. This built on Brezhnev's lead: Brezhnev had said in 1981 that it was "impossible and inappropriate to predict particulars" in the struggle to reach the lofty perspectives of socialism and communism. Chernenko added in 1984 that although socialism is bound to triumph over a "historically doomed" capitalist mode of production, capitalism still has "considerable and far from exhausted reserves of development." What realism!

A few weeks earlier Chernenko had made an important speech to the Central Committee, to call for greater activity and vigor in the soviets. He said that the 2·3 million members of the soviets across the USSR made insufficient use of their potentialities: "Generally speaking, there is a certain contradiction, a discrepancy between the greatest potentialities of the soviets and the way in which they are used in practice." Chernenko noted that only one in thirty soviet members bothered to use his official right to ask for information from various organizations. He said that the "main task" of the party was to guide the soviets, "to insure that their boundless powers, formalized in the Constitution, manifest themselves constantly and everywhere both in the content and in the style of their work."[17] What irony!

In 1980 Alexander Zinoviev's book *The Radiant Future* appeared in English translation. It begins with a declaration written by Zinoviev in Moscow in 1976, that is, before his outlook was affected by exile in Western Europe:

> Once I happened to overhear a conversation between Moscow intellectuals. One was a famous sociologist who had devoted titanic efforts to the development of Soviet sociology for the benefit of the party, the state and the people. Yet despite that, his group had been completely destroyed in the name of that same party, that same state and that same people. And he was

left with nothing to do, grateful merely that they kept on paying him. The other was a famous painter who had put no less effort than the former into the task of raising the Soviet visual arts to a world-class level, but who in the course of twenty odd years had not been allowed to stage even a small one-man show. I set down their conversation in full.

"What a bloody awful life it is!"

"Oh, f— it all!"

Zinoviev commented hopefully: "There can be no more definitive comment on the life we lead. And yet in that life we sometimes see some vague hints at something different. And those hints merit at least a moment's consideration." That is still the right problem: in a political culture built upon absurd truths can there be any political foundation for development "on the basis of Communism itself"?

PART TWO

Siege and Choice: Communist Development and Decay in Western Europe

4

Introduction to the Case Studies

The purpose of the following two case studies is to demonstrate that communist political development in West European countries can be read as an internal struggle waged essentially over the reform of democratic centralism, in its large rather than narrow meaning. The root issues, in other words, are those we have discovered in studying the development of ordinary Stalinism as the archetype of communist orthodoxy. (1) *Monolithism as the political ideal*, in which conception an absolutist prohibition of faction is both cause and effect, producing an intrinsic tendency toward totalitarian control from above. (Whether or not this tendency is actually realized, or rather to what extent it has been realized in any particular communist party, constitutes a problem of historiography rather than theory.) (2) Communism's ideological and historical goal of *transforming all politics into internal politics*. This issue raises all the questions of a West European communist party's relations with other institutions—its own "flanking" organizations (especially trade unions), other parties (especially the question of "unity" with socialist parties), and the institutions of government. (3) The consequent *impulsion* in West European communist parties historically (as in communist parties wherever they remain orthodox) *to be imperialistic, to extend communist internal politics to society as a whole, or to risk its own transformation*. In short, in contemporary West European communist parties the internal struggle over democratic centralism is the struggle over the meaning of communism as such.

In the politics of Italian and French communism the basic importance of democratic centralism to communist identity has suffused the past decade, as was demonstrated in the swelling and breaking of the Eurocommunist phenomenon. (The same is true for Spanish and Portuguese communism: cf. Mujal-Leon, 1983; Graham and Wheeler, 1983.) Broadly speaking, there have been two major

95

external pressures working at cross-purposes on democratic centralism. On the one hand, the discredit of international communism, which incites the West European communist movements to rely for legitimacy and appeal on the domestic claim of a superior form of organization. On the other hand, the strengths of West European societies, which pressure communist parties either to reform or to wither and decline. The Portuguese, Greek (exterior) and Cypriot Communist parties seem still able to stalemate the force of circumstance, a pyrrhic achievement which demonstrates the ecological coziness of traditional political culture, even for a Leninist-Stalinist warhorse.

To put the matter another way, the West European communist parties, it seems to me, are increasingly fated to suffer the effects of "Kirchheimer's rule," which means they will embody less and less the orthodox rules of democratic centralism, and more and more Michels's less devastating "iron law of oligarchy." As history (rather than theory) would have it, the results thus far are profoundly mixed, to which the following studies of "uneven development" in Italian and French communism testify. Although many factors interact, the nature of (1) the force of circumstance at work, and (2) differences in the quality of leadership, seem to stand out.

By way of preface it is useful to reexamine a passage from Henry Kissinger's influential June 1977 speech on Eurocommunism, a report to a high-level international policy forum. The speech, one should keep in mind, was given in the context of communist claims for governmental roles in Italy, France, and Spain, all at once, as well as the Portuguese party's failed Leninist strategy in 1974–5 and the brutal communist military victories in Vietnam, Laos, and Cambodia. Speaking of Eurocommunist parties, Kissinger said that:

Whether or not they are independent of Moscow, Communists represent a philosophy which by its nature and their own testimony stands outside the "bourgeois" framework of western constitutional history ... By the very nature of their beliefs, Communists will be driven to bring about institutional changes that would make their ascendance permanent ... We cannot know, with certainty, whether a fundamental change has occurred in these parties' goals and tactics. But their internal organization and management speak against such a view ... "Democratic centralism" ... is a doctrine of iron discipline, not a principle of free and open dialogue ... [The] key issue is not how 'independent' the European Communists would be [in government], but how Communist. (Kissinger, 1978, pp. 186–9)

Whether or not one agreed with Kissinger's policies, his formulation went to the heart of a particular analytical problem. Was not "democratic centralism"—still espoused by all the Eurocommunist parties even if they had rejected the "dictatorship of the proletariat" and "proletarian internationalism"—the sign of orthodox communism's identity and, therefore, its intrinsic intention? And was not an orthodox communist party, even if independent from Moscow, still a threat to free politics? These were pertinent questions, yet in Kissinger's apparently clear warning there lay a serious ambiguity: can a communist party's independence, its autonomy from Soviet control, be separated from its political identity and purpose in this manner? What is the relation between "proletarian internationalism" and "democratic centralism"? Is the retention of either a sign of second thoughts about having relinquished the "dictatorship of the proletariat"? Did the Eurocommunists still aim ultimately at a monopoly of political power?

Let us place against Kissinger's formulation of the issue the following more or less contemporaneous judgment of another experienced observer of West European and international communism:

The sympathy one feels for parties that combat the unitary views of Moscow and seek to consolidate independent national Communist policies should not blind one to the fact that such efforts are incoherent. To maintain a Leninist machine but to cut it off from the mystique of world communism and from the reality of Soviet [or Chinese] power is a contradictory undertaking that must fail. In warning [Eurocommunist] parties of this fact, Moscow [is] only being reasonable. The hallmark of a Communist party—the element that distinguishes it from Socialist parties of the Second International— is "proletarian internationalism," which means imbrication in a world movement with a national power base. Cut off from that movement and that stronghold, a Leninist party either backslides to social democracy or else degenerates into factionalism (if it is a non-ruling party) or warring cliques (if it is in power). (McInnes, 1975b, p. 45)

Neil McInnes in this passage set out what he aptly called "the characteristic heresy of west European communism" (McInnes, 1976, p. 28), that is, the conviction that a communist party could maintain the historical anti-capitalist and socialist revolutionary identity locked up in democratic centralism's organizational armor, while making concessions about, or even abandoning outright, the rest of orthodox communism's ideological and political baggage. Which has proven more correct: Kissinger's warning about the implication of democratic centralism, or McInnes's emphasis on the centrality of proletarian internationalism? There are elements of validity in both views, but as Chapter 3 demonstrated, the problem itself needs to be formulated differently.

From the point of view of contemporary political development the basic issue, as we shall see, is what orientation toward the future the nonruling communist parties will have. It has become anachronistic, for example, even to speak of them as "nonruling" parties—as if to imply that they will one day "rule," or necessarily will try to seize power. Yet while this is increasingly clear to the West European communists as well as to their adversaries, the question of "what is to be done?" remains to be given a new answer. During the years of Stalin, Thorez, and Togliatti the goal of communism, at least to its militants, seemed a "radiant future." One French Communist ode to Maurice Thorez, composed during his Soviet convalescence from a near-fatal stroke in the early 1950s, said this:

> Following your example, we have learned to love the Soviet Union, to love Stalin, and from that love, to love the future as it appears in its most radiant guise. (Quoted in Johnson, 1981, p. 44)

Today even the orthodox West European communists have become profoundly ambivalent in their sentiments about the Soviet Union and about Stalin, when the latter is not simply hated, like a treasonous lover. In such a situation local communist leaderships cannot escape the responsibility to manufacture some new hope, some new program which is also some new love for the future. In the circumstances this can hardly be a new messianic myth, and so much the better. But at the same time it must be something worth struggling for because, given the character of communism's appeal, remove the opportunity for moral struggle and the sources of enthusiasm for it run dry. What remains can only be the shell of a Michelsian bureaucracy.

5

The Reform of Italian Communism

Introduction

In 1984 there is a political quaintness in saying the Italian Communist Party neither wants nor is capable of making a revolution. Its declarations concerning a *terza via*, a "third way" society different from Soviet communism and Western capitalism alike, in their vagueness lead one to wonder whether, for Italian Communists, socialism is any longer a tangible goal, a set of changes which would transform Italian society for the better.[1] In Italy the very idea of socialism as an inspirational image seems to have withered. At the PCI's most recent Sixteenth Party Congress in March 1983 its reserved yet popular leader Enrico Berlinguer (whose unexpected death in June 1984 at the age of 62 provoked an equally unexpected outpouring of genuine national grief) posed the question: "Does the objective of socialism still make sense?" His answer—contrary to the orthodox communist litanies still intoned elsewhere—consisted of several involved paragraphs of explanation which ended in a call for "less ambitious, more empirical" policies. The great drama at this Congress, however, was Berlinguer's judgment of the final failure of Soviet socialism. "The exhaustion of the propulsive thrust of the Soviet model," as he called it, was a historic declaration by the party; yet it had been debated and accepted, "by vast majorities almost everywhere," throughout the PCI's organizations (*Italian Communists*, no. 1, 1983, p. 19). As journalists remarked, the Eurocommunist Berlinguer seemed almost embarrassed to speak positively of a socialist program. In replying to him later, Armando Cossutta, the only remaining openly Sovietophile leader, gave tough criticism of the new party program, which, he alleged, rested on "immature or

99

vague" conceptions. Cossutta stressed the basic danger to communist belief when party members are left to "define communist identity essentially in the negative" (*L'Unità*, 6 March 1983). The Congress, despite last-ditch resistance from a rump Sovietophile group, none the less voted to close an epoch: The judgment that "the propulsive force of the Soviet model is now spent" (*L'Unità*, 3 March 1983) was a leitmotif under whose sign Italian communism's future must be interpreted. Berlinguer's successor as General Secretary, Alessandro Natta, was chosen quickly in June 1984 to continue the policies which had led to this epochal judgment about communism's political development.

From the vantage point of the 1980s the ambiguous history of Italian communism in the 1960s and 1970s is now recognizable unmistakably as a story of reform from above. This secularization and liberalization of the Italian Communist movement has been a highly self-conscious and elaborated policy with four goals: (1) to achieve legitimacy in Italian political life, thus moving the PCI off an historical dead-end strategy by making it an acceptable ally and, ultimately, government partner; (2) to justify disengaging Italian communism from the Soviet-controlled international communist movement, thus enracinating the PCI in Italy and in West Europe, and abandoning the priority formerly given to relationships with other communist parties; (3) to reeducate the party bureaucracy and rank-and-file to accept the Italian Republic, and liberal parliamentary democracy generally speaking, as intrinsically desirable and permanent rather than temporary and instrumental, thus eliminating the fear that the Italian Communists want to impose an alien regime on Italian society; and (4) to preserve internal equilibria inside the party during this period of deep change, in order to avoid a party split and to maintain, in so far as is consonant with the reform itself, party unity, militancy, and popular support.

Palmiro Togliatti, Italian communism's main leader during the last Stalin decade and the ten years following his death to 1964, at the end of World War II coined the term *partito nuovo*. The idea of a "new party" in Italy, while recalling Lenin's "party of a new type" cliché, came to mean something different: a communist opposition mass party, with new ideas and organizational modes appropriate to the struggle for socialism in the very particular Italian conditions. During the 1950s and 1960s Italian communism reached a measure of independence in foreign policy, made certain inroads into the parliamentary process, and developed within itself a measure of organizational complexity and "uneven development" which reproduced Italian social structure and economic geography rather precisely (cf. Blackmer, 1968; Tarrow, 1967; Blackmer and Tarrow, 1975). Togliatti summed this up by saying that the PCI was sort of a political "giraffe." The 1970s term Eurocommunism was less metaphorical and also meant more in the way of reform: an Italian Communist "giraffe" might simply have evolved a characteristic peculiarity for the purpose of achieving an unchanged function; a Eurocommunist party was, in principle, something "new," almost a new identity. In the 1980s Giorgio Napolitano, a front-rank Italian Communist, and by common agreement one of Italy's most intelligent and subtle political leaders, calls the PCI a "unicorn" (cf. Belligni, 1983). This newest metaphor is not quite apt either— because Napolitano wants to imply that the "new" Italian Communist Party is not some mythical beast, but however difficult for adversaries to believe a truly liberalized communist party.

Whatever the failures of metaphor, in the early 1980s the PCI seems in fact the first incontrovertible instance of a genuinely reformed communist party of major size and influence which has not split or lost its popular following in the process of political development. The PCI continues to carry the name "communist" party, although its leaders have seriously discussed whether to change the label. Many experienced observers of Italian and international communist politics, such as the eminent historian Norberto Bobbio, say the PCI is already a "socialist" party. The words do matter, since they organize our perceptions. But only politics itself will provide the new name.

The secularization and reform from above of Italian communism, whatever the ultimate result will be called, has in other words been a policy which has not dared speak its name, or at least not too loudly or too aggressively, for the political reasons already stated above. The PCI's substantial decommunization has thus occurred as a sort of protracted tacit leadership "conspiracy" to transform the political culture of the hierarchy and the mass membership, a reform from above which has evoked a reawakening of the political instinct, and a toning down of orthodox bureaucratic habits.

The leadership has acted with consistency over a period of twenty to thirty years, as most studies demonstrate. Should the PCI leaders have acted radically, that is, have launched a classic communist revolution from above, this would have created a double danger: that of destabilizing not only the party, but also Italian politics as a whole. And a sudden, radical turn, without preparation and with no possibility to evaluate the consequences adequately is precisely the Leninist or Stalinist behavior the PCI's leaders have sought to expunge from the party's mode of operation. Italian politics moves in a process of infinitely slow mutual adjustments which is either faintly praised as the best of a bad situation or condemned as a system of mutual veto powers and governmental immobility, rendered inevitable by an irresponsible and corrupt *sotto governo* network of clans and factions. Whichever view one accepts, the incrementalism and self-conscious dedramatization at almost every point in Italian communism's ongoing secularization must be understood as a conscious intention of the leadership to give assurances: to demonstrate the genuineness of the avowed motives of its policy by refusing a Stalinist method of de-Stalinization. The Italian Communist Party's generally constructive role over the past several years—in Italian and European parliamentary affairs, in trade union life, and above all, in the agonizing struggle of the Italian state during the 1970s against both "red" and "black" terrorism—is, all things considered, very strong evidence that the leaders have permanently invested the party's future in the Italian parliamentary republic. Today, in other words, the goal of Italian communism is in no way to destroy or to revolutionize all established institutions. Italian Communist policy no longer makes confident or arrogant claims about creating "irreversible" changes in society and politics, and its strategy and ideology, in spite of continued references to Antonio Gramsci's theory of winning "hegemony," are now far from aimed at a monopoly of power in some hazily foreseen "higher stage" of development.

Altogether in the 1970s the Italian Communists brought to fruition a process of self-examination without equal among the West European communist movements (Hassner, 1980). Thus not for nothing was the Italian Communist "new look" a growth industry, occupying university researchers, journalists, foreign policymakers and other communist parties alike. The Bettino Craxi government of 1983 has for the moment toned down the daily scrutiny of Italian communism's behavior and declarations. Craxi, the first socialist to head an Italian government since the advent of fascism in 1923, is not simply seen as a striking innovation from the point of view of the political "right"; he also manifests the Italian Socialist Party's (PSI) hope to turn the tables historically on the Italian Communists as the French and Spanish Socialists have done recently on their respective *frères-ennemis*. And whereas in the French case the Socialist Party's strength had to be built up in *alliance* with "its" Communist Party, in the Italian as in the Spanish case, the

Socialists place a premium on avoiding national-level entanglements. Thus the present political situation, despite the PCI's continued internal reform and continued external popularity, is dangerous for the Communists: today any comparisons between Italian communism and fabulous unlikely beasts are a throwback. After the Sixteenth Party Congress, *The Economist* rightly reported (12 March 1983, p. 29): the PCI "once the bright young thing of Italian politics, has bags under its eyes."

Yet the fact remains today that of all the West European communist parties only the Italian Communist Party in 1984 still seems likely to have a serious political future. And here the "giraffe" and "unicorn" images are helpful to communicate what is after all one of the rarest of phenomena in contemporary politics: genuine decommunization.

Eurocommunism and Universal Reconciliation: The PCI's "Golden Dream"

In order to place the Italian Communist reform of democratic centralism in its fuller context we, first, must sketch other aspects of what Pierre Hassner has vividly termed "Eurocommunism and universal reconciliation . . . the PCI's golden dream of 1975–9" (see Hassner, 1980).

The Soviet-led Warsaw Pact invasion of Czechoslovakia in August 1968 had a tremendous negative and demoralizing effect in the Italian Communist Party. The Italian Communists, with few exceptions, had been extremely sympathetic to Alexander Dubcek's policy and to the general notion of "communism with a human face" as the reformed Czech Communist Party program was called. The PCI's leaders, it is true, had accepted and endorsed the Soviet action to put down rebellion in Hungary in 1956: despite a tough debate within the ruling group, it was still at this time basically a Stalinist crowd. However, the PCI condemned outright the "Prague Spring's" destruction and, unlike other initially opposed communist parties (such as the French) never muted this criticism thereafter. The leadership at that time vowed that "never again" would Soviet military imperialism be condoned, and after the Jaruzelski coup against Solidarity in December 1981 the Italian Communists moved quickly to what was called *lo strappo*: it is in this context that the Sixteenth Party Congress's resolution separating the PCI from even the Russian Revolution must be understood.

103

Gradually during the 1970s the PCI's leaders disengaged the party from its attachment to the Soviet Union and to the orthodox international communist movement, shrinking but still Soviet-dominated. A double policy was developed: on the one hand, insisting on respect for autonomy and mutual tolerance in relations among communist parties (as party documents put it, meaning a repudiation of orthodox "proletarian internationalism"); and on the other hand, reaching out for contacts and cooperation with Italian and West European political forces. In particular, this meant, in Italy, courting the Socialist and, above all, the Christian Democratic parties in search of the famous "historic compromise" coalition of Italy's three main political tendencies, which would bring the PCI into the national government. At the European level this meant seeking out new partners, especially the German SPD of Brandt and Schmidt, and François Mitterrand's revivified French Socialist Party, whose endorsements could help the PCI to gain legitimacy in Italy as well as to build a political role at the European level, in the European Community institutions and generally in European-wide political negotiations (Serfaty and Gray, 1980; Sassoon, 1981).

Already in the first years of the decade neither the Soviet link nor relations with other communist parties, generally speaking, any longer *dominated* the PCI's priorities, although at this point they seemed still equal in importance with concerns of national strategy and party organizational interests (Blackmer, 1975). As Donald Blackmer pointed out incisively, however, this relative balance of concerns could endure only so long as the goals were not mutually contradictory. Only a few years later the PCI's goal of legitimacy had clearly assumed priority over good behavior as a Soviet fraternal party, as was vividly demonstrated in the tense and genuinely antagonistic two-year negotiation to stage the International Communist Party Conference finally held in East Berlin in June 1976 (cf. Tökés, 1978; Hassner, 1976; Carrillo, 1978). At this time the so-called "autonomist" parties (the Yugoslav, Romanian, Italian, Spanish, and later, the French) bridged the European divide through their common desire to reject Soviet control, and the term "Eurocommunism" emerged as the label for those parties which sought not simply autonomy, but also internal reform (the Japanese party thus was added and the Romanian party dropped from the above list).

Within Italy the PCI pushed hard in these years for the "historic compromise," first announced by Berlinguer in articles analyzing the Allende government's destruction in Chile in 1973: Berlinguer's conclusion was that, given the goal of making substantial changes in society, "51 percent" was not an adequate basis for power in a government including the Italian Communists. (However, in rejecting a strictly "leftist" alliance the implicit political problem in the "historic compromise" was evident: how much innovation would be possible in a coalition government which included the powerful, corrupt, and internally highly factionalized Christian Democracy? Also a "historic compromise" government could weaken Italian institutions further, by missing the opportunity to establish a definite "alternation" in government and thus some principle of genuine electoral representativeness and competitiveness, Pasquino, 1982.)

The "historic compromise" strategy was a formula for an inter-party coalition, but in addition it implied some general reconciliation of Italy's three major political–ideological subcultures: Christian Democracy, and a lay socialism and communism. In such an alliance, dangerous to the Communist pretension to uniqueness, the PCI would want its own mass base as strong as possible. Thus a second element, of both defense and offense, was necessary; a strategy of "social alliances." One aspect of this was grassroots, that is, a multiplication of Italian Communist local and functional (for example, cooperative and mutualist) organizations, and their strengthened involvement with other groups. The other aspect, of decisive importance, was the trade union movement. Here a sort of "historic compromise" was indeed reached, a "confederation of federations" within Italian trade unionism among the communist-oriented CGIL (with its large Socialist minority), the Christian Democratic CISL, and the Socialist-Republican-Independent UIL. The Italian trade union movement, like the French and other Latin European syndicalisms, has been divided politically more or less along party lines, a division whose roots are historical, to be sure, but whose postwar persistence (as opposed to some form of reunification) owed more to communism specifically, as both cause and effect, than to some inexpungeable Italian inclination to political fragmentation.

In the 1970s a considerable electoral gain for the PCI, from about 27 percent to over one-third of the vote, weakened adversaries' claims that the PCI was illegitimate as a government partner in the eyes of public opinion (Sani, 1979a). Weak governing coalitions, faced with insistent PCI demands for participation, finally resulted in the Communists being given half a loaf by the Christian Democrats and Socialists: during 1977–9 they were accepted within a

105

"national solidarity" parliamentary majority, while still held outside the government itself. It was evidently a form of testing, to which the PCI responded well. The PCI in this period endorsed the government's "austerity" policies (unlike the French Communists *vis-à-vis* the Barre government), and criticized the government's failure to keep its promises. The PCI also took uncompromising and, in fact, rather exemplary positions in the desperate struggle against Red Brigades' terrorism (in particular, during the devastating kidnapping and execution of Aldo Moro). These stands substantially eliminated allegations that red terrorism was somehow linked to the PCI, although many argued that left-wing violence could not help but have roots, historically speaking, in the Italian Communist political culture and in left-wing defections from it.

In this same period the PCI made a substantial political investment in the institutions of the European Community (Sassoon, 1977; Amendola, 1979; Sweeney, 1984). Its European parliamentary participation was widely praised and despite a setback in the first direct elections to the European Parliament in 1979, the PCI sent an impressive delegation to Brussels and Strasbourg (some party leaders even thought the PCI delegation was excessively prestigious and made the party seem overanxious to please).[2] The PCI also made an explicit commitment not to challenge Italy's membership in NATO, although adversaries observed that the PCI voted against or criticized most NATO force improvement decisions, especially the December 1979 "two-track" decision to pursue arms control talks while modernizing NATO's intermediate-range nuclear forces. In any case, various statements indicated that the PCI's leaders were satisfied to be on the Western side of the NATO-Warsaw Pact frontier. Finally, the PCI's foreign policy tried to profit from disengagement from the Soviet Union in order to seek a role of mediator in East–West détente. This was a foreign policy of diplomacy rather than power, which seemed to fit well with the established orientation of Italian foreign policy generally (the Craxi government's stronger role in NATO affairs recently is a departure on this score). The PCI leaders, because of the combination of their experience and commitments, thought they had a potentially unique role to play in mediating between East and West as well as between right and left in the European Community.

In sum, the PCI's "golden dream," as Hassner says, was "universal reconciliation": an "historic compromise" in Italy and in Western Europe as well as, ultimately, between East and West, ending the twentieth-century religious war between liberalism and communism through a general secularization of world politics. As Hassner astutely pointed out, the main weakness in this noble project was the lack of an alternative for the PCI itself in the all-too-likely event this grand mediating role failed to materialize.

As we know, the expected occurred, and in mid-1984 the Italian Communist Party was in a lonely democratic opposition to all the other "democratic arc" parties which are part of Craxi's government or support it in Parliament. (This excludes the MSI, which is nearly neo-fascist, and the maverick radical party, the PR.) The PCI's failure over a decade to force its entry into the government, despite optimistic and, without doubt, earnest concessions and sacrifices at the altar of compromise and solidarity, has, not unexpectedly, been accompanied by an organizational decline. The membership is down by over 200,000 from the 1978 high point of 1·8 million or so, and down 40,000 in 1982 alone. Its electorate, after a high water mark of over one-third of the vote at the end of the 1970s fell to 30 per-cent, although it was back to over one-third in the 1984 European Parliament voting. The union membership, cooperatives, and party press, which are other usual indicators of Communist organi-zational strength and influence, likewise show an erosion of strength, all of this due in some considerable part to the strategy's failure to produce and to the demobilization which is a natural result, magnified by the political hardships of Italy's economic problems and the Craxi government's relative success in producing results.

Important as these facts are concerning the play of Italian politics, two other facts strike the observer more forcefully with respect to the problem of Italian Communist political development. First, for a Communist party leadership even to conceive such an ecumenical and mediating policy as reconciliation is in itself to emerge from an orthodox mentality. Secondly, the PCI leadership's seriousness of purpose, whatever part the leaders thought actually was achiev-able, can be judged by its persistence in Italianization, Europeani-zation, and Westernization in the past few years despite the break-down of both East–West détente, the West European basis of Eurocommunism, and its national strategy. During the 1970s the main features of Italian Communist policy became the primacy of domestic considerations over international communist affairs and a concomitant foreign policy and diplomatic role, while attempting to avoid an open split with the Soviet Union. In the early 1980s the break with the Soviet Union—historic, cultural, and institutional—was largely made final in the PCI's reaction to Eastern bloc policy in the struggle with Solidarity over the desirable, or at least permissible, limits of communist political development.[3] Domestically the Italian Communists shifted first from the near-complete ecumenism of the "historic compromise" proposal to the less promiscuous leftist "democratic alternative" formula, whose main characteristic, as opposed to the former, would be to build a government on a Communist–Socialist axis, excluding the Christian Democrats. (The Craxi government, by its mere existence, for now leaves the PCI without any credible governmental alliance strategy.) Yet while the PCI hammers home its line that sending the DC into opposition and dismantling its clientelistic network is "the moral question" of contemporary Italian politics, and while its opposition to Craxi's austerity policies recently included a tough, two-week filibuster in the Assembly, this is no return to some orthodox sectarianism. The paradox of the PCI's present situation is that its very electoral strength is still an excessive threat to its natural alliance partner, the PSI (Tamburrano, 1978). And in any case, the Craxi "experiment," which includes the possibility of building a stronger Socialist Party which could at some future date deal with the PCI, must run its course. At bottom, the present PCI strategy can be only *pazienza*: all the surprises of Italian politics are not yet played out.

Ideology and Secularism

Gramsci
The Italian Communist attitude toward democratic centralism as a principle of communist praxis and identity has usually been enunciated under the sign of Gramsci's authority. In an often-quoted line from *The Modern Prince* (1957, p. 179) Gramsci wrote that "Democratic centralism provides an elastic formula, which lends itself to many embodiments; it lives to the extent which it is continuously interpreted and adapted to necessity." This could, of course, mean almost anything: it might be a restatement of prerevolutionary Leninist ideas, or it might be a Trotskyite critique of Stalinism (indeed Gramsci's writings were often Italianized or West Europeanized interpretations of whatever vague understandings existed of Soviet practice in the 1920s). Such a worthy sentiment could even exculpate the most orthodox parties, always engaged in that harmless, minor tinkering with the organization long recognized as an efficient way to occupy militant energies and to divert attention from real problems.

It is none the less true, however, that Gramsci here, as generally in his theory, insisted on the importance of adapting general ideas of Bolshevism and communism to local conditions: "This continuous effort to separate the 'international' and 'unitary' element from the national and local reality is in fact concrete political action, the only activity which produces historical progress." But he also emphasized that a unifying conception of "centralism" was necessary in the international communist movement, without "which we end up with no unity ... but a 'sack of potatoes'," (a reference to Marx's famous metaphor of the nineteenth-century European peasantry). Gramsci warned further against letting centralism become bureaucratic, which occurs, he said, "because of a lack of initiative and responsibility from below." This bureaucratic centralism he opposed to "organic" or "democratic centralism," by which he meant a practical and experimental view of strategy, tactics, and procedures, in contrast to a "rationalistic, deductive and abstractive process ... peculiar to pure intellectuals (or pure asses)" (ibid., p. 178). Thus Gramsci arrived at a definition which would have pleased Lenin, and worried Stalin, greatly:

> democratic centralism ... is "centralism" in movement, so to speak, that is a continuous adjustment of the organization to the real movement, a tempering of the thrusts from below with the command from above, a continuous intrusion of elements which emerge from the depths of the masses into the solid frame of the apparatus of rule, which assures continuity and ... regular accumulations of experiences. (Gramsci, 1957, p. 178)

This decisively action-oriented and grassroots-oriented view is quite unconcerned with formal rules, let alone such a rule as a permanent, absolute ban on factions in the party. To give priority to a discourse on rules violated Gramsci's understanding of how "organic," healthy politics work. (Not for nothing was he himself nearly excluded from the Italian Communist Party for nonconformism before the fascists imprisoned him in 1926.) One supposes that Gramsci, like Lenin, thought of democratic centralism basically as a convenient name for the kind of freewheeling, comradely politics he already had in mind: Gramsci's party politics, like those of Lenin, could be summarized as hard debate, "correct synthesis," and "unity in action." Both, because their political views always remained steeped in revolutionary rather than in governmental political culture, underestimated or perhaps simply neglected the needs of large organizations for procedures and institutions, even—or rather especially—democratic political organizations.

A final interesting point in Gramsci's view is that his concern about bureaucratic centralism was not, like Trotsky's, anti-*Stalinist*, but rather anti-*liberal*, in a seemingly provincial Italian usage which is the defect of his otherwise virtuous emphasis on the importance of local conditions. As examples of "bureaucratic" centralism he cites Piedmontese supremacy in the first decades of Italian unity and also, curiously, the League of Nations; whereas his examples of "organic" centralism are the French Revolution and, curiously again, the Third Republic (ibid., pp. 177–9). Gramsci, on the basis of such judgments, generalized from the weak Latin European liberal tendencies as to the danger bureaucracy poses to liberal politics:

> The essential importance of the division of powers for political and economic liberalism: the whole liberal ideology, with its strengths and weaknesses, can be summed up in the division of power, and the source of liberalism's weakness becomes apparent: it is the bureaucracy, i.e., the crystallization of the leading personnel, which exercises coercive power and which at a certain point becomes a caste. (ibid., p. 186)

As a generalization about liberalism this postulate is more in error than enlightening. However, with reference to Italy one can see in this view an intellectual root of the Italian Communists' traditional concern with continuing the unification and centralization of the Italian state (meaning first of all to integrate the *Mezzogiorno* effectively), and perhaps also of their Italian, rather than orthodox, communist reasons for wanting to prohibit factions. Divided power for Gramscian communists is historically liberal and bourgeois; and one of Italy's weaknesses as a modern state has been the weakness of its bourgeoisie. In this sense "unity" in Italian Communist political culture is a modernizing and patriotic theme as well as the basis of a communist party's "unity and effectiveness."

A Secularized Dogma
Today, however, Italian Communist leaders rarely resort to essentialist contrasts between so-called "bourgeois" and "proletarian" politics to justify preventing the crystallization of internal party factions. The main argument against the deep factionalism in all the other Italian parties is, to be sure, that factions are a main source of

political corruption and clientelism, now the major distinguishing mark of Italian Christian Democracy's four-decades-old *sistema di potere* and *trasformismo* policies of rule (cf. Di Palma, 1977; Zuckerman, 1979). Factionalism in other parties, the PCI leaders say, is the cause of their degeneration as political parties. And because this corrupts the function as a whole, factionalism is the cause of the republican system's general corruption in Italy.[4]

Everyone in Italian politics, including the Christian Democratic Party's leaders, is willing to say that factionalism is excessive and corruption is the result. Although those who benefit the most have made certain not to harm their own interests by timely reforms. Against this government inaction (though Craxi has successfully muted the fragmentation in his own party) the Communists have tried with some success to become the "party with clean hands." In the past few years they have sought to counter the remaining ideological prejudices against them—above all the Soviet connection, the so-called "K factor" in Italian politics (Ronchey, 1982)—by raising "the moral question" against the DC, and therein vaunting the positive aspects of democratic centralism. The PCI's claim to be the natural replacement for the DC as the focus of an alternative government coalition is thus the implicit meaning of Giorgio Napolitano's typically oblique and understated declaration:

> The degenerative phenomena found in the relations between ... certain parties and the state as prescribed in the Constitution, as well as in these parties' general behavior, are linked tightly to the proliferation of tendencies and power groups in some of them, above all in the Christian Democratic party, and to the extreme virulence of factional struggles ... No one can deny the significance of the presence [in Italian politics] of a large party not divided into opposed factions, not torn by struggles between tendencies, and untouched by the forms of degeneration which accompany them. (Napolitano and Berlinguer, 1981, pp. 14–15)

Yet Napolitano is careful to add that democratic centralism, the PCI's undoubted special character or *diversità*, is to be understood as a practically proven method of party internal life: it is no longer to be considered, even secretly by the Communists themselves, as a sort of amazing grace inherent in the Communist revolutionary oversoul. Gramsci again provides Napolitano with the appropriate authoritative mantle of, one wants to say, "tradition" rather than "theory," in which to wrap this continuing secularization of the historical communist obsession with forms of organization:

> Gramsci already taught us to conceive of democratic centralism as a "general scheme" which not by accident lends itself "to many incarnations"—as distinctive in our party as in other [communist] parties—and which must be "continually interpreted and adapted to necessities." It is a general conception for regulating the life of a large mass and combat party like ours, not an ideological merit badge. (Napolitano, 1981, p. 37)

At the 1983 Congress, where the main issue of debate was precisely internal party life and democratic centralism (see below, *passim*), Enrico Berlinguer's report even argued that because democratic centralism was evidently no longer an ideological totem, several local organization resolutions calling for an *official* abandonment of democratic centralism were now themselves "ideological." In any case, the congress adopted a revision of the party constitution in which democratic centralism was designated a "method" rather than a set of "principles." Regional and local party organizations had debated this issue extensively before the national congress. The leadership's general line—to demote democratic centralism from an ideological essence and "an emblem on a flag" to a set of clearly parliamentary rules, with increased rights and guarantees especially for local party instances and individual members *vis-à-vis* the party's central authority—was widely accepted, even though an "ordinary Stalinist" tendency had the majority in a number of party sections.

This desacralization of democratic centralism was a culmination of a broader policy of secularization. At the 1979 Congress this broader policy had been given a stamp of permanent approval in the solemn declaration that the PCI was now a "lay" party. Such a declaration, of course, had a particular resonance in Italian political culture. That is, it referred not only to the abandonment of a traditional communist ideological world-view, but also was an implicit criticism of the Christian Democratic Party's continuing Catholic culture, whose historical roots are in a Catholic integralist philosophy which seriously matters still, for example, in Italian primary and secondary education. With respect to the PCI itself, becoming a "lay" party implied the intention to base policy no longer on doctrine, but on a reading of current realities in the light of certain values. These values remain to be adequately explicated, but this is a different issue.

The 1979 Congress also eliminated the statutory obligation of all party members to "study" Marxism–Leninism (which most members, as the specialists have long known, ignored already anyway). But what counted here was more the effect this had on the habits and mentality of *party cadres* and *militants* as opposed to the simple card-carrier. They were being, in effect, told two things: (1) that party policy is not a function of a scientific application of a scientific doctrine; and (2) that it is no longer necessary to explain or to defend PCI policy as a function of the world political development scenario worked up in Moscow and ratified in international communist documents and meetings.

It is not an exaggeration to say that the 1979 Congress resolution, in effect, abandoned the position that Marxism is a coherent theory at all. The redrafted party constitution places Italian Communist political thinking very vaguely "in the cultural and conceptual tradition whose roots and conceptual inspiration come from the teachings of Marx and Engels." It is no longer necessary even to be a "Marxist" in order to hold office in the party, and a special admissions screening procedure has been established for those who seek to join the PCI after holding high positions in other parties. In 1978 Berlinguer had said:

[They tell us that] if you do not renounce Lenin from A to Z, if you don't break your ties with the CPSU, you are Asians not Westerners. Do you think it would stop there? No, because from the repudiation of Lenin, Marx would be next. From the break with the CPSU, one would have to recognize the October Proletarian Revolution as an error! (*L'Unità*, 18 September 1978)

The 1979 Congress resolution stated that Leninist ideas and action had given "an impulse of historic importance" to the PCI's tradition. But this turned out to be a last hurrah for Leninism, repudiated definitively in the 1983 Congress's declaration that the Soviet model, and even the Russian Revolution as an inspiration, have exhausted their "propulsive force" (cf. PCI, 1979b). This conclusion, one can say, was a direct result of the radically unsatisfactory outcome of the "Polish August."

These are emblematic examples of what has been a protracted disengagement of the Italian Communist political culture, from an ideological conception of politics as a struggle for truth to a secular, lay, and pragmatic outlook. Berlinguer's caution that Italian Com-

munist pragmatism is not the "rearguard, non-revolutionary empi-
ricism" of social democratic reformism seems, as the well-known
Italian editorialist Giorgio Bocca commented (*La Repubblica*, 3 March
1983), the estimable expression of a "tenacious will to believe, in an
age when no one any longer has either the will or the time to
believe." In Bocca's evaluation the PCI's idea of socialism is "now
little different from a metaphor." The term has become honorific
because there is no longer an existing model, even an imperfect one,
to follow; nor does the PCI itself have even a set of convincing
intermediate-range goals. Thus the Italian Communist militants are
being weaned from the convictions that "communism" is human-
ity's only hope and that communist parties are inherently superior
to other parties.

The PCI's rejection of "proletarian internationalism," now fifteen
years old, was again firmly stated by Berlinguer at the 1983 Congress. Among the communist parties there is, he said:

> No leading party or state, no strategic or juridical center, no
> privileged relationship, no binding links of organization or
> discipline, but rather equality and autonomy of every political
> party based on the goals of socialism and communism; (there
> is) freedom of judgment and freedom to seek those points of
> convergence and cooperation which implement, or can lead to
> joint positions and objectives. (*L'Unità*, 3 March 1983)

Indeed, in the reference to parties "based on the goals of socialism
and communism" Berlinguer implied a blurring of the distinction
between socialist and communist parties. As Pierre Hassner (1980,
pp. 31–4) argued several years ago, the Italian Communists now
believe they have more in common with certain socialist and (in
their jargon) "democratic" parties than with most other communist
parties. The gradual devaluation of the international communist
movement as an influence and a reference point in the PCI's policy
process is both an absolute rejection of proletarian internationalism
and a redefinition of even the slogan of "internationalist solidarity"
with which the "autonomist" and "Eurocommunist" parties have
replaced it: the distinctiveness of communism as an international
political movement is blurred in Italian Communist declarations
these days. It is as if the PCI is seeking to make the name "communist" itself a label of convenience rather than an ideological badge, at
least in Italy. If this occurs, it would resolve what Peter Lange calls
the dilemma of identity v. legitimacy, that is, the contradiction

between maintaining a communist identity and yet achieving full political legitimacy in Italian politics (see Lange, 1979, 1980).

The slow, consistent, and laborious weaning imposed on the party by its leadership has disadvantages, not all of which are the defects of its virtues.

The party has often been criticized for avoiding decisive, totally unambiguous positions on tough issues. Some of the residual Italian and Western mistrust of Italian Communist intentions arises from the PCI's unquestionable attempt to please everyone, or at least to displease the least (including the Soviets, with whom PCI leaders such as Berlinguer and Pajetta have none the less had very hostile meetings). The PCI's refusal openly to support NATO is one case in point. Even *lo strappo*—the PCI's violent reaction to the "Polish December"—did not become an official and formal abandonment of the international communist movement, that is, a formal break with the Soviet Communist Party. Yet the PCI refused to attend the April 1980 Pan-European meeting of communist parties on "Peace and disarmament" (evidently to be directed against the NATO nuclear force modernization plans) cosponsored by the Polish Communist Party and the recidivist French Communist Party. Besides holding to the Eurocommunist position of refusing to attend such meetings anymore (a position the PCF gave up) the PCI asked why a meeting on détente should be confined to communist parties only, and why the invasion of Afghanistan should not be discussed at such a meeting.

Democratic Centralism outside the Party: The Reflux of "Internal" Politics

Over a period of twenty years the *scope* of democratic centralism in Italian communism has been radically reduced. This is precisely the organizational change one would expect, consonant with the PCI's overall secularization: ideology and organization, once again, demonstrate their mutual cause-and-effect relationships. The orthodox idea that democratic centralism (that is, monolithism as the form of "unity" combined with the party's "vanguard" role) applies as far as the party can extend it has been abandoned. Today democratic centralism in Italian communism refers only to the party itself. And even inside the party, as has already been suggested, it has been reworked from a political culture of totalitarian discipline into a constitutionalized set of rules, with some ordinary Stalinist residue here and there. It is symbolic that the PCI's statutes now contain a section called "On internal life and party democracy," of which democratic centralism is only one article, whereas the equivalent French Communist statutes carry the title "Internal party life: Democratic Centralism" (Pasquino, 1980c, p. 4).

In a nonruling communist party democratic centralism outside the party itself, in the orthodox version, has four elements: (1) subordination and absolute discipline, including permanently monolithic voting, of the communist parliamentary group; (2) control of a trade union and its use as a "transmission belt" both in the sense of a political weapon and a mechanism for leading trade unionists into the party; (3) maintenance of a series of permanent auxiliary or "flanking" organizations for youth, women, sports, culture, vacations, and so on; and (4) an entrepreneurial activity, in which commercial businesses (often import–export operations dealing with Eastern bloc counterparts), financial institutions, and agricultural and industrial cooperatives produce resources for the party, while remaining loyal but not necessarily directly controlled by it.

The first characteristic one notices about the Italian Communist Party's Chamber, Senate, and European Parliament delegations is that voting remains basically monolithic. But this fact in itself is misleading. On the one hand, very high degrees of party discipline are to be found in several types of European political party, right-wing as well as left-wing. On the other hand, the principle of permanent unanimous voting is a principle of political virginity: once broken, the essential is irremediable. (In 1982 the PCI's Chamber delegation was once permitted to vote as individuals, a first-time experiment which showed considerable division on the subject of East–West relations.) Instructed voting remains the rule, but other innovations have occurred which indicate the reflux of party control. The PCI's parliamentary candidates, for example, are no longer imposed by a central party committee operating secretly and with the infamous "biographies" which are a standard Stalinist operational tool. In fact a significant degree of decentralization has often given local party organizations autonomous power in choosing candidates, with the shifting of loyalties and paths of instruction that this would imply.

Really of greater significance than the habit of unanimous voting is the manner of participation. For decades Italian Communist deputies and senators have been deeply involved in the byzantine negotiations which produce legislation in Italy. They are experienced, pragmatic politicians in the Italian parliamentary labyrinth, possessed of a necessary degree of autonomy which makes them hardly available for the orthodox communist luxury of using Parliament basically for general denunciations of "bourgeois" government, and as a tribune to make propaganda for ulterior purposes.

In the Chamber and Senate Standing Committees where most Italian laws are voted and in which the requirement of a two-thirds majority makes PCI support almost indispensable, already in the period 1948–68 the Italian Communists negotiated and voted almost three-quarters of the Bills. In the cases of very important or controversial Bills requiring floor debate (and provoking general party-line voting, not just among the Communists) the PCI still voted 40 percent of them (Pasquino, 1980c; Cazzola, 1974; Di Palma, 1976). The PCI has worked hard and successfully to achieve a positive voting record in the European Parliament as well (Sweeney, 1984). One consequence of all this has been to demonstrate that the Italian Communists are not isolated, but rather have become part of the mainstream pushing and shoving of both Italian and West European politics. Italian and European parliamentarians who have had ample experience with the PCI recognize that its representatives are no longer party robots talking an orthodox, uncompromising line, but rather delegates whose habits are no longer radically different from others and who try to act constructively (within the limits imposed by real policy differences and the implacable necessities of competing for votes).

There is, however, one remaining distinctive characteristic of Italian Communist parliamentary practice, which arises, significantly, from the ban on factions and the Communist tradition of unanimity. The absence of organized factions makes for a greater sense of solidarity and collective responsibility among PCI deputies than exists in other parliamentary groups. One positive example was the PCI's steadfast policy against terrorist blackmail in the late 1970s, when other parties—particularly the Christian Democrats and the Socialists during the Aldo Moro kidnapping—were violently shaken by factional infighting.

The PCI still runs a set of flanking organizations—for women (UDI), peasants (ANC), youth (FGCI), and others—and still exercises a strong influence in the Italian "peace movement." A few years ago the emphasis was on rebuilding the FGCI as a way to reinvigorate the party itself from below. Most major West European parties have their own youth movements, one should note, often at odds with the party establishment, as is the FGCI. The FGCI's renewal has been lagging, and at the 1983 Congress Berlinguer talked lamely of "certain signs of recovery in the Young Communist Federation." (One importance of this issue is that the PCI's vote losses in the past few years have occurred in areas of previous strength: among young people, and also in the northern and central urban areas.)

If party members in these organizations still see their purpose as support of PCI general influence, this is less and less their *first* purpose. From the other side the party leadership no longer has a purely instrumental view of these organizations, and fewer demands for obedience have led to an accretion of organizational autonomy and a habit of negotiating policies. The UDI women's movement leadership, for example, was able to negotiate a more anti-clerical party policy on divorce and abortion in 1974–5, whereas the original party policy took less militant positions in order to favor the "historic compromise" offer held out to the Christian Democratic Party (Napolitano and Berlinguer, 1981, p. 41).

Over a period of years the PCI leadership has strongly promoted the women's movement in Italy, accepting that it be largely autonomous from party control, both on the substance of the issues and because liberation (that is, at least separating traditional women from the political control of their husbands) can prove a major new source of Communist support.[5] At the 1983 Congress Berlinguer's report put women's issues on the same footing as labor problems and the Mezzogiorno, a laudable stand, yet for some commentators also a sign of the party's current eclecticism.

But, of course, the most important issue of democratic centralism relative to the PCI's real internal/external boundary concerns the labor movement. What has Italian communism done with its trade union influence? It has disengaged the "transmission belt."

The Italian General Confederation of Labor (CGIL) contains a majority of Communist sympathizers and a strong Socialist minority, with other smaller minorities plus a residual group for whom the union is a useful advocate and not a declaration of political beliefs. The CGIL's disengagement from a "transmission belt" relationship with the PCI can be traced back in one sense to the 1950s. At that time the Communist Party leadership feared being totally marginalized in Italian politics because of the Cold War, once its "anti-bloc" alliance with Pietro Nenni's maverick Socialist Party broke down in 1956. This concern led to the strategy of using the

CGIL to keep contacts with others, at least in the factories. There was also the hope of having some continued, through CGIL–CSIL contacts, indirect influence in the Catholic working class, a characteristic approach of the Gramsci–Togliatti social alliance strategy. The CGIL itself, because of its own dwindling organization, had an autonomous interest in reaching out beyond constraints of its identity as a Communist tool, and this set of circumstances began a process of emancipation which took approximately two decades to complete.[6]

By the late 1960s the CGIL was already heavily engaged in traditional union action rather than acting, first of all, as a propaganda and recruitment wing of the Communist Party.[7] Its joint actions with the Catholic CISL and the Socialist and independent UIL eventually led to demands that the CGIL break its organizational connections to the PCI. After several years of resisting, the CGIL's 1969 Congress— this was the year of Italy's "hot autumn," following the French May 1968, and a time when trade union leverage was rising rapidly— accepted the demand, albeit unwillingly. As part of the inter-union agreement the CISL and UIL also broke ties with the DC and PSI. The CGIL's General Secretary, Agostino Novella, as well as several other top leaders, however, rejected the agreement (therein demonstrating its genuineness), and decided to keep their positions in the party's leadership by giving up their union jobs. The new CGIL leader, Luciano Lama, was committed to the idea of some sort of inter-union organization, and therefore also to autonomy for the CGIL. Thus, while remaining party members, the new top CGIL leaders (for instance, Lama and Bruno Trentin) all resigned their positions in the Communist Party leadership.

In 1972 a loose United Federation of the three main union confederations was created. In spite of an often stormy history, the Federazione has thus far survived. Its failure to eliminate the political division of Italian unionism has been somewhat compensated by the autonomy of unions from parties which it reinforces. The main issue, of course, has been the CGIL's autonomy from the Communist Party.

In the mid-1970s one American study found the CGIL's Communist leaders to be acting generally in a union rather than party partisan manner (Weitz, 1975), and a few years later an Italian expert judged: "Today, CGIL–PCI ties are probably less intense than those between the Trades Union Congress and the Labour Party." (Pasquino, 1980c, p. 82). Others have compared the CGIL–PCI relationship to that of the DGB and the SPD in West Germany.

As we have said already, the CGIL combines a generally dominant

Table 5.1 Party Affiliation of the CGIL Executive Committee

	1960 (%)	1965 (%)	1969 (%)
PCI	53	55	32
PSI	47	27	24
Other	—	4	32
PSIUP	—	14	12
	(N = 32)	(N = 22)	(N = 37)

Communist presence with Socialist and other minority groups. This is of special relevance in the leadership, of which Sidney Tarrow wrote in 1975:

> The factions in the CGIL are easily misinterpreted. While they are partisan in identification, they serve primarily to organize internal CGIL politics and not to transmit party directives to the CGIL. The presence of these factions has been severely criticized in recent years, both by other forces in the labor movement and by Socialists *and* Communists within the CGIL. While the factions have been formally disbanded, partisan identification still serves as the basis for promotion and occasionally for developing positions on important issues. (Tarrow, 1975, pp. 554–5)

Tarrow gives a table which shows the important change in the CGIL leadership in the years 1965–9 (Table 5.1).

The 1970s were a decade of growth and inflation, during which union power in Italy grew extremely strong: the remarkable wage indexation agreement, won from a Confindustria led by Gianni Agnelli, came in 1975. Labor market conditions on the whole were favorable to the Federazione's joint policy stands, and therefore also to the CGIL's autonomy from the PCI (Lange *et al.*, 1982; Regalia *et al.*, 1978). The labor unions at this point even were invited to discuss government policy as a whole (for example, IRI investment policy and the Cassa per il Mezzogiorno's operations) (cf. Couffignal, 1978). One commentator suggests, not unreasonably, that the DC and the Confindustria were satisfied in this period to deal with the Federazione on a wide range of policy issues as a way of keeping the PCI attached to the "national solidarity" coalition of 1977–9, therein obliging the Communists ever more to share responsibility for

120

government without actually letting them inside (Bugno, 1982, p. 263).

The sharp 1979–80 recession knocked the wind out of the Federazione's political sails, however. The disastrous failure of a major strike at Fiat in 1980, when tens of thousands of workers staged a back-to-work demonstration which disavowed the unions, was emblematic of a period of retrenchment for unions in Western Europe generally. Within the Federazione joint stands have become increasingly difficult to achieve, since it involves taking the blame for unpopular reforms of wage-indexing, seniority increases, pensions, labor mobility, job guarantees, and so on. Membership and union activism are down sharply, and the CGIL, CISL, and UIL each has attempted to shift the responsibility for unpopular positions to the others.

Yet the CGIL's independence has never seriously been called into question. This was evident in the controversy of January 1983 focussed on a major tripartite agreement between the unions, the Fanfani government, and the Confindustria to reduce wage-indexation increases (the *scala mobile* had leaped from base 100 in 1975 to 335 in 1983!). The Communist Party leadership was widely reported to be urging rejection or at least a much harder negotiating position. Yet not only did Lama's CGIL leadership sign the agreement; at the March Party Congress Lama criticized the "vagueness" of the party's program for a "democratic alternative" and rebutted Berlinguer's assertion that the CGIL was tempted by "pansyndicalism"—that is, taking over the political role of parties and Parliament by discussing all sorts of government policies normally out of union's purview. The CISL leader, Carniti, praised Lama for "explaining to Berlinguer what a union is," and the top Socialist leader in the CGIL, Marianetti, also recorded a *satisfecit* regarding the question of union independence.

In fact there is scant evidence to indicate the PCI leaders are attempting to regain control of the CGIL. This is not to say the CGIL's policies are anything but "left-wing" or working-class-oriented. But the "problem" of democratic centralism is rather specific with respect to the party–union relationship, and the PCI has disconnected the "transmission belt" mechanism, in the process abandoning the ideological and organizational premise of *What Is To Be Done?*.

Inside the Party I: The Problem of Structures

Compared to the study of other political parties, the Italian Communist Party's recent scholars have done it honor. There exists an enormous political science literature now on Italian communism, most of it produced after 1968 and concerned, explicitly or implicitly, with the issue of whether the PCI's Gramscian "war of position" strategy was winning for the party, or whether, to the contrary, the party's "presence" everywhere in society did not provoke classic degenerative phenomena: absorption of the conqueror by the conquered, and *trasformismo*, the Italian version of a party trading its principles for a share in power.

The reflux of Italian communism's political project has already been demonstrated in two respects: secularization of the party's ideology and program, and the abandonment of democratic centralism networks outside the party. It remains to study democratic centralism inside the party itself.

It is useful to begin, as always concerning Italian politics, with geography. The Rome headquarters of the party has permitted, even encouraged, a significant decentralization of authority. But this was surely inevitable, an example of the force of circumstance, in any party in which a single provincial federation, Emilia-Romagna, provides approximately one-quarter of the total national membership and militants! As with parliamentary candidacies, candidates for party office are no longer imposed from above, and the relevant party committee (which in the French Communist Party still produces "correct" candidates) was abolished years ago, as have been the notorious autobiographical records requiring detailed, incriminating information from every member. (It is significant that Giorgio Napolitano was the secretary for organization in the 1970s; in this position he was able to do much to implement liberalizing policies.)

Provincial (federation) and regional committees now also possess significant autonomy not only in terms of choosing their own personnel, but also in policy terms. A rather considerable local PCI political life, anything but robot-controlled from the party's center, has built up in the Italian regions, where the relatively decentralized structure of the Italian state has created substantial political foci. Several years ago one specialist (Tarrow, 1975, p. 610) even saw potential local and regional factionalism in the PCI, as opposed to the possibility of factions coalescing around programmatic differences. This has been largely avoided by the leadership because of its skill in accommodating regional and local interests.

The PCI's role in Italian municipal government has been considerable for decades in the center and north of the country. And in the

1970s the PCI won control of the south's major cities as well, including the mixed blessing of trying to govern Rome and Naples. This put the Communists squarely into the struggle against camorra and mafia interests (a top PCI leader, Pio La Torre, was assassinated in 1981 by the Sicilian mafia) as well as against red and black terrorism. Communist manpower and other organizational resources in the process have been stretched thin and often ground down by these responsibilities. Many of the party's best administrators have been thrown into the "black holes" of Italian local politics (for example, Naples) to be worn out in day-to-day battles for mere survival, with no chance of that general reform of state administrative institutions which the PCI has long advocated, but which would require Rome's initiative—and the PCI is still excluded from the national government. It has even been suggested that there be "two" government coalitions: one for "politics" and another to take on administrative reform. The PCI would find this very difficult to accept, in particular, after the political sacrifices it has made to the cause of *governabilità* in recent years.

In terms of the usual *structures* of orthodox democratic centralism the most significant institutional change inside the PCI has been to abandon the *cell* pattern, that is, the capillary structure of horizontally isolated and vertically tight-controlled small working groups. Twenty-five years ago the PCI's cell structure already was suffering the diversionary effects of economic boom and the withering political commitments of the "decline of ideology" years. Probably no more than 20–25 percent of the membership was active at all in the cells in the 1950s, when their number peaked at 57,000 or so. Entering the 1960s, which promised continued economic growth and even the first signs of a possible East–West détente, the PCI's leaders seem to have drawn three conclusions: (1) the "Leninist" cell structure could no longer be the embodiment of a genuinely revolutionary intent; European stabilization and NATO had rendered this notion nugatory; (2) de-Stalinization was a good policy in any case, and had to be imposed in the party—if necessary over internal resistance from the orthodox nostalgics; and (3) the party's "war of position" strategy was ill-served by the cell network, whose self-absorption tended to *isolate* party members locally rather than create points of "presence."

In consequence, the *cell* structure was almost entirely dismantled over a period of years, the party being reorganized at the next-higher level, the *section*. A section in the PCI contains between 100 and 1,000 members, meeting only once a month or perhaps every two months. Within a section today perhaps 10 percent of the members attend meetings, and the business is done, as in all parties, by a handful of the committed who meet more regularly. In 1976 there were 11,875 sections for about 1·7 million members, and in 1978 at the party's high point of almost 1·8 million members there were 12,769 sections, including 226 in foreign countries where Italian workers have emigrated. In 1980 there were only 3,300 cells left, many of them large factory cells hardly different from the sections.

The shift from cells to sections in the 1960s and 1970s was a deinstitutionalization, even a deorganization of the PCI. The party became a large collection of local political clubs, as opposed to a working capillary network. The effect on individual party members was evident: disengagement from the international communist movement weakened the Soviet influence on the PCI rank-and-file; simultaneously, abandonment of the cell structure put the greater part of the membership largely outside the PCI leadership's own reach. Altogether the party membership outside the activist core was banalized, that is, effectively decommunized in any sense related to political militancy. There remained at best an often quite strong, but politically less and less relevant, sentimental attachment to what the party used to embody. Neil McInnes (1975a, p. 102) drew the obvious conclusion: "Plainly, this is the transition from the Leninist party with its cells to the ordinary party with its constituency groups, that is, from a party based on militancy to one based on electoralism."

Detailed studies in recent years have indeed shown a decline in the PCI's character as a mass working-class party, that is, a party with large numbers of strongly committed factory militants and a large, permanent, ideologically committed vote (*vota d'appartenenza*). In its place there is a substantial increase in opinion and "exchange" (self-interest) voting for the PCI (Parisi and Pasquino, 1979; Penniman, 1977, 1981). McInnes (1975a, p. 100) is correct in one sense to say that the cell structure "constitutes the CP. Without the cell, there would be no CPs, and if and when they lose their specific nature and become more like other Western political parties, the process will begin with the decline of the cell." This is a useful standard of judgment, concerning which an incisive consensus among PCI specialists had begun to emerge already several years earlier:

It is precisely where the party's organization is most efficient—in central Italy—that the party itself is most saturated by the bourgeois culture in which it operates. It is of course possible to argue that a Communist network is by virtue of its origins radical in nature, but in that case, one would have to demonstrate that the party structure that once insured its revolutionary élan—a structure of horizontally isolated party cells—was still intact. No empirical analyst of the PCI has been able to do that. In the absence of such a structure, the PCI is a mass party that is *of* Italian society as well as *in* Italian society. That is its leaders' greatest weapon, as well as their greatest curse. (Tarrow, 1969, p. 182)

The PCI's leaders surely realized the implications of abandoning the cell network. Their decisive implementation of this policy is the most incontrovertible evidence of their "conspiracy" to de-Stalinize the party's structure. Just as there is no democracy without genuine citizen participation, so there is no orthodox democratic centralism without the true believing and ever-manipulated militants.

Inside the Party II: Factions, *Correnti* and Purges

Disbanding the cell network precluded the leadership's capacity for dictatorship over the party by the simple device of putting most of the membership out of the leadership's reach most of the time: a true self-denying ordinance. Yet even this change still could have left the inner-inner party network—the cadres, apparatchiks, and militants—exposed to manipulation by the party's center. In this sense McInnes's argument that the cell structure "constitutes the CP" is insufficient, and we must move to the more fundamental problem of the ban on factions, that is, the problem of "unity" within the party's inner core.

The PCI's leaders have tried to remain true to tradition and the party's collective memory, while at the same time substantially decommunizing again: they continue to defend democratic centralism's ban on factions while allowing a substantial open pluralism. Berlinguer, in a major speech on democratic centralism in 1978, said:

The method of democratic centralism does not exclude in any way the broadest possible discussion and voting with majorities. However in the PCI view, an incorrect system would be one that would crystallize majorities and minorities, which in turn would impede the necessary unity and effectiveness of party action. (*L'Unità*, 21 December 1978)

125

This passage covers both ends of the argument: on the one hand, making a clear "reform" reference to the legitimacy of majority/ minority voting (in effect a rehabilitation), and on the other hand, restating the traditional concern with "correct" (and "incorrect") forms of organization, including the liturgical invocation of the "necessary unity and effectiveness of party action." The 1979 Fifteenth Congress "theses" made the argument, again, that democratic centralism is communism's particular originality: "The method of democratic centralism is appropriate to the objectives of a party that wants to transform the bases and class nature of society and the state."

The reality of "unity" and "factionalism" in the Italian Communist hierarchy is quite complex. But there is, none the less, a plain fact with which to begin: whereas permanently organized factions still are not permitted and do not exist, for almost two decades the party has been openly traversed by "tendencies" and "opinion currents" (*correnti*); and in recent years the top leadership has legitimized this uncrystallized yet public and permanent basis of free debate as its characteristic reform—a mechanism of pluralism without factionalism.

The problem of unity in the Italian Communist Party has been, therefore, to keep opinion currents at the level of informal tendencies. In his 1975 study McInnes made the following evaluation:

> The PCI . . . for all its desire to be a "party of a new type" is, in the manner of all Italian parties, chronically divided against itself. Quite apart from the *Manifesto* rebellion, the PCI has been potentially two parties for a decade. Giorgio Amendola and Giancarlo Pajetta, members of the secretariat, had suggested the recognition of "majorities and minorities" and of [tendencies] . . . from 1961, but this was rejected at Togliatti's insistence as incompatible with the Leninist structure. The existence of such [tendencies] became public at the Bologna congress in 1969 and has not been hidden since. (McInnes, 1975a, p. 136)

The main tendencies or "opinion currents" in the 1960s and 1970s were the so-called "right," associated with Amendola, and the "left," whose leading figure was Pietro Ingrao. The first favored an alliance with the Socialist Party, focussed on the goal of reforms in Italian society. The right's main political worry was the possibility that a left–center coalition of Socialists and Christian Democrats would isolate the PCI. Yet in order to have the support of the then much stronger ordinary Stalinist elements in the party, the right leaders talked a generally pro-Soviet line (for example, they wanted a less strong condemnation of the invasion of Czechoslovakia) and were lukewarm supporters of internal party liberalization. The left tendency wanted to turn party attention to grassroots organization, as opposed to the right's focus on a party alliance with the Socialists. This line was in the tradition of "radical democratic" communism (although its leading spokesmen were soon outflanked by the Manifesto group and took part in its exclusion in 1969), and could even appear neo-Trotskyist. Not surprisingly the leftists strongly criticized the Soviet Union, considered Amendola-style thinking to tend to "reformism," and pushed for inner-party democracy (the latter both as a matter of doctrine and because minority rights were for them a political advantage).

This was classic right- and left-wing "deviationism," in orthodox communist categories. And as McInnes points out, the classic schema seemed to fit the PCI well enough, since there were also "Berlinguer's 'autonomists' holding the ring, elaborating the bureaucratic compromises" (loc. cit.), the classic role of the general secretary in a Stalinist party. But the language of "deviations" no longer held sway, as the party leadership was already in the process of reducing Stalinism. Furthermore, there was an additional, characteristically Italian, peculiarity to the *correnti* structure. Beyond the "party alliance" v. "mass base" strategic disagreement between "rightists" and "leftists" loomed the Catholic question and, ultimately, the goal of the "historic compromise." The "left's" grassroots orientation wanted to go beyond socialist and "lay" working-class fraternization to reach the left-leaning base of Christian Democracy as well. This, in short, was the germ of a strategy to reconcile Italy's three political subcultures.

In elaborating the "historic compromise" proposal in 1973, Berlinguer was thus building, in a sense, on both main tendencies in party strategic thinking: he was combining the "right's" surmise that an inter-party coalition had to be the PCI's priority in opening some avenue toward a government role, and the "left's" certainty that Christian Democracy, at least in the Italian case, was of more political significance to the Communists than were the Socialists.

McInnes is correct to say that "Neither of these currents ran its full course" (ibid., p. 137). In fact in the 1970s and early 1980s a considerable modification occurred in the position of each tendency. The "right" tendency, whose chief spokesman has been Giorgio Napolitano following Amendola's death, adopted whole-heartedly the party's abandonment of the Soviet model and "proletarian internationalism." The "left" tendency became more complex, as an open pro-Catholic (sometimes practicing!) "sensibility" developed, for example, Franco Rodano; its policy was less to focus on the grassroots, and more to establish contacts with the left-wing factions of the Christian Democracy party, hoping for an eventual splitting of the DC.

In any case our purpose here is not primarily to follow out the various political logics of the PCI's *correnti* (even if we will shortly need to speak of the more recent emergence of an additional element: the Sovietophile tendency which developed in reaction to the PCI's break with the Soviet party). What is important for our analysis is to demonstrate how the PCI's special form of pluralism is at once maintained and contained.

An "opinion current" is not organized. It is a cluster of recognizable opinions and policy preferences, extending both horizontally through the party's territorial organizations and vertically through the ranks. Each "opinion current" has its spokesmen in the top leadership, and its characteristic points of view are well known throughout the party because ten years ago inner-leadership debates began to be publicized in *L'Unità* and the rest of the party's press. The nature of leadership differences of opinion, and some indication of the seriousness of conflict, are now reported regularly in party press accounts of Central Committee and Executive Committee meetings. This is a policy which was initiated, according to Napolitano (who was then the secretary for organization), self-consciously "differentiating ourselves from other communist parties" (Napolitano and Berlinguer, 1981, p. 38).

The 1983 Congress, following the lead of the "left" tendency, still headed by the now venerable Pietro Ingrao, adopted a series of reforms to increase internal democracy and to magnify the "transparency" of the PCI's decision-making processes. (The fact that these reforms were proposed in identical or very similar language by various "Ingraoist" local organizations was, incidentally, a nice indication of the freedom of horizontal communication in the PCI today!) The most significant of these changes commits the national leadership to putting fundamental policy-making authority effectively back into the *elected* rather than *executive* or *co-opted* party organs, that is, the Central Committee, as opposed to the Executive Committee and the Secretariat. This means, among other things, giving the Central Committee timely and adequate information to do its job. Additionally, the Executive Committee and the Secretariat are obligated to bring any broad internal disagreements (which are, as I have pointed out, now routinely known through the party press) to a Central Committee debate. This has already happened increasingly, in any case, because of the top leadership's somewhat surprising occasional use of the "leak" to conduct its internal politics, resulting in "questions" in Central Committee meetings. Furthermore, the top PCI leaders already for years have talked to the general press as well as appeared in television interviews, without trying to deny that there are internal differences. This has reinforced the evolution of characterized "opinion currents" inside the party, a personalization of both internal and external party politics—as contrasted with the orthodox communist charade of fully interchangeable personalities in a collective leadership, all leaders speaking the same line in the same words, with no political "face" of their own. In other words, the orthodox code, that communists should hide their differences and speak freely only among themselves, is largely a dead letter in the PCI. Italian Communist journalists have taken regular responsibilities in non-Communist newspapers and magazines—sometimes writing rather critically of the Communist Party (for instance, Alberto Jacoviello in *La Repubblica*). There are significant numbers of Communists working throughout the Italian media without creating political or ideological scandals, although it is true that some Italian and foreign observers still worry, overly so in my judgment, about subtle institutional and propaganda manipulations.

The Italian Communist Party clearly, in any case, is hardly an organization any longer based on secrecy. Nor is it based on monolithic opinion, or even on some less-constraining version of unconditional support for a party line. Whereas it is still a point of discipline in the French Communist Party to support the party line unconditionally in public, the observer has difficulty encountering an Italian Communist who is not somehow critical of the leadership and its policy. (How could it be different, when the leadership is publicly divided within itself?) Georges Marchais's flat, Stalinist assertion that "Correct policies need no opposition" remains characteristic of the PCF's mode of operation as a hierarchy; in Italy characteristic examples would be former General Secretary Luigi Longo's open criticism in 1975 of Berlinguer's "historic compromise" policy (in a Central Committee debate given wide publicity in the party press), and Berlinguer's comment on inner-party disagreement over the break with the Soviet party: "Certainly there are a certain number of comrades who don't approve. But my view is that they are many fewer than you think, and the fact that they exist has not influenced the clarity of our position." One might even cite the episode in which *L'Unità*'s party cell voted to propose an amendment to the 1983 Congress resolution to do away with democratic centralism entirely (see *La Repubblica*, 28 January 1983).

The main problem of democratic centralism in the PCI has thus changed from the imposition of monolithic unity to the formulation of a policy which a perennially divided leadership and bureaucracy will accept and implement, which will mobilize the party militants, and which has the potential to win new support. The fact that the whole process is still called "democratic centralism" might lead one to see here a "return to Lenin," that is, to the problem of "correct synthesis" and the political struggle to achieve decisive policies without coercing the strong preferences of large party minorities. Indeed, Berlinguer tried to give this impression:

> Democratic centralism is not just an empty formula. What is important is how a synthesis is achieved—in methods of organization, in behavior, in statutory regulations and in practice—between the rich variety of demands, initiatives and proposals, and a united line, clear and effective decisions, and firm, united implementation. (From a speech at Genoa, *L'Unità*, 18 September 1978)

A less exalted view of the significance of labels does not credit the PCI with some new democratic method, but only the usual dilemmas of any political party, which, I hasten to add, the PCI may deal with better than most.

There remains the question of "dissidents" and purges. In a party which has given up most of the political culture of the "combat party," which has become, in McInnes's good phrase, "an amalgam of voters and stair-climbers," it is a matter of some difficulty to become a "dissident." The party's mode of operation no longer provides the necessary power structure of secret policy-making and forced conformism with regard to which dissidence is defined.[8] Unlike public opinion about the French Communist Party, in which dissidence is clearly still a calling as it is in Soviet political life, there is only a rump anti-Communist audience in Italian politics which is willing to credit allegations of Stalinism in the PCI. And almost always such accusations relate not to policies so much as to the difficulty of internal democracy itself, that is, when frustrated party members confuse the normal Michelsian limits and occasional ruthlessness of internal party life with Stalinism.

To be sure, the Communist apparatus is still quite capable of excluding members, but its limited use of purge and exclusion today no longer sets the PCI off in a category separate from other Italian or European parties. Even when someone is excluded for obviously political rather than procedural reasons, there is generally a relevant judicial basis (for example, when the editor of a newly started Sovietophile magazine called *Interstampa* was excluded in late 1982 for "factional" activity, the issue was the party rule against independent minority publications). The series of exclusions of Sovietophiles during 1982, related to the PCI's break with the Soviet party over Poland and Afghanistan, was justified as resistance against Soviet infiltration of the PCI, surely a founded accusation. In any case, here was a historically paradoxical working of the ban on factions, that is, its use by a communist party to preclude an intimacy with the Soviets!

Democratic Centralism and *lo Strappo*

In this chapter and in Chapter 6 we see various connections between internal party organization and the kind of national strategy and foreign policy a West European communist party pursues (cf. Hassner, 1976). It is hardly surprising, in this regard, that *lo strappo*, the PCI's break with the Soviet party over Poland, came in conjunction with decisive steps in internal party liberalization. Precisely because of internal party liberalization—both in its form and its content—the inner-party conflict over breaking with the Soviets was much less devastating than had been expected. The terrain for this historic change had been well-prepared gradually over two decades and the turning-point was a double success for the PCI's leadership.

The Sovietophile minority wing in the PCI was forced into the open and into some coherence as an "opinion current" by the party's tough-minded support of Solidarity during 1980–1 and its absolute rejection of the Jaruzelski *coup d'état*. The anti-Soviet policy of the majority is indicated, in reverse, in two texts by the leading Sovietophile personality in the party, Armando Cossutta. One is a speech at a Central Committee meeting in October 1981, entitled "The USA and the USSR must not be put in the same category." The second is an editorial he published in *L'Unità* in January 1982, titled, candidly enough, "Why I am against a break with the CPSU" (see Cossutta, 1982, pp. 182–90).

The Sovietophile opinion in the PCI is, like everything else in this party, complex and nuanced. The Sovietophiles have little enthusiasm for the USSR and "the Soviet model," for one thing. Their main policy idea (see ibid.) is to rehearse the historic orthodox communist choice "against capitalism and for socialism," and to argue that despite the Soviet Union's "deficiencies" and "errors" it still embodies the world-historical rupture of capitalist development, and in foreign policy is still an effective counter to national and international capitalist pressures. The PCI itself, they argue, would not be so strong without the USSR's existence. Cossutta adds that the 1983 Congress's declaration on the "exhaustion" of Soviet political inspiration is particularly "destructive," both because it leaves the PCI without an ideological model with reference to which party unity must be organized, and because without the role of representing the Soviet Union in Italian politics the PCI inevitably weakens its bargaining position and mass support. It is worth quoting Cossutta directly on the mixed significance of the Soviet Union in his view:

> I think that among the Italian Communists there are neither a great many nor only very few who would like to live in the Soviet Union ... The Italian Communists rather want to build socialism in their own country ... [In Italy] the struggle for socialism would be much more difficult if there was not this extremely strong counterweight to the effect of imperialism which is—even with all its limits—the Soviet Union's role ... [and] despite everything, the USSR has worked more than any other country to bring humanity closer to achieving ... the most important goal for which communists struggle: equality. (ibid., p. 19)

Finally, it is clear that Cossutta is making an old argument: the main guarantees of Italian Communist identity and vigor are the Soviet link and democratic centralism. Abandoning these constitutes "revisionism." And at the 1983 Congress Cossutta hinted portentously that Berlinguer was steering a "liquidationist" course, leading the party toward "reformism," an exhaustion of the party's will to revolutionize capitalism in Italy.

In local party meetings to establish delegations and resolutions for the national congress, a series of Sovietophile amendments to the national draft resolution provoked a watershed innovation in the PCI's procedures. The problem of "factions," heretofore eluded by the device of *correnti*, finally was faced directly by encouraging majority/minority secret ballots at the *section* and *federation* preliminary congresses. (Secret ballots, requiring a request by 70 percent of the delegates, never had been used so often.)

In other words, here was the inner-party constitutionalism typical of liberal and democratic parties everywhere. Moreover, *not by accident the first legitimized "factional" grouping in Italian Communist history had turned out to be the party's historic center and ideological root—the Soviet connection—now shown by regular voting procedures to be reduced to a rump of orthodox "hardliners."* The Sovietophiles, when actually counted, indeed turned out to be a much smaller group than either outside experts or the PCI's own leadership had first suspected.[9] As against predictions of 20–30 percent, the so-called "Cossutta amendments" finally won 5 percent or less of the vote overall in 109 separate federation congresses (with a 15 percent maximum in the Milan federation). On the other hand, over one-third of the federations voted majorities for the "Ingrao amendments" to democratize democratic centralism. (This was a particularly remarkable example of local initiative, in that the Central Committee initially had rejected Ingrao's amendments in preparing the draft resolution.)

In sum, in the West European communist parties breaking with the Soviet Union goes hand in hand with internal party democratization. The vote on the Cossutta amendments showed the "K factor" had failed to polarize the Italian Communist Party internally and was unlikely in itself to produce a party split.[10] Moreover, Soviet attempts to sabotage the PCI's internal debate, no doubt with the intention of eventually splitting the party, had been pushed aside.

Conclusion

Despite all insistence that democratic centralism in the PCI—the party's originality or *diversità*—continues to mean, first of all, the absence of inner-party factionalism, it is hard to escape the conclusion that today this absence is a *lack* rather than a *ban*.

It is an interesting problem to study how the PCI has maintained leadership "unity" despite serious internal policy differences and relatively continuous public debate about them over a period of years. Panebianco (1982, p. 161) speaks for a large body of specialist research in his conclusion that there is "an incipient transformation of the traditional tendencies into factions." There are, it now goes without need for elaboration, many large points of conflict and disagreement over emphasis in PCI policy-making: the "historic compromise" v. the "leftist" or "democratic" alternative v. the current policy of attacking the Socialist Party in making opposition to the Craxi government; a grassroots emphasis v. an emphasis on party coalitions and a "political culture of governing" (the old difference between "social" and "political" alliances); an emphasis on reaching out to Catholics v. a "lay" strategy; pro-Soviets v. neutralists v. the profoundly ambivalent foreign policy pursued by the party's top leaders.

What explains the PCI's remarkable overall leadership cohesion in the face of such differences? On what basis has the leadership for years walked a thin line between a tacit conspiracy to liberalize the party and a descent into the "evils of faction"?

The Italian Communist leadership is still dominated by men educated politically during the historic period of communist unity as an international movement, say, despite the Yugoslav and Chinese splits, through the Khrushchev years. For such people party unity has a double value. As the cynics would begin, party unity maintains their jobs and their prestige. But party unity for them is also a validation of the moral superiority of the political enterprise in which they have invested all their adult lives. These are dedicated individuals, even though the identity of the undertaking has undergone remarkable modifications. However, this means also that the next generation of leaders will not necessarily be such good communists. The post-Berlinguer, post-Natta generation ultimately will refuse to subordinate legitimate differences over policy and position to "party unity." A future Cossutta will not withdraw his amendments voluntarily from a Congress debate, will not accept total defeat, and will not say,

> there are no Cossutta-men, there are no Ingrao-men, or others still. There are only communists. I am strongly opposed to the crystallization of organized factions . . . Our supreme objective must remain unity. (*L'Unità*, 6 March 1983)

The method of precluding factional struggle for the party's leadership by including the major points of view and spokesmen in the top group, in conclusion, is a structure of open debate but *without* the necessary institutional guarantees. It is, to put the point differently, inherently precarious. But while it lasts, the benefits of "faction" are had without many of the vices. Nevertheless, the top leaders need to meditate Gramsci's observation (1957, p. 151) that a party's leadership is to be judged not only on the basis of "what it actually does"—here the PCI's current leaders will be remembered for the machiavellian *virtù* of having created a second historical chance for the party[11]—but also "in what it prepares on the hypothesis of its own destruction." Gramsci added portentously that "of the two facts it is difficult to say which is the more important."

6

The Decay of
French Communism

Introduction: on the Fears of Leaders

In chapter XX of *The Prince* Machiavelli considers "Whether building fortresses and other defensive policies often adopted by princes are useful or not." After a discussion of several characteristically contradictory Italian precedents—among which this one is of remarkable connection here: "The so-called wise men among our ancestors used to say that Pistoia was to be held by factions and Pisa by fortresses"(!)—Machiavelli concludes: "the prince who fears his own people more than he does foreigners ought to build fortresses, but a prince who is more afraid of foreigners than of his own people can neglect them." To this flat rule of governance Machiavelli, however, did not fail to add a typically wise caution to those fearful princes who build fortresses:

> I may approve of those who build fortresses or of those who do not, depending on the circumstances; but it is a foolish man who, because he puts his trust in his fortresses, thinks he need not worry about the enmity of his people . . . Actually the best fortress of all consists in not being hated by your people.

Orthodoxy and Independence:
A Self-Contradictory Strategy

Under the erratic "chairmanship" of Georges Marchais, the French Communist Party's ruling group in the 1970s flirted, sometimes passionately, often frantically, but finally inconsequentially, with genuine liberalization of French communism's ordinary Stalinist political culture. This was called "Eurocommunism," when the PCF finally accepted the label in order to emphasize its avowed conversion to West European ideas, and "socialism in French colors," when the ruling group wanted to stress the party's newly taken autonomy from Soviet control. The reform ultimately failed not because it was rejected by a hostile Stalinist rank-and-file, but rather because of the inner clique's own panicky reaction in the 1977–8 crisis of its "union of the left" coalition with a resurgent Socialist Party led by François Mitterrand. In this moment of truth the top leaders showed that, unlike the leaders of Italian communism, they did not possess the political and psychological qualities required to carry through to fruition a political cultural renaissance.[1]

In the summer of 1977 the small inner-core Marchais ruling group realized that the coming 1978 legislative elections, which the left had every chance to win, could also be a historic defeat of the Communist Party by the Socialist Party within the left-wing victory as a whole. The Communists, having been the leading left-wing party since 1946, would come in far behind the Socialists and would join a left-wing government as a junior partner. Faced with the fact that its alliance strategy had unexpectedly produced a fundamental realignment of the left in favor of the Socialists, the ruling group made a recidivist choice to scuttle the "union" and gave in to disused but still powerful Stalinist reflexes both in its relations with the Socialists and in the governance of the party internally.

On the pretext of disagreement in "updating" the 1972 joint Communist–Socialist–left-wing Radical program (which the Communists caused by radically upping their demands in the negotiation concerning nationalizations, military policy, and the PCF's share in a future left-wing government), the alliance was split. Given the connection between internal party life, domestic strategy, and foreign policy, this sectarian regression was soon followed by a return to "splendid isolation" opposition in French politics, and to realignment on Soviet positions in foreign policy following a decade of steadily increasing French Communist independence. With respect to *le peuple communiste*—as the PCF's leaders called their rank-and-file with secret irony—the gates of the ruling group's Stalinist fortress were shut up again tightly. This time, however, the orthodox communist love of leadership was turned into hatred of the leadership.

These three remained the major elements of PCF policy between 1978 and 1981. Then, in May 1981, François Mitterrand's surprising late comeback victory in the presidential election put the Marchais group in the way of another paradoxical situation: in 1977–8 the Communists had snatched defeat from the jaws of victory, and were well enough contented with what they considered a narrow escape from a historic defeat. Now in June 1981 they found themselves obliged by circumstances to join the government, but from a still weaker position than would have been the case in 1978. And the fact that the feared historic decline of French communism has, indeed, materialized in the past few years reflects far more than a moment of bad luck in the 1981 throw of the electoral dice. Rather the PCF is suffering the consequences of its general failure to get off a dead-end path of political development.

The responsibility for this failure lies mainly with its own leaders. Gramsci was absolutely correct to say that in "all actions which demand sacrifice . . . after every defeat it is always necessary to look into the responsibility of the leaders" (Gramsci, 1957, p. 144). The Marchais group, in its fortress, used democratic centralism in a Stalinist fashion to escape scrutiny; the consequence has been French communism's decay.

Ordinary Stalinist Democratic Centralism: The Ideology's Persistence

In Volume 3 (1982) of his history of the PCF's internal affairs Philippe Robrieux, a former leader of the French Communist youth organization and a one-time protégé of Maurice Thorez, gives a concise definition of the party's Stalinism, still its dominant political culture at the very moment it signed the Joint Program with the Socialists:

> [To] be a Stalinist or to remain one is not necessarily to approve everything that Stalin said or did; rather it means to have a fundamentally monolithic conception of the international [communist] movement and of the parties which compose it, as well as the vision of the world and of politics which derive from it. Monolithism, leadership omnipotence justified by democratic centralism as practiced since the rise of Stalin—the murderous insanity left aside—the directing role of the Soviet leadership accepted in fact, even though denied for obvious propaganda reasons: This was still the official credo of the PCF at the beginning of 1973. (Robrieux, 1980–4, pp. 82–3)

One can say that the French Communist Party leadership decided to test internal party reform following its double crisis of 1968. First, the PCF's revolutionary pretense was stripped naked by its incapacity to take advantage of the May 1968 general strike. Whatever advantages the PCF's constituencies gained in the Grenelle agreements, and whatever political reinforcement the Communist-controlled CGT union would gain from settlement, the Communist Party itself left the battlefields of May and June with its prestige in tatters. It had neither provoked nor led the strikers; nor, as everyone knew, had it tried to take the strike to some radical conclusion. Rather the CGT leader Georges Séguy, who was simultaneously a member of the PCF's PolitbuMo, held secret talks with government officials to find a way to end the strikes and thus to regain control by the established political bureaucracies of a situation that had become anarchical. The strikers of May–June had evidenced a patent distrust of PCF and CGT sloganeering in the crisis; the Communists' ideology of a "transition to socialism" had been shown up badly, and the leadership's remarkable lack of contact with rank-and-file movements cast broad doubts on the Communist movement's overall political credibility.

One response was to open the party and go to the people. Hence the PCF's internal party reform first began with a genuine, if none the less opportunist, desire to try a new political road. Thus despite the very bad result of May 1968 from the Communist point of view, it produced, in one sense at least, a very positive consequence, which can explain the enthusiasm of the post-1968 period inside the party: there seemed to be a new beginning, and the party's top leadership seemed to be acting audaciously for a "progressive" policy.

The second crisis of 1968 was the invasion of Czechoslovakia. The PCF's policy had been in general very favorable to the Dubcek reforms, although under the leadership of a forward-looking but still very cautious former peasant, Waldeck Rochet, the party's ruling group remained deeply divided on this issue, even if democratic centralist discipline kept this disagreement almost entirely screened from public view. Waldeck Rochet's finest moment as the PCF's General Secretary was to achieve the Politburo's strong and immediate condemnation of the invasion of Czechoslovakia, in spite of internal opposition from, among others, Jeanette Vermeersch-Thorez, the widow of Maurice Thorez. This break with the Soviets was softened and rendered ambiguous in the next few years through conciliatory judgments about the "normalization" process in Czechoslovakia. It did, however, have a lasting effect: the PCF was launched on an "autonomist" foreign policy which would flower briefly in the party's very aggressive "Eurocommunist" phase in the middle 1970s; and increasing dissatisfaction with "proletarian internationalism" had a predictable effect on internal party reform as well.

In sum, the PCF's break with the Socialist Party in 1977–8 had its correlative movement inside the Communist Party itself in addition to the realignment of foreign policy on Soviet positions. Yet the most important fact in all this was that the radical zigzags in domestic strategy and foreign policy were possible *only because* the PCF internally had remained fundamentally Stalinist. Orthodox democratic centralism had survived, at least for a time, the challenges of "Eurocommunism" and "socialism in French colors." This confirmed Annie Kriegel's prediction (1974, p. 257) that democratic centralism would be the most durable of the orthodox communist holy trinity of dogmas, and that "the structure of the party itself" would prove the "least flexible" element of French Communist political development. To be sure, in addressing non-Communist audiences, leaders such as Marchais and the secretary for organization Paul Laurent (1977) tended to be coy about making orthodox claims about the meaning of democratic centralism. But inside the party at the same moment—among the cadres, militants, and internal "idéologues"—the old claims were reasserted with force:

> [D]emocratic centralism, while it expresses the revolutionary essence of the vanguard party, can never be justified in itself or at the level of abstraction. It finds its *raison d'être* in the concrete historical situation in which the revolutionary essence of the vanguard party is expressed ... This is essentially a political question, in the Marxist sense of the term. Being thus the organizational form which expresses the revolutionary essence of the vanguard party, it is possible to establish the scientific foundation of democratic centralism. Democratic centralism is not one possible organizational form among others for the French Communist party. This organizational structure, this principle of functioning, is the mode of existence of its revolutionary essence as the party of the working class. (Spire, 1977, pp. 78–9, 83)

This passage (from the PCF's official monthly, *Cahiers du Communisme*), which could have been from any Comintern or Cominform document, written perhaps by Stalin, Zdhanov, or Suslov, perfectly expresses the political culture of ordinary Stalinism. In it democratic centralism is an ideological badge—despite the sham invocation of "a political question, in the Marxist sense of the term"—whose purpose is to inflate true believership and to intimidate adversaries with the alleged intrinsic vanguard superiority of the Communists.

The French Communist Party in the 1970s was thus without doubt the best example of what Neil McInnes (1976, p. 28) called West European communism's "characteristic heresy": that "a party remains communist (no matter what else it gives up) as long as it retains the Leninist party machine, the practice of democratic centralism and absolute rule by a small group around the secretary-general who can change tactics brusquely and without explanation." At its 1976 Congress the party officially abandoned the "dictatorship of the proletariat" dogma, and in the same year at the international meeting of communist parties in East Berlin, it officially repudiated the doctrine of "proletarian internationalism." We shall see that despite all backsliding, on foreign policy especially, this sacrifice of symbols expresses also willy-nilly real political changes. What of orthodox democratic centralism in this context? We shall look closely, first, at the "Paris affair" and the purge of 1978–80, and then at the French Communist Party's behavior since enrolling in the ranks of Cabinet ministers and government bureaucrats.

The "Paris Affair": A Question of Deciding or of Implementing Policy?

As we have said, the PCF's internal party crisis erupted as a delayed reaction to the top leadership's seemingly inexplicable failure in summer 1977 to renegotiate the Joint Program successfully, and thus to reforge the Union of the Left coalition for the 1978 elections. Between the split in August 1977 and the March 1978 elections there was a sort of "phoney peace." Both the Communist and Socialist leaderships continued to say they hoped "unity" would be repaired (the small, left–center Movement of Left-Wing Radicals seemed above all relieved to be out of what had always been for them foreign territory). But ultimately no agreement was reached, and the elections were evidently lost already in the first ballot results. (A good summary analysis is found in Johnson, 1981, chs. 10 and 11.) The PCF, at 21 percent, conserved its electorate. The

PS, damaged by the combination of Communist attacks and internal demoralization over the failure to keep the PCF in a coalition, won 23 percent, but was far short of the 28–31 percent it had earlier been expected to win. For the Communists, the main point was that the Socialists led them only by 2 percent, not by the predicted 8–10 percent.

On the day following the first ballot the PCF, PS, and MRG leaderships suddenly, after almost a year of deadlock, announced that an agreement on the usual mutual withdrawals had been reached for the second ballot. The Socialists had been expecting to seek such an agreement, since they wanted Communist electoral support even without a program alliance. Yet they were rightfully astonished when the Communists agreed, almost without discussion, to the principle of second-ballot help. For the Communist leaders had said all during the campaign that there would be no agreement of any kind, even purely electoral, unless the Socialists accepted Communist proposals concerning the Joint Program. How could the top Communist leaders suddenly have abandoned their demands on the Socialists, merely for electoral purposes and in violation of the leaders' previous promises? And if the disagreements about program were not so significant as the Communist Party's bureaucracy and voters had been told, then why had the leadership not compromised with the Socialists *before* the elections, in order to win and then work from within to push the Socialists? Or as rumors had had it for months, was the Communist leadership's real purpose to *lose* the elections, in order to avoid helping the Socialist Party in a historic new dominant position on the left?

As one specialist has put it, after the first ballot showed the left could not win a parliamentary majority, the Communist leaders "had grounds for discreet relief" (ibid., p. 201). This is, to say the least, an understatement! Contrasted with François Mitterrand's gloom, Georges Marchais on the evening of the defeat seemed unexplainably placid. Then on the following day the PCF's Politburo issued a declaration whose two affirmations were patently outrageous (*L'Humanité*, 20 March 1978):

(1) The Communist Party had no responsibility at all for the PCF–PS split and its consequences; the "entire responsibility" rests with the Socialists.

(2) The party's strategic line had been absolutely constant in favor of "unity" with the Socialists since the Joint Program was signed.

Ten days later, after a period of silence from the leadership during which time the party's ranks went into turmoil, the second-ranking leader, Charles Fiterman (after 1981 the Transport Minister in the Mauroy government), spoke to an important meeting of the party's federation secretaries: "We did not want a defeat," he said, implying the pertinence of the question.

The central headquarters was deluged with protests from all levels—grassroots petitions from scores of party cells and sections, and also bitter attacks from party intellectuals in non-Communist newspapers (for instance, Louis Althusser and Jean Elleinstein in *Le Monde*). This, a direct violation of the unwritten rules of democratic centralism, came after *L'Humanité*, under instructions from the top, refused their articles. Most important, there began to appear a protest from within the upper levels of the party bureaucracy, from the *permanents* (apparatchiks) who for decades had been primarily responsible for enforcing the discipline of ordinary Stalinism.

As Althusser put it, the party had deserved a left-wing victory. The party had deserved a left-wing parliamentary majority, which could test the Fifth Republic's constitution and take control of the state away from the right in order to begin the long-promised "peaceful transition to socialism." But now the party suspected that its leaders had in truth *planned* a defeat, and had agreed to second-ballot withdrawals only after this primary goal had been achieved. There had been, Althusser charged, "a *secret* strategic turnabout, not explained but on the contrary hidden behind continuity of the old language" of left-wing unity (Althusser, 1978, p. 48). Althusser went to the central point, in a remarkable avowal and denunciation of the PCF's ordinary Stalinist culture. It was not that breaking the alliance was in itself Stalinist; rather the Stalinism was to lie, in the refusal to admit and explain why it had been necessary to betray the Socialists. The party, said Althusser, would have accepted the real reason, which was valid: the Communist Party could never abandon its historic vanguard position in order to help the Socialists. It would have been *Leninist* politics to be truthful, at least inside the party. But to the contrary, the Marchais group chose a Stalinist method: lying to the outside world and to the party alike. Why could the Marchais group not admit that its strategy of alliance had been a mistake, that it had helped the Socialists more than the Communists and needed now to be abandoned? The answer was simply that everything was at stake: the entire orthodox communist edifice of "correct" leadership—scientific socialism, policy infallibility, and party "unity":

[Because] a change in strategic line naturally leads to a critical analysis of the old line, *thus, of mistakes in strategy. And once one opens the chapter on mistakes, one knows where one begins but not where one may end up*: The new strategy may also be mistaken, because the old one was without it being realized . . . Without a doubt the old leadership reflex came into play: "the party (the leadership) is always correct"; "everything that has occurred has verified the correctness of our strategy"; "the party line has been constant." (ibid., pp. 50–1)

Althusser's attack on the party's leadership was a political bomb. As opposed to Jean Elleinstein, a "right" experimenter always viewed suspiciously in the party bureaucracy, Althusser was a party loyalist and a lionized Marxist theorist. Althusser's public accusation that the top leaders had betrayed the party was the first shot of a profound protest from within the PCF's upper ranks—the first of its kind since the Hungarian debacle in 1956.

The Unwritten Rules Are Mobilized

The Marchais group had one overriding goal now: to smother debate and squelch the protest. They had chosen a fortress strategy in a Stalinist reflex, but the choice once made, its implementing was a matter of consciously putting into operation the unwritten rules of ordinary Stalinist democratic centralism. They were, of course, past masters, having all been educated in Soviet party schools and begun their way toward the top during the Thorez years.

The same mechanisms which produce unanimity at Stalinist party congresses now were mobilized to produce unanimity in accepting the leadership's version of the left's defeat. As Fiterman told the federation secretaries, the issue had become a matter of "political" truth.

First, discussion was limited by ruling-group fiat to the party itself: Marchais explained that keeping debate among the Communists themselves would prevent harmful influence by adversaries from outside. Secondly, the ruling group itself provided all the documents for discussion: these were the Politburo's short declaration of 20 March after the second ballot, and Fiterman's 29 March report to the party's federation secretaries. No other documents could be discussed, and Fiterman's report was the sort of "accounting" from the General Secretary which is "accepted" with unanimous approval at a Stalinist party congress. Thirdly, discussion inside the party was compartmentalized in the usual ordinary

Stalinist manner: discussion in cells, with a filtering process of "correct" resolutions going up through the sections and federations to the very top of the party. In effect, this meant that the party's grassroots would debate in secret, and that only the *results* of these 10,000 or so individual discussions would be known, since the "outside" could not be present and since party members themselves were not to discuss Communist affairs with non-Communists. Moreover, the ban on horizontal communication meant that at all levels—cell, section, and federation—debate occurred without knowledge of what the rest of the party was saying. This made it impossible for "oppositionist" groupings at any level (meaning those who rejected the ruling group's explanation) to know how widely their views might be shared in the party (conceivably they could have even been a *majority* to start with!), or have the opportunity to advocate their views beyond their particular location in the network. Finally, the one public inner-party mass medium which could have provided a real debate of a sort—that is, the daily newspaper *L'Humanité*—was closed to this discussion. Contrary to the practice of running a "discussion tribune" (guest editorial columns) in preparation for party congresses and other important meetings, in this instance Georges Marchais announced that the party constitution prohibited "discussion tribunes" outside the party congress periods. In fact the party constitution says nothing about this: Marchais had simply invented another unwritten rule of democratic centralism. (And in any case, these guest editorial columns, when an ordinary Stalinist ruling group wants to keep the screws down, are censored so as to produce whatever result is desired: Marchais's reaction on this score seems to have been another Stalinist reflex.)

Those dissidents who continued during the initial period in March–May 1978 to publish attacks in non-Communist newspapers were, in relation to all this, out of control. And Marchais indicated the Stalinist line which the ruling group would take with *all* non-conformists, in a declaration (*L'Humanité*, 27 April 1978) which lumped together protesting intellectuals (always suspect in the party's *ouvriériste* culture) and loyalist critics in the bureaucracy: "It is easy," he said, 'to monolog sitting behind a desk and to write peremptory articles outside real life." This is "opportunist," which could lead "the party to liquidation."

In short, all the typical Stalinist clichés and all "the unwritten legislation of Stalinist democratic centralism" (in Robrieux's phrase, 1980–4, vol. 3, p. 332) were used to silence the party. The fortress strategy was designed to protect the ruling group before everything else, but an outside observer had to wonder at Marchais's capacity for creating crises which put the leadership in danger: in 1975–6 there had been the crisis with the Soviets; in 1977–8 there had been the crisis with the Socialists; now there was a crisis within the party itself. Not all regimes which govern by crisis are Stalinist, it goes without saying. Indeed, *weak* regimes often use crisis as the routine mechanism of making decisions. Stalinism, on the other hand, is a regime of awesome centralized power which *requires* crisis to maintain its vigor. Were the crises of the Marchais period thus primarily the result of a recidivist Stalinist mentality? Or did they result simply from weak leadership? Or seen from a more comprehensive point of view, were they not more truly a demonstration that de-Stalinization, especially half-hearted, cannot be accomplished through Stalinist methods? Marchais's policies, in their incompetence and inadvertence, had misused Stalinism and de-Stalinization alike.

The "Paris Affair"

The protest in the PCF in spring 1978 began with a roar, but died down after only a few months. The rapid restoration of control in the party by the top leaders—Georges Marchais took his month-long holiday as usual in July—surprised most observers (including myself at the time), given the initial situation. The lack of a sustained grassroots action against leadership was partly a matter of the typically sporadic and temporary character of rank-and-file initiative throughout political life, but one also needs to account for the fact that an initially outraged party bureaucracy allowed itself quickly to be "normalized" by pressure from above for Stalinist discipline. Here Neil McInnes seems again to have had the French Communist Party specifically in mind among the Eurocommunist parties when he wrote (1976, p. 46) that "a party long unused to liberty does not know how to use it when it tries." Contrasted with the PCI leadership's patient cultivation of lower-echelon responsibility and sense of integrity, the Marchais group's tardy, hectic, and ambivalent Eurocommunization of the party in the middle 1970s could not possibly in so short a period produce a bureaucracy capable of resisting its political leadership—least of all at a moment when it could legitimately be claimed that the party was in danger, another historical cliché of orthodox communism, but none the less true for that.

Nonconformism inside the party thus rather soon after the initial outburst became localized in two places. On the one hand, there

were the dissidents. To some extent the PCF's recent dissidents—
for example Roger Garaudy in the late 1960s, Elleinstein, and
Althusser more recently—had been the typical right and left "deviations" in an orthodox hierarchy in which Stalinist conformism is
the "correct" line between "opportunism" and "sectarianism." In
addition, a durable Sovietophile tendency emerged as well in the
1970s in opposition to the policies of foreign policy independence
and rejection of the Soviet Union as a model.[2]

Yet the dissidence of the Paris affair was something different: a
revolt inside the "machine to manufacture unity" itself, in which a
group of high-level apparatchiks worked orthodox democratic centralism back to its untenable premises.

In the flattest terms of bureaucratic infighting the Paris affair was a
conflict between the Marchais ruling group and the eight-member
secretariat of the PCF's Paris federation. The Paris federation is one
of ninety-five, but obviously it is quite special. The party's most
characteristic ordinary Stalinist federations are those in the
working-class "red suburbs" of Paris; by contrast the Paris federation cannot help reflecting its own environment to some extent. In
the 1970s the Paris federation was the party's most Eurocommunist
federation, and the one whose leadership had become most committed to and dependent on the alliance with the Socialists.

It was not surprising that the Paris federation should have been
the source of some of the most aggressive opposition to the national
leadership following the 1978 elections. Its first secretary—Henri
Fiszbin, a former factory worker, long-time *permanent*, Central
Committee member, and also the party's mayoral candidate against
Jacques Chirac in 1977—has written a detailed account of the
episode. This remarkable book, *Les Bouches s'ouvrent*, is the best of a
considerable list of insiders' accounts.[3] It is the old story of a "good
communist," as he puts it, a pure product of 35 years of party
membership, of loyalty, of action in the service of the working class
and of the vanguard party" (Fiszbin, 1980, p. 16).

Henri Fiszbin: The Disillusion of a "Good Communist"

Shortly after the 1978 elections, as the initial revolt reached
momentum against the Politburo's cynical agreement with the
Socialists and its denial of all responsibility, the Paris federation's
weekly newspaper published a summary of a violently critical
debate in one of its local organizations. Marchais, alert to the fact

that the Paris federation had never really digested the policy of breaking with the Socialist Party a year earlier, saw the danger. Instructions were issued throughout the party press network not to make any reference to this article, and not to produce any others of its type. Furthermore, instead of an open "discussion tribune" in *L'Humanité*, which Marchais had already vetoed, the party's federation secretaries were then instructed to write "summaries" (trumped-up and fit for the occasion) of discussion in their organizations.

Fiszbin's turn came. "The readers of *L'Humanité* until then had mainly been given refutations of positions which had never been stated themselves," he wrote later (Fiszbin, 1980, p. 37). So Fiszbin published a "summary" which gave some of the questions as well as the "correct" answers to those who had not yet "understood" the national leadership's explanations. Was it possible, he wrote, that the Socialists were "entirely" responsible for the split, and the Communists not at all? Had the Socialists really "turned to the right" in their proposals for an updated Joint Program, or had the Communists suddenly upped the ideological stakes? Why, given the party's new Eurocommunist commitments to democratic methods, as stated emphatically at the 1976 Congress, was no open debate permitted now? Why had the leadership made the issue one of *absolute* agreement with *every* aspect of the party's line, resulting in a division of the party into "good communists" who "understand," and those who "refuse to understand"? As a responsible federation secretary and a good communist, Fiszbin gave the "correct" answers, to be sure, but this display of loyalism, which got the article through censorship, could not repair the audacity of publicly formulating the burning questions themselves.[4]

At the next Central Committee meeting (April 1978) a few Paris federation committee members unexpectedly asked questions of Marchais's peremptory analysis of responsibilities and proclamation that the line had not changed since 1972. Fiszbin, a long-time Central Committee member, says "This was the first time that certain members of the Central Committee had found themselves in the presence of criticisms or disagreements" in a meeting (ibid., p. 44). According to the unwritten rules of orthodox democratic centralism, however, this important and truly representative internal debate was held secret. Only the "official" resolution—meaning Marchais's report—was published, unanimously voted. Fiszbin, despite his criticisms still basically a loyalist, voted with everyone else in favor of the ruling group. His justification is worth quoting at length, for it brilliantly, if inadvertently, conveys the insider's reasoning about orthodox discipline:

> I therefore voted [yes]. Why? It's all the more a legitimate question in that I seriously questioned what attitude I should adopt. I hesitated for a long time: vote against? abstain? In the discussion I had spoken my mind: I don't need to reproach myself for not having had the courage of my convictions. But [disagreement] remains private, internal. However to break unanimity with my vote would have been something else. I am not certain, even today, that a [dissenting] vote would have worked toward what I wanted. As a practical matter all the party's internal life excluded the hypothesis that a federation secretary, a Central Committee member, could refuse to vote the report presented. What would have been my situation had I, for example, abstained in the vote? Theoretically there is no problem: I vote according to my opinion and thereafter I implement the decisions. But I know the rest by heart: the 15 [other] Central Committee members belonging to the Paris federation would rise to defend the Central Committee's position in the face of the federation first secretary "who doesn't agree." It is unendurable, even more for the federation than for myself. The problem is unresolvable. (ibid., pp. 51–2)

Among the 147 Central Committee members Fiszbin felt himself "as if in a surrealist soccer match trying to score goals between goal posts protected by 146 goalies" (ibid., p. 184).

Despite (and in part because of) Fiszbin's reluctance to break Central Committee unanimity at the April meeting, the Paris federation for a time continued to be the major pocket of institutional resistance to the national leadership, eluding "normalization." Then in January 1979 the Politburo finally put the Paris secretariat on the carpet. There were four classic, Stalinist cliché accusations: "laxism," "opportunism," "lack of resoluteness" in defending the party's line, and "lack of proper class spirit" (ibid., p. 21).

At a confrontational meeting the eight Paris federation officials, led by Fiszbin, should, according to the rules, have collapsed in political obeisance. However, against all tradition and past behavior (several of them had two or three decades of loyalist service) they resisted. They argued that criticisms of the leadership's recent behavior toward the Socialists, and of the truncation of internal party debate, were meant to reestablish "correct" applications of the national leadership's own policies. Fiszbin, seemingly still not quite clear at this point about what really was at issue, explained the conflict in terms of problems of democratic centralism:

> The "Paris Affair" was in my view an error of the leadership. It derived precisely ... from objective difficulties encountered in the application of our strategy, from uncertainty about the means for overcoming them, from hesitation to discuss the questions posed openly with all the Communists. (ibid., p. 206)

Put differently, Fiszbin wanted to interpret the conflict as disagreement about how best to implement an agreed policy. That the Marchais group would not let it go at that signified not only, to recall Alfred Meyer's point, that "Lenin erred in drawing an insufficient distinction between making and executing policies," but more important, that Stalin had shown communist bosses only too well how to manipulate the rules of democratic centralism to achieve absolute dictatorship over the party.

After a violent confrontation at this meeting, Henri Fiszbin resigned in protest as first secretary of the Paris federation (by November 1979, ten months later, the other seven secretariat members all had resigned as well). The ruling group explained his resignation in the party's newspaper so as to make Fiszbin seem an isolated dissident (the other resignations were never even announced); soon thereafter rumors were spread linking Fiszbin's "eccentric" behavior to a real, but irrelevant, illness, the point of which was to suggest, Soviet fashion, that "reformism" is a "disease."

The ruling group's attention to dissidents, however, was not limited to the best-known ones. There was, indeed, a characteristic Stalinist meticulousness (to take the Paris federation as an example) in a campaign of "personal visits" to all party members who had signed the so-called Aix-en-Provence Protest Petition (see Barak, 1980), or who were members of the 116 cells and sections in the Paris federation which had voted critical motions, or sent critical letters to the national headquarters. Fiszbin himself (1980, p. 17), despite his internal opposition and before resigning as first secretary, worked loyally at this task ("Yes, I believe in discipline; I'm committed to it as the only way to act effectively"). Under his authority a census of factional activity pinpointed 200 resisters; 169 were contacted (the rest were out of town or refused to meet). The result, Fiszbin reports, was that slightly less than one-half refused to change their positions; some of these vowed even to continue their public protests. The majority, however, "admitted that their actions had had prejudicial consequences" for the party, and accepted "normalization" (ibid., pp. 59–60).

In November 1979 Fiszbin—no longer the Paris federation's first secretary but still a member of Central Committee—cast a lone negative vote against organizational secretary Paul Laurent's Central Committee report which, in part, repeated the ruling group's accusations against the Paris federation leadership. A Central Committee member since 1967, Fiszbin says that this was the first time in twenty-two years that even a single dissenting vote had been cast. He then resigned also from the Central Committee, an act without precedent in the entire period since the PCF's Bolshevization in the 1930s. (Maurice Thorez, it is reported, had once rejected an attempted resignation in 1949: "One doesn't resign from the Central Committee".)[5]

To the end, as Fiszbin says of himself, he never quite escaped the dilemma of the true believer: what he believes is decided from above, and thus can legitimately be changed from above. To refuse to agree is to lose one's identity as a true believer, as a "good communist." In other words, while Fiszbin accepted, in accordance with the logic of democratic centralism, the possibility that the Marchais group might have reasonable criticisms of the Paris federation's *application* of policy, he was disoriented totally to be accused (after thirty-five years of loyalty!) of betraying the party, of rejecting a strategy—"unity"—which he profoundly endorsed. One ruling group leader told him that "contrary to what you said . . . most of the [Paris federation] debates did not come from the desire to implement the 22nd congress strategy better, but rather from the desire to combat it." Marchais made the same accusation in his more brutal style: "You, I know you disagree with the party's line and you just refuse to admit it!" (ibid., pp. 94–5). The thought that the ruling group *itself* had done a secret about-face on the strategy of alliance with the Socialists was hardly formulated before being dismissed as unthinkable. The loyalist critic could not accept it without "liquidating" the very idea itself of the communist party in his own mind. The result was necessarily intellectual and political confusion:

> Any criticism is said to be opposition to the party's policy and to the leadership . . . It is true that certain comrades have made a very personal interpretation of the 22nd congress [strategy].

But what should be done? Prove that these comrades are not in agreement, even when they affirm their desire to support the 22nd congress? Or, much to the contrary, to create a good and proper interpretation with all those who say they are in agreement? (ibid., p. 46)

Fiszbin's problem was, however, something less complex and more terrifying: the classic dilemma of the "good communist" caught in a Stalinist system, that is, in the totalitarian trap built into the language itself of Stalinist thinking: "What was unendurable was not the criticisms . . . but the questioning of what each of us holds most dear: His resolution to give all his energies in the service of his party's policy" (ibid., p. 93).

An Ordinary Stalinist Purge

"The purge," Annie Kriegel (1972, p. 146) says, "is the mode by which a Stalinist power demonstrates it is a power never shared." This is true, but incomplete, for there are high Stalinist and ordinary Stalinist purges.

After the ruling group's exclusion of Roger Garaudy in 1970—a last gesture of disdain for the "infantile communism" of May 1968—Georges Marchais said there would never again be exclusions from the party for political reasons, to enforce monolithic discipline and leadership fiat. In order to keep this "promise," while doing the contrary, the purge methods used in 1978–80 adopted a classic hypocrisy of the Great Purge, originated by Stalin's prosecutor, Andreii Vishinskii. This involved saying that those who question the party's line *exclude themselves* from the party: they "voluntarily place themselves outside the party," by breaking the unwritten democratic centralist rules of discipline and fealty. At each level of the party—a cell, if it is a question of an individual dissident; a section, if the matter is accusation of a dissident cell; or a federation or even the Central Committee itself, if there is a charge of factional behavior extending horizontally beyond local boundaries—the relevant party organ simply adopts a resolution "taking note" of the "fact" that a member or group "has placed itself by its own actions outside the party."

This was the method used against Fiszbin and others involved in the "Paris affair" and the anti-Stalinist Jacquerie of 1978–80, generally speaking. Hundreds were officially excluded in this ordinary

Stalinist purge (a purge without executions), while others resigned in advance and thousands more dropped out of the party by not renewing their party card. Literally dozens of now "unreliable" journalists were fired from the party's major press organs— *L'Humanité, Cahiers du Communisme, La Nouvelle Critique*—while *France Nouvelle* and many local newspapers were liquidated outright in addition to the purge of personnel.

As we shall see, there were, not surprisingly, also drastic repercussions in communist influence outside the party, in the CGT and in the party's flanking organizations. With regard to the party's membership, it is impossible again today, as it used to be years ago, to have an even approximately truthful answer from party sources on the size of the organization. Falsification is once again the unwritten rule regarding membership statistics. But certainly the party was devastated after 1978. It lost perhaps 200,000 of its claimed 700,000 members in the two years following the 1978 elections, and its current membership is probably between 200,000 and 300,000.

Fiszbin and other dissidents organized themselves outside the party, once they lost a determined battle to resist becoming victims of what might be called Vishinsky's revenge on Eurocommunism. Their little political club (the RCH) tried hard to organize "communists outside the party," that is to say, former Communists. They wanted one day to be strong enough to challenge the official Communist Party leadership's legitimacy to "represent" the communist impulse in France. But this courageous attempt to remain "communists" without being any longer "Communists" has waned in quixotic frustration.

French Communism in the Mitterrand Presidency, 1981–4

Accommodation
The French Communist Party's government role after 1981 was an experiment in political accommodation. Since the outbreak of the Cold War, which pushed the SFIO into the Fourth Republic's centrist coalitions, the PCF's leaders had been able to state the terms in which left-wing politics were conceived and discussed. For thirty-five years Communism's simultaneous political unacceptability and vanguardist superiority complex made any Union of the Left policy unthinkable, of which fact the PCF made a virtue by assuming a position of "splendid isolation." The SFIO, cumulatively compromised by the weakness of French government, demoraliz-

ing colonial wars, and the rally of its leaders to General de Gaulle for the first years of the Fifth Republic, suffered communist ideological and organizational intimidation. The Communists, and the CGT union they controlled, were an awesome if pent-up political force; the Socialists, by contrast, were weak, internally divided, and as usual caught between their nostalgia for a radical program and the routine margins of Establishment government policy.

All this was reversed in the Socialist apotheosis of 1981. The reinvented Socialist Party won an absolute parliamentary majority by itself (only the Gaullist party, in June 1968, had accomplished this previously). Moreover, the PS beat the Communist's electoral score by 23 points (39 to 16 percent) and had an advantage of over 200 parliamentary seats! From the point of view of policy President Mitterrand arrived in office with a list of "110 propositions" of which many were "structural reforms"—nationalizations in banking and industry; decentralization of the state; a renewal of industrial planning; self-management innovations in big enterprises—which the Communists had already endorsed in the Joint Program. In this situation the PCF would have had to take large risks, immediately and from a weakened position, if it wanted to outbid Mitterrand politically in 1981 as it had done in 1977. Furthermore, among all the Socialists and the other leaders of what had symptomatically been called the "nonconformist left," François Mitterrand was the most difficult to intimidate, and the most experienced in dealing with the Communists. In a sense he was fundamentally an anti-Communist, notwithstanding his genuine respect for Communist activism and grassroots dedication. The PCF's leaders remembered with chagrin Mitterrand's declaration in 1972 at a Vienna meeting of the Socialist International that a revivified Socialist Party in France could hope to rebuild itself "on the terrain of the Communist Party itself," ultimately winning over most of the Communist vote.[6] In short, in joining Pierre Mauroy's government in June 1981 the Communists entered a profoundly more dangerous stage of their half-century rivalry with the Socialists. Moreover, as President of the Republic, Mitterrand now could bargain and threaten the Communists much more strongly so as to limit the possibility for any repeat of the Communists' radical betrayal of 1977.

All things considered, the Communist Party was a relatively pliant government partner for the years 1981–3. Its main goal was to cut its own political losses, through the appearance of loyal behavior. (This was the major difference from 1977–8.) However, even more than its reversion to criticism of Socialist policy in 1983–4 the

154

Communists' *previous* bad behavior continued to have its effect on public opinion. The result was that the PCF lost heavily again at the 1984 European Parliament elections. At 11 percent the PCF now is in real danger of permanent political marginality. Current gossip that its leaders plan to profit from a big Socialist defeat in 1986 in order to return in strength in the 1990s is a sign of desperation more than anything else. The CGT's influence also has seriously diminished, both in an absolute sense and in relation to the rest of the labor movement. Unexpectedly in the Mitterrand presidency, the moderate Workers' Force (FO) union has pulled up about equal in strength to the Socialist-leaning CFDT, both no longer so far behind the CGT's strength of numbers. Altogether it would be a mistake to see the Communist accommodation 1981–3 as anything other than the consequence of weakness.

At the time of writing (summer 1984) it is too soon to draw firm conclusions about the less evident results of French communism's three-year government role on its practice of democratic centralism. What we can do, considering the facts, is to suggest an analysis of how government burdens and opportunities have affected aspects of the PCF's internal structure and its recidivist Stalinist political culture.

"Flawless Solidarity": The Work of Communist Government Ministers

In the agreement signed in June 1981 by Socialist and Communist leaders, founding their government coalition, the Communists had to promise "flawless solidarity." This clause referred to a past history filled with Leninist and Stalinist aggression on the Socialists by the Communists. Not only the betrayal of 1977, but the unexpected Communist attacks on the Socialists in 1975 (including the publication of Marchais's secret 1972 report), the merciless Communist treatment of the SFIO during the Fourth Republic, the Communist infiltration and seizure from within the CGT in 1945–6—in other words, the entire history of Communist–Socialist relations, going all the way back to the PCF's Ministry of the Masses during the Popular Front and the "class against class" tactics of 1921–8 were reflected in the Socialist demand for "flawless solidarity" from the Communists. Furthermore, it was specified that solidarity did not stop in the councils of government; it extended also to the factories. The CGT thus also was affected by Mitterrand's kept promise to bring the

155

Communists into the government: in a sense Mitterrand now proposed to manipulate the Communist Party's control of the CGT, to make democratic centralism work for the Socialists just as he had used the PCF's Union of the Left strategy!

Inside the government the Communist ministers behaved indeed with near to "flawless solidarity," aware that they were watched closely for subterfuge or a double game.[7] The Communist ministers were "tracked" on two sides: the Socialists, on the one side, put their own people in positions to spot Communist political abuse of office; on the other side, Communist ministerial Cabinets were filled with Communist Party members, some of whom, it must be assumed, reported to internal party organs. Several were PCF deputies defeated in the 1981 debacle, and others were Communist journalists laid off because of austerity in the party's press network. So government membership, for the Communists as for all parties, provided patronage, welcome in the party's recent hard times, to maintain loyalists (Frèches, 1983, pp. 450–1).

With minor exceptions, the Communist ministers accepted all the controversial Socialist foreign policies—including support for INF deployment of Pershing and Cruise missiles in Western Europe, and the strong anti-Soviet declarations concerning Poland and Afghanistan. The Communist Party, as a party, sometimes took a different line. But what was surprising is not that two parties in a coalition should disagree on certain policies (the Giscardist–Gaullist coalition ran for years on this basis), but that the Communist Party accepted the political humiliation of separating its ministers' voices in the government from party policy. (This could even be seen as a perverse working of democratic centralism: the ministers must vote against the party's policy in order to preserve the party's discipline!) Yet it would be disingenuous not to recognize that the PCF was not a "usual" example here, and that disagreement within the left was potentially more explosive and damaging in the French government than was disagreement between the UDF and the RPR. None the less, the fact of "flawless" Communist ministerial solidarity was evidence that the PCF's leaders accepted the rules of a certain institutional framework, or were being obliged to abide by them. This does not change any basic policy conflict between the Socialists and Communists, especially in East–West relations, but it well demonstrates that the Communists completely lost the political initiative.[8]

156

Beyond this the Communist ministers avoided taking positions publicly on issues outside their ministerial purview, and inside the Cabinet the Communists generally spoke only concerning their own dossiers, unlike other ministers, who offered opinions across the board according to the Socialist Party tradition. This prudence was, again, no doubt simply a function of political weakness. (In addition, however, Mitterrand and Mauroy discussed general policy and coalition politics privately with Fiterman.) Until 1984 the Communist parliamentary group also was reliable in support of the government's policies, despite a certain amount of expected criticism of the switch to austerity and an oppositional position when the Socialists did not insist on solidarity. The main task in Parliament was to avoid the impression that the PCF had become a political doormat for the PS. Yet this terrain was dangerous: when Communist criticism of the government's austerity and industrial reorganization plans (cutting jobs, cutting subsidies, allowing weak firms to go under, especially in steel, automobile, and shipbuilding industries where the PCF has a strong political investment on top of everything else) reached a maximum point in spring 1984, Mitterrand and Mauroy put an issue of confidence before Parliament which, after some histrionics, the Communists voted unanimously on 2 April.

All this said about ministerial solidarity and parliamentary support willy-nilly, the Communist Party remains "unlike the others" in the sense that its government ministers and parliamentarians still acted first of all as Communists, on the rules of orthodox democratic centralism. The ministers were controlled, in general, and in any particular controversy, by the party's ruling group. At the same time, there inevitably developed a large "technical" sphere in which the ministers acted autonomously, a degree of autonomy which increased as they gained experience and influence. In addition, the Communist ministers and officials moved in a wider circle of contacts than the Communist apparatus could control (and Charles Fiterman, with his special link to Mitterrand and Mauroy, seemed often a case apart). Several of the top Communist government officials, for example, used foreign trips to create a minuscule "foreign policy" which no doubt had some personal aspects (for example, Fiterman's trips to negotiate in Algeria). But on the whole, whatever transpired inside the PCF top hierarchy, it remained a "black box" as far as the outside world could see. Only at the end, in the spring and summer of 1984, was there clear evidence of sharp internal factionalism.

Spoils System or White-Anting?

The Communists surprised neither adversaries nor friends by taking full advantage of the chance to put party people in influential positions, and to give loyal militants civil servant jobs, to provide a basis for certain forms of influence in French public administration even now that the party is out of government. It is in regard to this, in addition to the increase of CGT influence in company boards and administrations, that most accusations of "white-anting" arose from those who believe that having taken the Communists into the government was a long-term miscalculation.

Despite the Communist movement's visible decline, some are concerned that it still has latent potential for influencing economic policy and political cultural conceptions through its penetration of public administration organizations and the media (cf. Frèches, 1983; Jeambar, 1984). There are really two issues here. One is the actual extent of new Communist influence; the other is whether Communist appointments and patronage constituted a classic strategy of "packing the ministries" to infiltrate government, or whether this was a typical instance of the spoils system at work. In 1944–7, it is beyond doubt, the French Communists hoped to gain permanent control of the internal civil service networks (Tiersky, 1974, ch. 5). However little chance this had to gain control of the state, the French Communist true believers thought themselves engaged in a long-term positional strategy of Communist advance in France as part of a general Soviet geopolitical strategy.

In the 1981–4 situation a number of appointments to significant positions in public administration need first to be cited. Besides the four Communist Cabinet-level positions and the patronage attached directly to them, Communists were named to head the Paris RATP Metro system, the national coal board (the Charbonnages), and one division of the national health services administration. Several observations can be made about these appointments. First, in giving the Communists these sorts of Cabinet and administrative position Mitterrand kept them away from international affairs and military security matters. Secondly, in any case, Soviet espionage did not have much to learn from French Communist leaks from the government. Moreover, the Cabinet did not discuss security policy in its weekly meetings. Thirdly, the Communists were given jobs which made them responsible for economically and politically difficult sectors, often pitting Communist administration against the party's electoral and militant rank-and-file. The PCF was thus obliged to

158

"deliver" its constituencies in the service of its government privileges, and the party had to share responsibility in the eyes of public opinion for economic and social results that profoundly discouraged left-wing expectations.

The RATP, under the Communist Claude Quin, was in general run admirably enough, and even improved the Paris Metro (more attention to transport in and between working-class suburbs, economies of time, greater comfort, and savings for the less well off). In addition, Quin adopted a policy of not spending all the government's subsidy for the RATP, which in 1983 produced a budget surplus of 55 million francs. An economist as well as a Central Committee member, Quin said that assured government subsidy of budget deficits was "demobilizing" for a workforce and, more generally, that France's "mixed economy" is "durable" (*Les Nouvelles*, 12–18 April 1984, pp. 64–5). Charles Fiterman, in another case of Communist enthusiasm for efficient management, took the politically courageous decision to authorize Air France to buy American-made Boeing 737 planes, following years of stalling by the French pilots' union which refused the consequent reduction in cockpit staff from three to two (see de Closets, 1982, pp. 314–15).

The national coal board had disastrous results from the point of view of saving jobs, which was the initial government priority. French coal resources already had declined precipitously, falling from 61 million tons produced in 1958 to 23 million tons in 1980. The number of mine-connected workers declined from 242,000 to 62,000 in the same period, with less than 27,500 actually digging coal. Despite huge deficits—the French state paid a 2-billion-franc subsidy in 1980 and almost 6 billion francs in 1982—and despite much cheaper and more abundant foreign coal as well, pressure from unions, especially the CGT, obtained a relaunching of the coal-industry *forteresse ouvrière*, while Giscard d'Estaing was still President. The left-wing government coalition came into office promising to revivify the French coal industry in the northeast, and the Charbonnages was initially given large increases in funds to subsidize this renewal. By 1984, however, Mitterrand and Mauroy could no longer reject arguments made by the Finance Minister Jacques Delors, and a plan for sharp reductions in jobs and state financing was announced. The Communist director of the national coal board, Georges Valbonne, resigned, and the CGT staged unsuccessful street protests.

The Communist Party's relation with the French mass media was a particularly bloody terrain of struggle after June 1981. The mass media posed a double problem: they were simultaneously a target of opportunity for the Communists—who hoped to place journalists and propagandists in the "ideological war" which remains a fundamental element in the PCF's political culture (cf. Jouary *et al.*, 1980)—and a target of criticism, in the sense that the Communists, even from the government, continued to perceive the media as "bourgeois" and, therefore, "viscerally anti-Communist." Thus the PCF never abated its attacks on nationalized television and radio news presentations of the PCF's policies, of Soviet foreign policy, and of the Eastern bloc regimes.

At the same time, after 1981 a significant number of Communist journalists obtained jobs in the radio and television system, after total exclusion during the long Gaullist/Giscardian political tutelage of the media against both the Socialist and Communist parties. Those who condemned the decision to bring the Communists into the government obviously worried about their potential influence in the media: "The Socialists are obliged to accept a political sharing of patronage which reinforces Communist positions in the most sensitive sectors [of public life]" (Frèches, 1983, p. 459). Any such conclusion now seems exaggerated. For example, several Communist journalists were part of radio and television news teams, yet despite much attention, on the whole without political scandal. In addition, the Communists in 1983 failed in a campaign to get one of their people the top job at Radio-France; and a Communist film director named to the new High Authority governing board of the nationalized radio and television networks adopted an empty-chair policy against the board's refusal to change personnel and programming policies he alleged were "anti-communist."

Finally, what was most striking about French communism's relation with the media in 1981–4 was the inability (or unwillingness) to accept new opportunities from the point of view of a government party. The PCF was *in* the government as well as responsible *for* the government, like it or not. But psychologically, because old habits of mind are hard to change, the Communists were never *of* the government. In fact the PCF's old "countersociety" position in French society was paradoxically *updated* in 1981–4, and in many respects even worsened, despite being in the government. Above all, the ruling group's perception that it is desperately isolated in French politics and society (just as now inside the PCF itself) seems not to have softened much. Thus in 1982–3 it made psychological and political sense to find the PCF's leaders acting so vigorously as local relays for Soviet attacks on alleged misrepresentations of Soviet policy in the Western media. Although the old PCF–CPSU ties are undone, the French Communist leaders must feel solidarity with the Soviet ruling group's isolation in international affairs and in Soviet society. The PCF's leaders, with a few exceptions, like the Soviet bosses have only "allies," no real friends.

On "Unity": The Remains of Democratic Centralism outside of the Party

In the 1950s S. M. Lipset made this observation of modern left-wing politics in Western Europe:

> A look at the political history of Europe indicates that no mass lower class-based political party, with the single exception of the German Communists, has ever disappeared or significantly declined through losing the bulk of its votes to a party on its right. The loyalties once created in a *mass* left-wing party are rarely lost. (Rejai, 1971, pp. 87–8)

This is now proven to be no longer true. The French Communist movement is in general reflux, having lost one-fifth of its electorate in the Gaullist landslide of 1958, another 25 percent of its voters in the 1981 presidential and legislative elections, and now an additional increment in the 1984 European Parliament elections. Its membership is also at a crisis level: Louis Althusser has written sardonically about the PCF's past membership crises, that whenever a radical zigzag tactic, or the necessity to digest a Soviet "error," had put the leadership at odds with its rank-and-file, rather than changing the leadership in the PCF "the leaders elect a new party." Annie Kriegel wrote in the same vein a decade ago (1974, p. 199): "During each crisis the party lost a fair share of its members. Like a sponge abandoned by the ebbing tide, it became dry, shrunken, and hardened, but it was always capable of swelling up again when the tide returned." But even a sponge ultimately wears out and disintegrates. Today the membership is decimated and demoralized and it is difficult, given the decline of French communism across the board, to imagine the conditions of a serious renewal. In the 1983 municipal elections, to take yet another example of decline, the Communist local government bastions were severely weakened, especially in the "red belt" areas where the party historically had been strongest and most fortress-like. Then a series of annulments (for fraud and other reasons) of Communist victories in these elections reduced even further the PCF's local presence, which was cut overall in a year by over one-third. And finally, the hard core of the hierarchy, the PCF's structure of permanent apparatchiks, those with long training and large dedication, has also been much reduced, as a repercussion of the "Paris affair" and the general demoralization in which the party has sunk progressively since 1977. Henri Fiszbin gives one reason for the "exit" of many of the old hard-core militants:

> During my activity as a leader I knew a very long period in which the core of the party, from the section level up to the Central Committee, reacted to great political events spontaneously in an identical manner. From the cell secretary to the federation secretary, everyone knew more or less what the national party's positions would be. Today the trouble is very deep. Between the party's policy, set in the Congresses, and the manner in which the leadership reacts [to circumstances], the margin of uncertainty is increasing. The resulting situation is strange: The Communist militants are often surprised by the positions of their party. (Fiszbin, 1980, p. 208)

The ruling group's policy inconsistency and unpredictability has thus weakened not only the party's capacity to renew its large marginal turnover membership, but more important, now the forty-year-long genuine ideological unity of the party's inner militant core. This was the significance of Fiszbin's resignation—what Hirschman terms the "exit" option—and those of many others in upper-level apparatchik positions:

> A new practice has been created little by little: the leadership believes that it is normal that the Communist militants, in a first period, don't comprehend its decisions ... The party [however] should not be divided into those "who understand" and those "who don't understand". (loc. cit.)

This "degradation of consensus in the party," as Fiszbin calls it, is in fact the historic decline of orthodox communism as an ideology. What is left is orthodox democratic centralism, but only as a practice. The ordinary Stalinist ideology which sustains it over the long term has already substantially withered away even in the French Com-

162

munist Party. In consequence, orthodox democratic centralism in 1981 was something of a bluff waiting to be called: François Mitterrand, by a combination of skill and luck, did just that.

What is left? Like declining or relatively insignificant communist parties elsewhere in Western Europe (for example, in Spain or in England), the main reservoir both of organizational resilience and political force in French communism is its trade union, the CGT, which is also declining. Yet there are reasons why communist trade unionism will, in Western Europe, ultimately outlast communist partyism, *pace* Lenin.

Historically whenever the Communist Party went through a dry period, it relied on its union affiliation to sustain it until the waters returned to swell up the sponge of organizational capacity. This was certainly part of the ruling group's plan (or hope) on entering the government in 1981. But the years that have elapsed since that time have revealed a CGT caught in a doubly paradoxical situation which threatens even its remarkable capacity to play again a familiar part. First, as always, Communist use of the CGT for political ends has been a central point of attention since 1981. The Communists years ago officially abandoned the "transmission belt" dogma, but few even among the most sympathetic, have any doubts that the CGT is still substantially controlled by its Communist elements for Communist ends (cf. Lavau, 1981, and Ross, 1982, for different analyses which reach substantially the same conclusion).[9]

In the three years of Communist participation in the Mitterrand government the CGT was rather less aggressive than its adversaries had feared. The clause on "flawless solidarity" which the Communists signed and—more important—knew Mitterrand would enforce was undoubtedly at work. The number of strikes was unusually low, although the government did face brutal strikes in its second year (the autoworkers' strikes at Renault and Citröen in early 1983) and in early 1984 (the steel industry and again the auto industry). The CGT's behavior overall 1981–4 expressed how, because of democratic centralism, it was hopelessly torn between its representative role, which obliges the union to strike, and its role as an arm of the government, through its desire to serve the political goals of the Communist Party.

The second paradox in the contemporary CGT was revealed through the first, that is, the strikes which could not be prevented but which were not fought through with the usual aggressiveness by the leadership: this second paradox was the revelation of the extent to which the CGT, particularly in certain heavy industrial bastions, has become a union of immigrant workers. Media coverage of the strikes tended to show the CGT in the factories in the form of brown or black shop stewards with African names and accents making loudspeaker demands for increased political organizing rights.

Race prejudice in France, as in Germany and other European countries faced with high unemployment and large numbers of "guest workers," has become a politically powerful issue, and the French Communist Party has tried to win new support by calling for an end to guest-worker "economic immigration." The Communists have pointed out, correctly, that foreign workers cluster in working-class municipalities, often PCF local governments, and that Communists have a particular reason therefore to speak out. However, after a series of racist incidents in such municipalities, the party has been taxed with a reputation for anti-Arab and anti-black racism, in addition to its traditional *ouvriérisme* and Gallocommunist xenophobia.

Though an important new factor, this politics of race cannot be studied in detail here. Suffice it for our discussion to remark how the difference between, on the one hand, the CGT's new social composition and, on the other hand, the PCF and CGT leaderships' traditional political cultural characteristics, amounts to a new form of isolation of orthodoxy in the French Communist movement. It would be interesting to know (though the PCF's return to secretiveness makes it impossible) what the real percentage of non-French is in the current party membership. One suspects that the ordinary Stalinist leadership of French communism is less and less *chez soi*.

The "degradation of consensus in the party" described by Fiszbin is, in other words, a more profound change than a decline of internal policy agreement. At stake is the very character of French communism. The fortress of ordinary Stalinism is crumbling from within, because the dangers which it was constructed to withstand are no longer those with which it is faced today.

PART THREE

The Struggle of Two Logics:
Decay or Development?

7

Conclusion: The Force of Circumstance

The Imperative of Change

To be understood dispassionately, communism must be understood in many ways, for it has many "faces." Communism is simultaneously a certain kind of political system; an economic system; a political ideology, culture, and philosophy; a superpower influence in world affairs; and an international military–economic coalition. This book has focussed on the specifically political face of communism: as a unique form of politics, as an ideology of organization, and as an organization of ideology. My intent, through an analysis of democratic centralism as praxis, has been to provide an evaluation of the issue of communism's deadlock and of its prospects for political development.

Orthodox communism today is a routinized form of Stalinism. It is ordinary Stalinism. In political terms the methods of high Stalinism—the great violent purges and the mad political campaigns which mobilized tens of millions of people in the service of impossible ideals and their own moral and human destruction—are in general long gone. Yet the political *goal* of ordinary Stalinism remains that of high Stalinism: monolithic unity. Imperfections in achieving the principle of unanimity do not alter the goal in any substantial meaning.

What Bagehot could have called the "efficient secret" of contemporary orthodox communism is the ideology and practice of democratic centralism. We have seen, however, that democratic centralism was originally only one of three fundamental political dogmas of Stalinism which were so many versions of the same primordial metapolitical goal: "democratic centralism," "dictatorship of the proletariat," and "proletarian internationalism" all were translations of *monolithic unity as a means and as an end*. In this sense Stalinist communism is, speaking theoretically, in *all* its forms and extents *a regime of internal politics* which functions with the same working principle everywhere. Thus we can now state the real "secret" of communism: *Communism, as communism, is a simple regime*. And "simple governments," as Burke (1955, p. 37) said, are "fundamentally defective." They are intrinsically fragile. *Complexity*, according to a tradition which spans the history of politics as a disciplined study, is, to put it differently, the secret of political *stability*. Thus because communism is a simple regime, it *must* change profoundly, no matter how long its development or decay can be retarded by mitigating factors—whether the geopolitical imperialism of the Soviet state, local and historical–cultural complexities folded into communism's simplicity in any given country, or the patriotic defense of communism instigated by the rest of the world's hostility.

On the Destruction of Symbols and Privileges

The philosopher Ian Hacking gives us a rule for thinking through the potential for communist decay, as opposed to development. "Groups of different internal structures," he says, "will fall apart in different ways, and so will perceive different kinds of risk." He adds that, "Ecology teaches that an organism armed against a specific list of dangers responds poorly to new kinds of threat" (Hacking, 1982, p. 30). With respect to the French Communist Party's imperviousness, Philippe Robrieux might have had this very premise in mind: The PCF, he writes, is "an organization which was conceived and elaborated for decades in order to resist pressure from outside, so much and so well that—helped by its ideology—it has ended by becoming almost totally impermeable to influences and information coming from the outside" (Robrieux, 1980–4, vol. 3, p. 463). Indeed, one could take this as a characterization of orthodox communism generally speaking.

Yet beyond a certain point, as Hacking's formulation implies, even communism's originality loses its special force of resistance. Communist organization was conceived precisely to *resist* certain kinds of change but ultimately it, like all constituted groups, becomes prey to the force of circumstance of "new kinds of threat," involving "different kinds of risk." Communist parties are, after all, in a sense bureaucratic hierarchies like any other. And even the most longstanding, hidebound commitment to communist parties, as commitment to any hierarchy, can be altered decisively in two ways, as Walter Lippmann said (1922, chs. 14 and 15): by destruction of sacred *symbols*, and of the *privileges* of belonging.

The Thesis of Parallel Fates

Within the Soviet bloc and among the Soviet Union's client states outside, the intrinsic decay of communism's ideological symbols is retarded, if hardly masked, by Soviet economic support and its geopolitical and military intimidation. In the nonruling communist parties, however, the objective disintegration of orthodox ideology is less inhibited and thus more advanced. Furthermore, the dissident directions of West European communist party development are favored by the fact that the self-interest of these parties is contradicted by the Soviet habit of "paying for" only those communist advances which it can hope to control. In this sense the West European communist parties have long been told to wait for the very long term, and they are in general no longer willing to sacrifice their own futures, in order to serve Soviet causes.

The "thesis of parallel fates" is the proposition that the basic symbols or dogmas of orthodox communism ultimately live and die together. Because communism is a simple regime and a simple ideology, its primal symbols being organically linked, the destruction or withering away of any one is in principle the death of them all. The rest is a matter of time and of details.

The thesis of parallel fates, furthermore, is implicitly a forecast of the withering away of communist ideology from the periphery toward the center: from the nonruling parties toward the ruling parties, and from Western Europe and other outlying areas of Soviet influence past and present (therefore including China) toward the Soviet Union itself. As a tendency, communist world political development thus has entered an epoch we might call "communism in single countries." And in the long run the thesis of parallel fates is, in logic, a forecast of the Soviet Union's return to ideological isolation, of not "socialism in one country," but rather "Stalinist communism in one country."

Would the Soviet leadership allow itself to be isolated ideologically? Or given such a trend, would Soviet leaders become at some point a decisive force themselves for the reform of commun-

169

ism in the Soviet Union? The next section provides a framework in which to set this problem.

The Possibility of Structural Development

The starting-point of the present book was that communist political development is, generally speaking, in a situation of historical deadlock. By this I mean that despite a few exceptions which indicate possible paths of significant adaptation, communist politics as a form of government has become a dead-end option; this self-limiting principle, intrinsic to communist policy, is a crucial explanation of communism's near-universal decay. The conclusion can now be drawn: communism's likeliest future is decay rather than development.

This does not mean, as I have indicated in the Preface, that in my analysis there are no possibilities apparent for political development as opposed to political decay.

Various paths of communist development are conceivable. A characteristically liberal or "Western" hypothesis has been that economic development will spill over into the political system and eventually lead to political pluralism. Though not a hypothesis to be excluded, it is intellectually dubious if only because the supposedly "necessary" or "inevitable" pluralizing and democratizing effects of economic development have proven chimeric before, as in the projects for rapid Third World "modernization" in the 1950s and 1960s or of more direct relevance, in the theories of East–West "convergence" fashionable in the same period. As Brzezinski and Huntington long ago forecast (1963), economic viability was more likely to *reinforce* the particular characteristics of liberal and Soviet regimes than to efface them. This has proven to be the case.

A second hypothesis of communist development asserts, perhaps in desperation, that the ideological, bureaucratic, and historical–cultural impediments to change are so great that the only possible solution to communism's historic developmental deadlock is charismatic leadership. *Only* a new Lenin, in this view, could possibly rescue communist parties from the consequences of inertia and hidebound orthodoxy. This is a desperate conclusion about development because it implies an impossible *prediction*—of the appearance of a certain extraordinary *individual*, and in a *catastrophic circumstance*.

To take such a point of view regarding the issue of development is in effect to abandon the field intellectually.

The common characteristic of both hypotheses, as indeed of many similar scenarios that one could inventory (there are shelves of books on "the future of communism"), is the supposition that communist hierarchs will continue perpetually to resist reform, or at least that their self-interest *is perceived by them* to necessitate all possible resistance. This supposition is probably a fallacy. Whatever the continuing influence of orthodox ideology, it is intrinsically more plausible—*especially* in a theory of self-interest—that the continuing pressures on the parasitic role of the party, and on its unsustainably regimented organization of society, will eventually produce a communist Burkean conservatism: a resigned willingness to make the changes necessary to preserve some semblance of communist rule without keeping the entire system perpetually at stake in what can ultimately only be a losing cause.

Once again communism's historical development would, in such a case, be affected decisively by the force of circumstance. And once again the process of reconstitution would be organic and historical, an issue of making choices in given circumstances rather than the working out of somebody's "theory." The attempt to realize in practice absurd slogans about the nature of reality, or else to circumvent the absurdity intrinsic to ordinary Stalinist thinking about development—through secrecy, corruption, occasional heroism, or even "hare-brained schemes"—would give way to some appropriate mechanism of adaptive change already existing within communism itself.

To begin to think cogently about the political development of communism, in other words, it is necessary to drop the idea of dropping communism from the equation. Consider Alexander Zinoviev's formulation of this premise:

> There are people in the world who hope that the Soviet Union and other Communist countries will return to their pre-Communist state. These hopes are vain. Communism is not a temporary historical zig-zag. It is an epoch. It is not a political regime which can be discarded and replaced by another while the country's social order is preserved. Communism itself is a profound social order on which everything else is based. One can remove and replace "everything else," but not that which forms its basis. Communism amounts to

such a revolution in social organization that its reversal via an evolutionary return journey is logically excluded. (Zinoviev, 1984, p. 259)

Absent some unpredictable cataclysm of communist power—the "physical destruction of the Communist bloc" in Zinoviev's apocalyptic language—the likeliest path of communist political development, he says, will be "a struggle for the blessings of civilization on the basis of Communism itself" (ibid., p. 259).

To the extent Zinoviev simply means a slow, rearguard political relaxation which would result indirectly from the combination of (1) a generalized desire among the people for a higher standard of living, and (2) political tired blood in the communist hierarchy, his insight that communism will change within its own terms is incapable of distinguishing development from decay. The issue really is whether communism is a social order with a political superstructure, or whether it is a political system which creates a certain type of social structure.

It is possible to show, as I have here, that communism is at its root a political system, and that communism contains, within itself, the potential mechanism for significant political development. This mechanism is the doctrine and practice of democratic centralism, and, in particular, reforming the prohibition of faction. Orthodox communism is, so to speak, a "Stalinist Gothic" political edifice: in this architecture democratic centralism is the Gothic arch, and the prohibition of faction is the keystone.

Our analysis of Soviet development in the years 1917–21 explained the original constitution of orthodox communism as a fundamentally *historical* problem—as a problem of circumstances, choices, and unintended consequences—rather than a sociological determinism or the "inevitable" consequence of applying certain general Marxist and Leninist values. (Whatever role Russian political culture had in this initial development of Soviet communism— a role I have neglected here and about which there would be much to say— the fact remains that the Soviet regime must be understood historically, and not as a foregone conclusion.) And if the Italian Communist example in itself can prove nothing about communism generally, let alone the specific case of Soviet politics, our study of its development produced useful insights into the *logic* of communist development generally.

How could the prohibition of faction be altered within communism's own terms, yet so as to change the nature of ordinary Stalinist regimes? Here it is worth a prefatory comment on what is referred to as the "interest group theory of communist politics."

It has gone almost without saying throughout this study that, notwithstanding the ordinary Stalinist fetish of monolithic unity, in practice, communist parties and regimes everywhere only achieve this goal very approximately; in other words, communists have always struggled with disagreements, conflicts of interest, and factional divisions. One scholar has summed up the history of East European communism precisely in this vein:

> The Eastern European communist parties have never been as united as propaganda and theory assume, and leaderships have always been divided into factions seeking power and advocating conflicting policies. Such factions are in a certain sense a surrogate, in a one-party state, for parties within a multi-party system. (Skilling, 1972, p. 85)

I would suggest that the interest group theory of communist politics draws the wrong conclusion from this fact.

Factional groups running essentially through the communist party, but extending beyond the party into the various realms of society while retaining their focus within the party, are indeed "a surrogate, in a one-party state, for parties within a multi-party system.' By focussing on factional coalition-building, in the communist sense of the term, we suddenly perceive a natural, intrinsic location, in communism itself for the *political* development of *public pluralism*. By looking for factionalism, to put it differently, instead of interest group structures in the Western sense (which do not exist in communist regimes), we can account convincingly for a real phenomenon—the instigation, into policy-making and politics generally speaking, of bureaucratic and other interests—without forcing it into a conceptual frame—the liberal theory of interest groups as the basis of democratic pluralism—which violates the meaning of this behavior in its own political culture. In short, to analyze an "interest group structure" in communist systems is to begin with an error of comparative method, an example of false reasoning by analogy. The result, in my judgment, is not simply an inadequate but a fundamentally misleading, because alien, understanding of communism. The consequence is thus a mistaken perception also of the potential mainsprings of communist political development.

Altogether no one would deny that communist monolithism is far

173

from pure, even in the Soviet Union and the French Communist Party, which historically have set the standards in the matter. The issue here is rather how to conceptualize the real situation most fruitfully for analysis and to piece out the forms political development might take if the operative mechanism were indeed to alter the meaning of the prohibition of faction, still within communism's own terms of discourse.

Although it is certainly to give hostages to fortune, let me suggest two ways in which such development is plausible.

First, a communist party might begin to move from hidden and fragmentary political competition to public pluralism by establishing multiple candidacies for elections to party and state offices. The Hungarian party's Central Committee adopted such a change in July 1983. While in an initial period, as in the Hungarian Central Committee directive, candidates are all obliged to support the party's electoral manifesto, later on support for the "same" program and policies could lead to more or less open and institutionalized partisan coalitions based on the democratic centralist distinction between making policy and implementing it. (This might even be endorsed as a new form of "socialist competition" and "socialist emulation"!) One need not be an expert in Hungarian politics to see how this sort of political step is congruent with the Hungarian party's better-known interest in economic reforms. How a broad and far-reaching public pluralism might be elaborated on the basis of inner-party factionalism is impossible to foresee in any detail; but the already established dogmas of "nonantagonistic contradictions" and "nonantagonistic classes" in communist ideology could easily be extended to adopt a notion of "nonantagonistic factions." This would presumably permit permanent, structured coalitions built on "horizontal communication," a pluralism based on cross-institutional interests and solidarities, linked through the communist party's own internal structure. Thus in a vague sense the principle of the party's "vanguard role" could be safeguarded, even as the bureaucratic centralist and reactionary orthodox communist *parti unique* would give way to a reformed and forward-looking *parti unifié*, a single-party regime of "parties within the party" such as exists already today in several regimes of cultural levels roughly comparable with the most Stalinist communist hierarchies.

I offer the above speculation merely as an example of one possible form of *development from within*. One can also imagine development as a *reaction to external circumstances or events*. In the case of a *long-term* development (China?) the reaction to persistent environmental

174

pressures might take a form similar to what I have already described. In the case of development as a reaction to *crisis* one can cite the precedent of the League of Yugoslav Communists, which became a "unified" as opposed to a monolithic communist party as a result of its struggle with the Soviets in order to rally a heterogeneous and hardly formed society around its political leadership in the face of an evident external danger. In any case, so far as Eastern Europe is concerned, it seems clear that Soviet power forecloses the possibility that one of its client regimes can simply abandon communism. The durable developmental tendency in European communism is thus Italian and Hungarian reform, not Polish revolution.

Even so, reform once launched in a communist hierarchy might proceed with unexpected quickness. This would be true, I think, mainly in the controlling and/or most orthodox centers of communist power. Ordinary Stalinism is a Leviathan whose coercive apparatus is awesome but basically fragile. In the Soviet Union this fragility of communism is compensated by the character of Russian political culture as well as many other factors. The Soviet developmental deadlock, despite all the pressures put on it from within and without, seems likely to resist the longest, unless some totally unforeseeable trend or event intervenes.

Could there be such a factor? A second path of development, as I said above, indeed seems conceivable; it would involve a genuine debate in Soviet politics on the meaning of democratic centralism as a constitutional doctrine. This is not at all unthinkable. As we have seen a defined Soviet tendency toward legalism and the "constitutionalization" of democratic centralism already exists. This can be interpreted as one more means of routinizing regimentation (which it undoubtedly is) but it seems to be not only this. Samuel Finer remarks how provisions of the Soviet constitution and legal codes have been used by dissidents to challenge the legality of their persecutions, and even by ordinary, if braver than usual Soviet citizens with a complaint, in an attempt to close the gap a bit between Soviet law and Soviet reality. Konstantin Simis, a recent émigré who was himself a Soviet lawyer, also emphasizes the relevance of Soviet laws, if not of the rule of law as such:

> Yet—apart from the stillborn constitution—there are a multitude of laws and codes that really do operate in the Soviet Union. It is on the basis of these that the courts decide on disputes between citizens, try crimes, resolve labor disputes,

and so forth. Nevertheless, the principle of legality does not operate in the Soviet Union . . . [because] the regime does not consider itself to be bound by the law. (Simis, 1982, p. 28)

Over a period of time, the habit of legalism could evolve into an intellectual–political–moral climate favorable to a genuine constitution. Thus contrary to the opinion that only a new Lenin could redeem the Soviet Union (spare the Soviet peoples another do-gooder such as Lenin!), what would be required is perhaps, as Sidney Hook (1984, p. 365) suggests, a "Soviet Aquinas," but even more likely a communist James Madison. A Madisonian communism would be a prodigious synthesis. Its possibility is that of which Emerson said, "Genius is the activity which repairs the decay of things."

In short, a second mechanism of political development based on democratic centralism could be some grand interpretation of democratic centralism itself so as to safeguard stability and most privilege, while at the same time providing the intellectual basis upon which communist hierarchs could then shift the course of development out of its historical cul-de-sac. In citing Madison, of course, I do not have in mind some sudden "liberal conversion" of communism. A limited communist pluralism, probably neither profoundly liberal nor profoundly democratic, may have to suffice in the Soviet empire "for a long period" (to use a communist cliché). What would be primordial, to go back to Lippmann's point, would be to end the *monopoly of privilege* which binds a communist hierarchy into a tacit bond of implacable solidarity *vis-à-vis* the "exterior," meaning both its own population and the rest of the world. And the only privilege which a renaissance of communist political thinking must absolutely delegitimize would be *the privilege of having no public opposition*: make the notion that "correct policies need no opposition" the equivalent of "taxation without representation," and a key to communist political development would have been found.

The Banality of Decommunization

In the long term communist political development is inevitable and the real issue is not whether, but when. To be sure, Keynes's aphorism implying the futility of thinking about the long run remains as valid as ever—meaning it is questionable whether he had the right idea. In any case, this book has not been written only with

176

an eye to the long run. My hope is to influence the mood of current thinking about the possibility, and even the desirability of communist development as opposed to communist decay. I think we must begin to find the right terms for the task of analyzing decommunization.

Pessimism and cynicism are natural temptations for statesmen and policy-makers, both because such a mindset makes action less complicated in the real world of international relations and because it can plausibly be read as the appropriate conclusion to draw from the lessons of history. It is thus unsurprising to find in the views of our politicians not only an objective pessimism about the prospects for communist development, but almost what might be called a professional preference for communist decadence rather than development. If this is so, I would say that while from the point of view of the immediate dilemmas of world politics we must necessarily be worried by Soviet vigor, from the point of view of democratic political development, and the peaceful management of international relations in the medium and long term, we ought to prefer communism's development to its decadence.

Notes

Chapter 1

1 In other words, Polish Catholicism historically has been a source of resistance to Poland's domination by other states, in particular, Russia and now the Soviet Union. Moreover, Polish Roman Catholicism, like Polish nationalism, has linked Poland's destiny to "Europe," as Milan Kundera pointed out in explaining his reevaluation of the potential political value of religion as an institution, *New York Times Review of Books*, 29 April 1984, p. 47:

> I began to see that the force of Catholicism in a place like Poland had to do with asserting that you are a European when you live on the frontier between the two churches—Western and Eastern—that in fact divide Europe from the East ... I understood that what the Russians were forbidding [Poland] was really Europe, that Catholicism and skepticism were the two poles that defined Europe, and that Europe, so to speak, was the tension between them.

Chapter 2

1 It is always worth recalling, in order to emphasize the genuineness of belief in Marxist doctrines, that a few intransigent Bolshevik leaders actually rejected the plan to seize power in order to move the revolution to a socialist program, precisely because this contradicted established party theory. Kamenev and Zinoviev, fearing a "historic error," even took the astounding risk of publicizing the decision to stage an insurrection, hoping to head it off! (It is worth recalling also, to emphasize the nature of discipline, punishment, and forgiveness at this time, that Zinoviev and Kamenev were kept in the leadership and held high positions in the postrevolutionary regime. They were both purged later by Stalin.)

2 Lenin's more usual idea appears in a characteristic passage from *What Is To Be Done?*, given in *Christman*, (1967, pp. 159–61):

> What is the use of advancing "broad democratic principles" when the fundamental condition for these principles ... full publicity ... *cannot be fulfilled* by a secret organization? ... Try to put this picture (i.e., the desire for internal party democracy) in the frame of our autocracy ... It is a useless toy because, as a matter of fact, no revolutionary organization has ever practiced *broad* democracy, nor could it, however much it desired to do so. It is a harmful toy because any attempt to practice the "broad democratic principles" will simply facilitate the work of the police in making big raids. ...

3 It is true that there still was sharp ambiguity in Lenin's words and actions on this score. For example, in 1912 Lenin called a meeting of the Bolsheviks which he falsely represented as a congress of the whole party. The "liquidator" tendency,

meaning Mensheviks who wanted to deemphasize the illegal, revolutionary underground, was condemned, marking the irrevocable split of Bolsheviks and Mensheviks. At the same time, Lenin and Trotsky continued polemics on questions of organization. In 1914 Lenin criticized Trotsky's refusal to accept the 1912 Congress's decisions and his continued "factionalist" behavior. He had no qualms about deciding himself the legitimacy of others, yet he was also genuine about the problem of "correct synthesis":

> Since 1912, for over two years, there has been no factionalism among the organized Marxists in Russia, no controversies in tactics in *united* organizations, at *united* conferences and congresses. There is a *complete* break between the Party, which in January 1912 formally announced that the Liquidators *do not* belong to it, and the Liquidators. Trotsky often calls this state of affairs a "split" ... But it remains an undoubted fact that the term "factionalism" is *misleading* ... Although he claims to be non-factional, Trotsky is known to everybody ... as the representative of "Trotsky's *faction.*" Here there is factionalism, for we see the two essential symptoms of it: (1) nominal recognition of unity and (2) group segregation in fact ... Where the *majority* of the class-conscious workers have rallied around precise and definite decisions there is *unity* of opinion and action, here is Party spirit, and the Party.

This passage is quoted in Daniels, 1960b, pp. 64–5; from Lenin, "Disruption of unity under cover of outcries for unity" (May 1914), *Selected Works*, vol. I, book 2, pp. 249–51, 255–6.

4 Compare this with Lenin's declaration that a "revolutionary Social Democrat is a Jacobin who is indissolubly bound to the organization of the proletariat and aware of its class interests" (the Trotsky and Lenin quotations are both from Knei-Paz, 1978, p. 199).

5 The just-founded French and Italian Communist parties, whose history in the 1970s is studied later on in detail, posed particular problems of homogenization: see Tiersky, 1974, chs. 1–2, and Blackmer, 1968, for accounts in English; and also read Ignazio Silone's short memoir of his trip with Togliatti to Moscow in the late 1920s where both had to face Stalin's now dogmatic demand for unanimity (in Richard Crossman's *The God that Failed*, 1949). Silone resisted, whereas Togliatti after some internal torment became a loyalist.

6 It is worth quoting *in extenso* the "On party unity" resolution to point up both the general frustration with factionalism and the sense of a response to grave circumstances, in Daniels, 1960, vol. 1, pp. 207–9:

> Even before the general Party discussion on the trade unions, certain signs of factionalism had been apparent in the Party, viz., the formation of groups with separate platforms, striving to a certain degree to segregate and create their own group discipline. Such symptoms of factionalism were manifested ... both by the so-called "Workers' Opposition" group, and partly by the so-called "Democratic Centralism" group. All class-conscious workers must clearly realize the perniciousness and impermissibility of factionalism of any kind, for ... in practice factionalism inevitably leads to the weakening of team work and to intensified and repeated attempts by enemies of the Party ... to widen the cleavage and to use it for counter-revolutionary purposes. The way the enemies of the proletariat take advantage of every deviation from the thoroughly consistent Communist line was perhaps most strikingly shown in the case of the Kronstadt mutiny, when the bourgeois

counter-revolutionaries and Whiteguards in all countries of the world immediately expressed their readiness to accept even the slogans of the Soviet system, if only they might thereby secure the overthrow of the dictatorship of the proletariat in Russia ... Criticism of the Party's short-comings ... is absolutely necessary [but] everyone who criticizes must see to it that the form of his criticism takes into account the position of the Party, surrounded as it is by a ring of enemies.

7 *Underground* factionalism within the formal party organization continued for a time, as was seen at the Eleventh Party Congress (March–April 1922); see Trotsky, 1941, p. 351: "During the intervening year ... the oppositionists had gone underground and had organized clandestinely so well that a number of the resolutions sponsored by the ruling group at the 11th Congress were voted down overwhelmingly enough to preclude any fraudulent 'revisions' of the ballot." Moreover, the entire period 1921–8 was shot through with fierce leadership struggles which have long been the usual focus of political histories of the period.

8 From this point of view the Soviet economy's continued separation into growth sectors (essentially the Soviet military-industrial complex) and stagnating sectors (nearly all areas of consumption as well as agriculture) may involve a leadership strategy (conscious or unwitting) to defuse the natural social plura-lism produced by economic development. By the same token, the political implications of socioeconomic development can be cited as one of the forces of circumstance which press for communist political development, as opposed to decay (see Chapter 6). Let me here express an intellectual debt, on this point and generally speaking, to Richard Lowenthal's studies of communism, above all, regarding the issues of "development v. utopia," the "disintegration of a secular faith," and the postrevolutionary rationalization of communist politics in a Weberian sense.

Chapter 3

1 I have taken much from Alfred Meyer's studies of Marxism, communism and Soviet politics. As is evident in Chapters 2 and 3 in this study, Meyer has been one of the few scholars to write about the implications of democratic centralism: see, first of all, his book on *Leninism*, 1957. And it is not surprising that he should have written a general account of Soviet politics: *The Soviet Political System*, 1965, which interprets that system as "bureaucracy writ large," that is, as a sort of single "corporation" in which, to use my terms, political life is entirely internal. It is worth quoting a passage *in extenso*; see pp. 467–70:

the USSR is best understood as a large, complex bureaucracy comparable in its structure and functioning to giant corporations, armies, government agencies, and similar institutions ... in the West. The Soviet Union shares with giant organizations everywhere the urge to organize all human activi-ties rationally, from professional life to consumption patterns and leisure activities ... Organization seems still to be far stronger than pluralism; command and duty, superior to interests and rights. Despite the ever more frequent and open disputes among the various elites, the Soviet system will doubtless be able to present itself (for some time to come) as a unified bureaucratic command structure to the outside world as well as to its own citizenry.

This prognosis, written now twenty years ago, is still valid. Yet so is the evident problem in his conceptual interpretation of Soviet politics which, with character-istic fairness, he presented himself; see pp. 472, 475:

> To be sure, one might argue that in the process of being writ large, bureaucracy as we know it in Western societies undergoes a very significant change: it becomes virtually all-powerful . . . Surely, a bureaucracy which encompasses all human endeavors must be different from one that func-tions within a markedly pluralistic constitutional system.

Exactly so!

2　I must give some definition to the distinction I make between "high Stalinism" and "ordinary," routinized Stalinism. (The distinction as such, however, should not be controversial in the least, whether on the left—in whose writing I first encountered the term "ordinary Stalinism"—on the right, or, I hope, among political theorists.)

High Stalinism is, first of all, a *temporal* reference—the years when Stalin was the Soviet "Egocrat" (as Solzhenitsyn says), between 1929, or, in a stricter usage, the middle 1930s, and his death in 1953. As for *substance*, in the high Stalinist period Soviet society was permanently mobilized by a charismatic party and a charismatic, increasingly monomaniacal "great leader" to whom, as Dostoevsky would have said, "everything is permitted." Soviet politics was lived as a continuous battle—both real war and Cold War, and a militarist internal social mobilization (1) to *implement grand policies* (heavy industrialization, collectivi-zation of agriculture, political purification, and Russification), and (2) to *destroy* massive groups of supposed *internal enemies* ("the kulaks as a class," "bour-geois remnants," and a motley collection of "saboteurs, wreckers and para-sites"). High Stalinism, in short, deserves to be thought of as a political *epoch*.

By contrast, routinized, ordinary Stalinism is a conceptualized understanding of orthodox communism after Stalin's death. Ordinary Stalinism crystallized politically once the confusion was lifted as to how seriously Khrushchev's de-Stalinization policy was meant, and how far it would or could take hold: Khrushchev's largely authenticated memoirs—2 volumes, 1970 and 1974—are required reading. Ordinary Stalinism is thus a "model" of orthodox communism in the Brezhnev, Andropov, and Chernenko years. To use the names of Soviet leaders implies that the Soviet Union itself is the main reference point; but the term refers to post-Stalin communist orthodoxy wherever it is found. The concept's premise is that, notwithstanding all national, regional, historical, cultural, ethnic, and other differences, a generic analysis of communism is possible, within which each communist phenomenon is a greater or lesser approximation of the model. This is not to conclude *a priori*, however, that "communism" always dominates other phenomena.

3　This premise can become the basis of a critique of the "interest group theory of Soviet politics": see the concluding Chapter 6 of this study.

4　I am indebted to conversations ten years ago with Professor A. Kriegel for the original elements of this formulation of communist ideology.

5　There have been four Soviet Constitutions in all. The 1977 Constitution is the revision of the 1936 Constitution, which had two predecessors, those of 1918 and 1924.

6　Article 6, which concerns the party reads: "The leading and guiding force of Soviet society and the nucleus of its political system, of all state organizations and public organizations, is the Communist Party of the Soviet Union. The CPSU exists for the people and serves the people." Article 7 is also of some relevance: "The Communist Party, armed with Marxism–Leninism, determines the general perspectives of the development of society and the course of the home and foreign policy of the USSR, directs the great constructive work of the Soviet people, and imparts a planned, systematic and theoretically substantiated character to their struggle for the victory of communism": all quotations from the Soviet Constitution are from the official English translation; cf. Soviet editions or Finer, 1979.

7   The original Soviet sources used by Waller are: A. S. Fedoseev, *Demokraticheskii tsentralizm—leninskii printsip organizatsii gosudarstvennogo apparata*, Moscow, Yuridlit, 1962; V. M. Lavrichev, *Demokraticheskii tsentralizm—dialekticheskii printsip organizatsionnogo stroeniya*, Moscow, Mysl', 1971; CPSU–SED, *Printsip demokraticheskogo tsentralizma v stroitel'stve i deyatel'nosti kommunisticheskoi partii*, Moscow, Politizdat/Berlin, Dietz Verlag, 1973; V. I. Vasilev, *Demokraticheskii tsentralizm v sisteme sovetov*, Moscow, Yuridicheskaya literatura, 1973; V. G. Afanasev, *Nauchnoe upravlenie obschchestvom*, Moscow, Politizdat, 1967; and N. A. Moiseenko and M. V. Popov, *Demokraticheskii tsentralizm—osnovnoi printsip sotsialisticheskoi ekonomikoi*, Moscow, Lenizdat, 1975.

8   Conceivably this is a disguised new form of the historical struggle of most East European peoples against Russian dominance, and now also against Sovietization. If this were so, studies of East European regimes from the point of view of democratic centralism, and of constitutional and legal questions generally, might lead to significant new knowledge about undercurrent movements in political struggle and evolution. Indeed, a new concern with Soviet and East European law is one of the promising fields of communist studies today.

9   These mechanisms are familiar to all who know the communist parties' internal operations. The best and most detailed accounts we have of the Soviet and East European parties date from the Stalin period. The recent "dissident" writings are also revelatory but they usually are not written by "insiders." My own understanding, in addition to reading in this literature, derives from observing the French and Italian parties. The Soviets, of course, invented the schools which taught all foreign communists the workings of Stalinism.

10 This insider's view—the speaker is Paul Thorez, the son of Maurice Thorez—is confirmed by Leonard Schapiro in a passage taken from the distinguished historian's review of Roy Medvedev's biography of *Khrushchev*, 1983, p. 7:

> Khrushchev [was] much more of a problem [than Stalin, Brezhnev, or Andropov]. The trouble is that he was something almost unknown among leading Soviet politicians—a human being ... He was "real" not only because of his peasant earthiness, his proverbs, and his vulgarity; he was "real" because he behaved as if he knew what reality was, and was not just mouthing ideological claptrap. In spite of the fact that he left the country so much better off than he had found it when Stalin died, he was not widely respected there [because] the Soviet public most likes its leaders to conform to patterns. Let outward, ideological life follow its dreary course, let leaders be dull, prim, and hypocritical in the way that has become established: at the lower levels life goes along its normal way of endless fiddling and grousing.

11 In a recent report on three research visits to the Soviet Union in 1983–4 during which he saw high-level leaders Seweryn Bialer, 1984, p. 6, emphasized that "words" continue to matter greatly even in the realpolitik realm of contemporary foreign policy:

> No one who seeks to understand the political culture of Soviet Russia, not to speak of its historical tradition, should underestimate the potency of words. Among the Soviet elites, who have spent much of their lives manipulating

the nuances of ideology, words are taken very seriously. They use an elaborate rhetoric to convey existing attitudes and shifting policies and they expect no less of the adversary's rhetoric. For Soviet leaders and high officials President Reagan's decision to use bellicose language ... [the] administration's self-righteous moralistic tone, its reduction of Soviet achievements to crimes by international outlaws from an "evil empire" ... was and is a political fact that amounts to a policy pronouncement.

12 Trotsky should have added, although it was not in his polemical interest to do so, that the maneuver also served to legitimize the Communist Party (and Stalin himself) among masses of previously hostile people, by giving them a stake in the party's and the regime's survival.

13 In the French Communist Party's abortive internal development during the 1970s one innovation was officially to limit this monastic mental discipline to the ruling group and the *permanents* (the apparatchiks). Lower-level party members, in other words, were allowed a little freedom of political conscience (literally a Stalinist liberalism!), though they still were obligated to maintain absolute discipline in their behavior. Fiszbin, 1980, says the PCF's old-timer, hard-core membership took this as a serious change in policy.

Lest an uninitiated reader think this simply peculiar, let me cite the equivalent step forward in the Yugoslav party, which came not earlier than the Eleventh LYC Congress in 1978. The revised statute on democratic centralism began by recalling "the obligation of members whose opinions and proposals remain in the minority in an organization or organ of the League of Communists to accept and carry out the decisions adopted by the majority," *now adding* "with freedom to retain [their] own opinion": Burg, 1983, p. 317. Burg does not say whether this was simply a codification of practice—the LYC's internal discipline has long been authoritarian rather than Stalinist—or whether on this particular point there was a real Stalinist obstacle to knock over. (I doubt it.)

14 Stalin had already dogmatized this lesson in his *Foundations of Leninism*, 1932, pp. 118–20:

The opportunist elements in the Party are the source of Party factionalism. The proletariat is not a closed class ... petty-bourgeois groups somehow or other penetrate into the Party, into which they introduce an element of hesitancy and opportunism, of disintegration and lack of self-confidence. To them factionalism and splits, disorganization and the undermining of the Party from within, are principally due.

15 Meyer returned to this discussion in *The Soviet Political System*, 1965, from which I permit myself two extended quotations:

The conflict between democratic and bureaucratic principles is reflected in ... "democratic centralism" ... Once it was committed to any line of action, the Party could tolerate no dissent or debate. In this sense, all decisions were, almost by definition, unanimous. The Party statutes make this policy explicit by interpreting the principle of majority rule so as to make it a majority dictatorship. The minority must submit, and by submitting make any decision unanimous. But once a decision has been adopted unanimously, it becomes difficult even to question the manner in which it is being carried out, because every such discussion comes close to interpreting the unanimous decision itself ... Theory and practice, decision and execution, are so closely linked that insistence on unanimity and loyalty virtually prohibits all discussion. More particularly, it becomes impossible for individual members or groups—or indeed for entire subordinate organizations—to argue that a decision or policy should be re-examined ... In effect, therefore, the will of the membership cannot even place something on the agenda for discussion. (pp. 154–5)

And:

In fact, all the inconsistency of "democratic centralism" is revealed in the implicit assumption that a political issue can ever be closed—that there can ever be a problem that must no longer be debated because a vote has been taken and the Party has been committed to action. *The entire process by which discussion simply died in the Party is attributable to this idea that a matter remains settled unless the highest agencies of the Party, perhaps the General Secretary himself, declare it once again to be debatable"*. (pp. 190–1; emphasis added)

Meyer's conclusion is overdrawn. But the point is of great importance.
16 cf. Chafarévitch, 1977 and Zinoviev, 1984.
17 These quotes are found in reports in the *New York Times*, 11 April and 26 April 1984, pp. A12, A15; and *The Economist*, 5 May 1984, p. 41.

Chapter 5

1 A representative sample of recent Italian Communist program documents is found in PCI, 1978, 1979a, 1979b, *Italian Communists*, nos. 1 and 2, 1983; Gruppi, 1979; see also the interviews with Giorgio Napolitano, done by Eric Hobsbawn, *The Italian Road to Socialism*, 1977. The PCI's Foreign Section publishes noteworthy party documents in English, French, and German translation in a periodical called *Italian Communists*.
2 At the Sixteenth Party Congress in 1983 the Dutch Socialist Piet Dankert gave an address—breaking precedent—as the European Parliament's president. The speech was a remarkably warm endorsement of Italian Communist support for European institutions.
3 For summaries of policy declarations, and of the range of PCI leaders' and intellectuals' statements regarding the Soviet Union and international communism generally, see Valenza, 1978; Pajetta, 1978; Galluzzi, 1983; and Spriano, 1983. Cossutta, 1982, is the Sovietophile leader's "combat book" in preparation for the March 1983 Congress; its bias does not negate the book's additional interest as a survey of the recent period including elements not emphasized in other books. Blackmer, 1968, 1975, is still essential on the earlier period, and a forthcoming study by Joan Barth Urban is to deal with the full history of Italian Communist relations with the Soviet Union.
4 As postwar Italian politics turned into a *partitocrazia*, a regime in which party interests and factional power struggles dominate the functioning of nearly all public institutions, the multiplication of factions inside the governing parties themselves was promoted by the opportunity of winning control of special patronage networks, which required the capacity to blackmail current party leaders and other factions. The *partitocrazia* became a combination of spoils system and pork-barrel politics taken to an extreme, which in turn only increased yet further the evident usefulness of factional networks. Ministries and even the highest government positions, including the prime ministership and the presidency, became prizes of factional struggle within and across party lines.

Thus proposals for "nonparty," technocratic governments have been one persistent reform idea in Italian politics. And the fact that choice of the Prime

Minister had been for years a function of the DC Party's internal factional struggles gave not only a political, but also a properly institutional, character to the successful fight in 1981 to have the first non-Christian Democratic Prime Minister since the end of World War II: this was the Republican Party's leader, Giovanni Spadolini.

5   Even in less practicing Catholic France, the PCF has undergone a sociological "feminization" in the past decade, limiting its devastating decline somewhat.

6   Leaving aside for a moment the problem of the CGIL's Communist Party connection, Alessandro Pizzorno, 1980, p. 173, observes that there have been two other important reasons for Italy's politically divided labor movement: (1) the Italian system's need to isolate, or at least to divide the labor movement in order to reduce its wage and social security demands to an already elevated minimum, in comparison with other countries; and (2) labor militants generally have a strong political commitment prior to joining a union; the most politically intense militants generally provide the pool for union leadership; thus a politically divided labor movement in Latin European countries is to some extent a consequence of a strongly partisan party system in which several parties have substantial working-class social bases.

7   The CGIL had several organizational advantages which furthered its primacy in the union movement. Of particular interest to us is the fact that, beyond the usual communist enthusiasm for organizational work, CGIL leaders and militants were also favored by the PCI's ban on factions. That is, CISL and UIL leaders, in addition to union and party activities, were also deeply involved in factional struggles inside the DC and the PSI: cf. Pizzorno, 1980, pp. 178–9; and Sivini *et al.* 1968, p. 39.

8   In this regard one can juxtapose the cases of the Italian Communist intellectual Salvatore Sechi: cf. 1979, 1980; and the French Communist intellectual Jean Elleinstein: cf. 1981. The former's case against the PCI was basically a Michelsian problem: and though Sechi became a minor *cause célèbre*, he never really could become a "dissident," even though he was finally excluded. Elleinstein, on the other hand, tried hard to stay in the party, whose case against him was basically a matter of nonconformism on the "right." In a classically Stalinist episode he was asked by the leadership, during its flirtation with Eurocommunism to write critically of the Soviet Union, for which later he was attacked and eventually excluded.

9   The Manifesto group which developed in the political struggles of the late 1960s had been a much greater challenge to the party Establishment than the Sovietophiles turned out to be in 1982–3. But then Manifesto was also a more familiar and attractive challenge to a communist Establishment, that is, a classic "leftist deviation," which could rally radical communist democrats, neo-Trotskyites, Maoist sympathizers, and all other sorts of anti-Stalinist revolutionary socialists. In addition, Manifesto was organized as a true faction, publishing its own newspaper, holding separate meetings and raising its own funds. The Manifesto leaders were given "a fair and formal trial" in the party (McInnes, 1975a, p. 134), and expelled strictly according to the party rules. In the 1972 elections the Manifesto candidates were annihilated politically, while the PCI continued to make gains.

10   One liberal gesture was Cossutta's reelection to the Central Committee. A few weeks later, in a sort of new liberal apotheosis, he was named chairman of the Central Committee's commission to oversee party propaganda!

11   The June 1984 European Parliament elections put the PCI ahead of the DC for the first time. Though the PCI may not remain the largest Italian party, it is now crucial that the Socialist Party seems not to be gaining significantly. Among the Western European communist parties the PCI's future is indicated in the fact that

there are twenty-seven Italian Communist deputies in the European Parliament now as against a total of fifteen communist deputies from all the other nine EC countries combined.

Chapter 6

1   On these points and the rest of this section see, for example, Tiersky, 1979b; Robrieux, 1980–4, Vol. 3; and Annie Kriegel, *Le Communisme au jour le jour*, Paris, Hachette, 1979. For corroborating versions from inside the PCF see Fiszbin, 1980; Althusser, 1978; Hincker, 1981; and Spire, 1980.

2   The Sovietophile tendency has had several exponents (for example, Gaston Plissonier) among regular Politburo members, but when the party's policy became aggressively Eurocommunist, they had always to observe discipline. In 1981 Jeannette Vermeersch-Thorez became a public Sovietophile critic of what she (along with Althusser, Elleinstein, and various other internal critics) called "the Marchais group," breaking democratic centralist discipline by writing newspaper articles and doing a long television interview. Her justification for what was, for her, a desperate step was that Marchais's policies were ruining the party. She thought him an "opportunist" which, in her orthodox logic, meant he was at bottom a "social democrat." She also argues the past fifteen years' foreign policies, that is, since the denunciation of the invasion of Czechoslovakia, constitute a betrayal of the communist movement at the international level. The PCF's Sovietophile tendency, in other words, agrees with Marchais's "bourgeois" and "realpolitik" critics alike, that the PCF's return to alignment on Soviet foreign policy positions is pragmatism rather than a rediscovery of faith. On this she is certainly correct.

3   See also Balibar *et al.*, 1979; Barak, 1980; Belloin, 1979; Bouillot and Devesa, 1979; Daix, 1978; Elleinstein, 1981; Hincker, 1981; Kehayan and Kehayan, 1978; Molina and Vargas, 1978, 1979; and Spire, 1980. Althusser, 1978, is a machiavellian model of conciseness and incisiveness. One only wishes his politics had permitted him to write this devastating little book years earlier, when his considerable reputation in certain milieux might have had a more timely political effect.

4   Although a budding critic, Fiszbin's loyalist instincts permitted him, "naturally," to conceive the ruling group's justification of censureship, "The leadership judged the situation so difficult, the pressure to make the party responsible for the defeat so strong, the stakes in the struggle over the issue of responsibility so decisive for the future, and, finally, the party so poorly prepared to resist . . . [that it would have been] to put the party in danger, not only to open a public forum [in the party press], but simply to authorize summaries of the debate under way": 1980, p. 35. Clearly, a party which is "put . . . in danger" by *press summaries of what its members believe* ought to change!

In any case, the ruling group's commitment to reform was simply being torn to shreds. Paul Laurent, the Secretary for Organization, with Eurocommunist ingenuousness had in 1977 declared the PCF's new policy on truthfulness. In moving to reform the party, he said (in *La Nouvelle Critique*, April 1977; cited in *Le Monde*, 9 April 1977):

We came to the idea that to discuss seriously, to participate genuinely in decision-making, it was necessary to know the whole story. In consequence, the problem of giving complete information to party militants has become considerably more significant . . . There is a visible change [in the party] closely linked to evolution of its style, its leadership and its activists: This is the idea that the practice of withholding information on the pretext that a certain fact might help this or that campaign of our adversaries is disappearing from party policy.

Fiszbin's book shows that Laurent too had an entirely recidivist role in the "Paris affair."

5 In becoming the first PCF central committee member to resign in decades, Fiszbin not only broke a party taboo, but also went further in reinventing certain elements of democratic behavior out of his direct experience, "I am only rediscovering however what history has long known: that refusal is a form of action": 1980, p. 162. Pointing out that resignation is not forbidden in the PCF's statutes, but that the unwritten rules make resignation tantamount to an act of treason, Fiszbin specifies yet another way in which even *ordinary* Stalinism is equivalent to a permanent martial law regime; see Fiszbin, 1980, p. 193:

> But why should [resignation] be against the standards of acceptable conduct in the party? . . . The drama is . . . that resignation in the party is considered to be dramatic. Certainly it is not a banal matter. But is it a satisfactory situation that the resignation of a Central Committee member should be an historic event? Why build a system in which a militant can accept or refuse a responsibility, but once he has accepted he must allow to others exclusively the power to release him from his commitment, as in earlier times in religious orders?

6 While Mitterrand's statement was provocative, in two ways it was loyal to the alliance with the PCF which had just been signed. First, the declaration was public, and while perhaps not "fraternal," legitimately expressed the normal struggle of ideologically contiguous parties for the same social base. Secondly, Mitterrand made the statement outside France, which can be interpreted as political courtesy. The Communists operated differently. Just a few days after the Joint Program was signed, Marchais gave a secret report to the Central Committee, published only three years later as part of one of the PCF's intermittent regressions to Stalinist abuse of the Socialists. In that report he said: "It would be dangerous to have the slightest illusion about the Socialist party's sincerity or firmness of conviction" about "remaining loyal to the Joint Program" and not later making "one of those reversals of parliamentary majorities which constitute its entire history . . . At bottom the Socialist party's ideology is totally distinct from scientific socialism; at bottom [the PS leadership] refuses totally the necessity of taking a working class point of view in all situations": Marchais, 1975, pp. 93, 109–10. What this secret report embodies—beyond the mentality itself of secrecy and a Leninist–Stalinist instrumentalism regarding alliance partners—is the fact that inside the party the PCF ruling group's vocabulary was still saturated in orthodox ordinary Stalinist political culture (confirming Robrieux's description of the PCF's internal Stalinism already quoted above).

7 The four original Communist ministries (of a total of forty-two in the government) were Transport (Charles Fiterman, also given the extra prestige of a minister of state qualification); Health (Jack Ralite); Civil Service (Anicet Le Pors); and Vocational Training (Marcel Rigout). While some observers saw them initially as "strategic sectors": see Frèches, 1983, p. 448, others considered them "minor": see *The Economist*, 27 June 1981, p. 41. In fact despite some worries that Fiterman's Transport Ministry could have been problematic in providing auxiliary military logistical support in a crisis, after three years there was general agreement that they were "strategic," if at all, only in the sense of providing a basis for some Communist "white-anting" in the French state administration (see below). In the March 1983 Cabinet reduction the PCF kept its proportion of

ministerial seats (two out of fifteen instead of four out of forty-two): Fiterman and Rigout remained as ministers, while Ralite and Le Pors continued in their jobs, but demoted, like many Socialist ministers, to the rank of state secretaries.

8 The French Communist priorities were confirmed in April 1983 when, following the French government's expulsion of forty-seven Soviets as spies, Marchais declared "absurd" the hypothesis that because of *this* the Communists' membership in the government would be thrown into question.

9 Communists have nearly all the key CGT leadership positions, even though party members are a small minority of the total membership. All the departmental union secretaries without exception, and about 90 percent of the federation leaders are PCF members; this means that the Communists also control, through "election," the membership of the National Confederal Committee and the Executive Committee. In the Executive Committee elected by the Fortieth CGT Congress (1979), the Communists had a strong majority (sixty out of 100), with seven socialists, and thirty-three Christian Democrats or unaffiliated. The CGT has never disallowed the cumulation of union and party leadership positions (unlike the Italian CGIL), and in 1980 eight CGT leaders were also PCF Central Committee members, while three, including the General Secretary (Georges Séguy, replaced in 1982 by Henri Krasuki), were Politburo members. A PCF committee decides the nomination of Communist cadres in the CGT, and even decides *which non-Communist* candidates in the CGT the Communists should favor because of their susceptibility to influence. Assuming a large realm of autonomy in the workplace, it is none the less obvious that, overall, CGT and PCF policy comes from a single source. (Indeed, a minor scandal in the Mauroy government occurred in early 1983 when a Communist government minister was overheard in a telephone tap discussing the government's internal deliberations with the CGT leader Krasuki.) Altogether, despite internal cross-pressures the PCF's control of the CGT remains an expression of orthodox democratic centralist doctrine: trade union action is in principle a preparation for political action, which is the party's domain.

Bibliography

Abendroth, W. (1980), *La socialdemocrazia in Germania* (Rome: Editori Riuniti).

Accornero, A. *et al.* (1983), *L'identità comunista* (Rome: Editori Riuniti).

Afanasyev, A. (1971), "The CPSU and the theory and practice of scientific management of society," in, CPSU, *Development of Revolutionary Theory by the CPSU* (Moscow: Progress), pp. 237–57.

Almond, G. (1983), "Communism and political culture theory," *Comparative Politics*, vol. 15, no. 2 (January), pp. 127–38.

Althusser, L. (1977), *22e Congrès* (Paris: Maspéro).

Althusser, L. (1978), *Ce Qui Ne Peut Plus Durer dans le parti communiste* (Paris: Maspéro).

Amendola, G. (1979), *I comunisti e le elezioni europee* (Rome: Editori Riuniti).

Amyot, G. (1981), *The Italian Communist Party. The Crisis of the Popular Front Strategy* (London: Croom Helm).

Arendt, H. (1966), *The Origins of Totalitarianism*, rev. ed. (New York: Harcourt, Brace & World).

Aron, R. (1982), "Alternation in government in the industrialized countries," *Government and Opposition*, vol. 17, no. 1, pp. 3–21.

Baechler, J. (1978), *Le Pouvoir pur* (Paris: Calmann-Lévy).

Balibar, E. (1982), "Sur le droit de tendances," *Politique Aujourd'hui*, no. 12, pp. 90–7; also in G. Labica (ed.), *Dictionnaire critique du marxisme* (Paris: Presses universitaires de France, 1983).

Balibar, E. *et al.* (1979), *Ouvrons la Fenêtre, camarades!* (Paris: Maspéro).

Barak, M. (1980), *Fractures au PCF. Des communistes parlent* (Paris; Edisud et Karthala Editions).

Barbagli, M. *et al.* (1979), *Dentro il PCI* (Bologna: Il Mulino).

Bell, Daniel (1976), *The Coming of Post-Industrial Society* (New York: Basic Books).

Belligni, S. (ed.) (1983), *La giraffa e il liocorno. Il PCI dagli anni '70 al nuovo decennio* (Milan: Ed. Franco Angeli).

Belloin, G. (1979), *Nos Rêves camarades* (Paris: Seuil).

Belloni, F., and Beller, D. (eds.) (1978), *Faction Politics: Political Parties and Factionalism in Comparative Perspective* (Santa Barbara, Calif.: ABC-Clio Press).

Benedikter, H. (1978), *Eurokommunismus. Der grosse Bluff* (Bozen: Verlaganstalt Athesia).

Berlinguer, E. (1975), *La "questione comunista"*, 2 vols. (Rome: Editori Riuniti).

Bialer, S. (1984), "Danger in Moscow," *New York Review of Books*, 16 February 1984, pp. 6–10.

Bibliography

Biegalski, C. (ed.) (1978), *Révolution/classe/parti* (Paris: Union générale d'éditions).

Blackmer, D. L. M. (1968), *Unity in Diversity: Italian Communism and the Communist World* (Cambridge, Mass.: MIT Press).

Blackmer, D. L. M. (1975), "Continuity and change in postwar Italian communism," in D. L. M. Blackmer and S. Tarrow (eds.), *Communism in Italy and France* (Princeton, N.J.: Princeton University Press), pp. 21–68.

Blackmer, D. L. M., and Kriegel, A. (1975), *The International Role of the Communist Parties of Italy and France* (Cambridge, Mass.: Center for International Affairs).

Blackmer, D. L. M., and Tarrow, S. (eds.) (1975), *Communism in Italy and France* (Princeton, N.J.: Princeton University Press).

Bosi, M., and Portelli, H. (1976), *Les PC espagnol, français, italien face au pouvoir* (Paris: Christian Bourgois).

Bouillot, F., and Devesa, J.-M. (1979), *Un Parti peut en cacher un autre* (Paris: Maspéro).

Brown, A., and Gray J., (eds.) (1977), *Political Culture and Political Change in Communist States* (London: Macmillan).

Brown, B. (1978), *Eurocommunism and Eurosocialism* (New York: Cyrco Press).

Brunet, J.-P. (1982), *Histoire du PCF* (Paris: Presses universitaires de France).

Brus, W. (1972), *The Market in a Socialist Economy* (London: Routledge & Kegan Paul).

Bugno, F. (1982), "Sindacato grande malato," *L'Espresso*, 14 November 1982, pp. 260–3.

Burg, S. L. (1983), *Conflict and Cohesion in Yugoslavia: Political Decision Making since 1966* (Princeton, N.J.: Princeton University Press)

Burke, E. (1955), *Reflections on the Revolution in France* (Chicago: Regnery).

Burke, E. (1960), *Selected Writings of Edmund Burke*, ed. W. J. Bate (New York: Modern Library).

Carew Hunt, R. N. (1963), *The Theory and Practice of Communism* (Harmondsworth: Penguin).

Carrillo, S. (1978), *Eurocommunism and the State* (Westport, Conn.: Lawrence Hill).

Castoriadis, C. (1981), *Devant la Guerre* (Paris: Fayard).

Cayrol, R. (1978), "Courants, fractions, tendances," in P. Birnbaum and J.-M. Vincent (eds.), *Critique des partis politiques* (Paris: Editions Galilée).

Cazzola, F. (1974), *Governo e opposizione nel Parlamento italiano* (Milan: Giuffre).

Cella, G. P. (1979), "L'azione sindacale nella crisi italiana," in L. Graziano and S. Tarrow (eds.), *La crisi italiana* (Turin: Einaudi), pp. 271–301.

Chafarévitch, I. (1977), *Le Phénomène socialiste* (Paris: Seuil).

Chesnokov, D. I. (1971), "Contemporaneity and the Leninist teaching of the creative role of the socialist state," in CPSU, *Development of Revolutionary Theory by the CPSU* (Moscow: Progress), pp. 204–36.

Christman, H. (ed.) (1967), *Essential Works of Lenin* (New York: Bantam Books).

de Closets, F. (1982), *Toujours Plus!* (Paris: Grasset).

Bibliography

Cohen, S. F. (1975), *Bukharin and the Bolshevik Revolution: A Political Biography, 1888–1938* (New York: Vintage Books).

Cossutta, A. (1982), *Lo strappo* (Milan: Mondadori).

Couffignal, G. (1978), *Les Syndicats italiens et la politique* (Grenoble: Presses universitaires de Grenoble).

Dahl, R. (1961), *Who Governs?* (New Haven, Conn.: Yale University Press).

Daix, P. (1978), *La Crise du PCF* (Paris: Seuil).

Daix, P. (1982), *L'Avènement de la Nomenklatura. La chute de Khrouchtchev* (Paris: Editions Complexe).

Daniels, R. V. (1960a), *The Conscience of the Revolution. Communist Opposition in Soviet Russia* (Cambridge: Cambridge University Press).

Daniels, R. V. (1960b), *A Documentary History of Communism*, 2 vols. (New York: Vintage Books).

Debray, R. (1979), *Le Pouvoir intellectuel en France* (Paris: Editions Ramsey).

Di Palma, G. (1976), "Contenuti e comportamenti legislativi nel parlamento italiano," *Rivista Italiana di Scienza Politica*, vol. VI, no. 2 (April), pp. 3–39.

Di Palma, G. (1977), *Surviving without Governing: The Italian Parties in Parliament* (Berkeley, Calif.: University of California Press).

Doder, D. (1978), *The Yugoslavs* (New York: Random House).

Duhamel, O., and Weber, H. (eds.) (1979), *Changer le PCF?* (Paris: Presses universitaires de France).

Duverger, M. (1954), *Political Parties: Their Origin and Activities in the Modern State* (London: Methuen).

Eckstein, H. (1982), "The idea of political development: from dignity to efficiency," *World Politics*, vol. XXXIV, no. 4 (July), pp. 451–86.

Elleinstein, J. (1981), *Ils Vous Trompent, Camarades* (Paris: Belfond).

Fainsod, M. (1953), *How Russia Is Ruled* (Cambridge, Mass.: Harvard University Press).

Fallenbuchl, Z. (1982), "Poland's economic crisis," *Problems of Communism*, vol. XXXI (March–April), pp. 1–21.

Fedele, M. (1979), *Classi e partiti negli anni '70* (Rome: Editori Riuniti).

Fédoséev, P. (ed.) (1974), *Le Communisme scientifique* (Moscow: Progress).

Finer, S. E. (1979), *Five Constitutions* (Hassocks: Harvester Press).

Finetti, U. (1979), *Il dissenso nel PCI* (Milan: Sugar Co Edizioni).

Fiszbin, H. (1980), *Les Bouches s'ouvrent* (Paris: Grasset).

Frèches, J. (1983), *La France socialiste* (Paris; Gallimard).

French Communist Party (1979), "XXIIIe congrès du PCF," *Cahiers du Communisme*, special issue (June–July).

French Communist Party (1982), "XXIVe congrès du PCF," *Cahiers du Communisme*, special issue (February).

Galli, G. (ed.) (1968), *L'organisazione politica del PCI e della DC. La presenza sociale del PCI e della DC. L'attivista di partito* (Bologna: Il Mulino).

Galli, G., and Nannei, A. (1980), *Italia, Occidente mancato* (Milan: Arnoldo Mondadori).

Galluzzi, C. (1983), *La svolta – gli anni cruciali del Partito comunista italiano* (Milan: Sperling & Kupfer).

Graham, L. S., and Wheeler, D. L. (eds.) (1983), *In Search of Modern*

Portugal: The Revolution and its Consequences (Madison, Wis.: University of Wisconsin Press).

Gramsci, A. (1957), *The Modern Prince and Other Writings* (New York: International).

Gramsci, A. (1971), *Selections from the Prison Notebooks of Antonio Gramsci*, ed. Q. Hoare and G. N. Smith (New York: International).

Graziano, L., and Tarrow, S. (eds.) (1979), *La crisi italiana*, 2 vols. (Turin: Einaudi).

Gruppi, L. (ed.) (1979), *Teoria e politica della via italiana al socialismo* (Rome: Editori Riuniti).

Gruppi, L. (1980), *La teoria del partito rivoluzionario* (Rome: Editori Riuniti).

Guttsman, W. L. (1981), *The German Social Democratic Party, 1875–1933: From Ghetto to Government* (London: Allen & Unwin).

Hacking, I. (1982), "Why are you scared?," *New York Review of Books*, 23 September, pp. 30–41.

Haimson, L. H. (1955), *The Russian Marxists and the Origins of Bolshevism* (Cambridge, Mass.: Harvard University Press).

Hampshire, S. (1951), *Spinoza* (Harmondsworth: Penguin).

Harmel, C. (1977a). 'Le centralisme démocratique dans les statuts du Parti Communiste français," *Est et Ouest*, no. 599 (16–30 September), pp. 8–16.

Harmel, C. (1977b), "Le Parti Communiste n'a pas changé. Des changements qui n'en sont pas," (supplement), *Est et Ouest*, no. 601 (16–31 October), pp. 1–24.

Harmel, C. (1977c), "Le Parti Communiste n'a pas changé. Le centralisme démocratique," *Est et Ouest*, no. 603 (16–30 November), pp. 1–28.

Hassner, P. (1976), "Les stratégies de l'URSS et des partis communistes en Europe occidentale et méridionale," CERI, Paris, mimeo.

Hassner, P. (1980), "The PCI, Eurocommunism, and universal reconciliation: the international dimension of the Golden Dream, 1975–1979," in S. Serfaty and L. Gray (eds.), *The Italian Communist Party: Yesterday, Today and Tomorrow* (Westport, Conn.: Greenwood Press), pp. 211–32.

Hayek, F. (1944), *The Road to Serfdom* (Chicago: University of Chicago Press).

Hayward, J. E. S. (1981), *Surreptitious Factionalism in the French Communist Party*, Hull Papers in Politics No. 20 (Hull: University of Hull).

Hendel, C. (1953), *David Hume's Political Essays* (New York: Liberal Arts Press).

Herzog, P. (1982), *L'Economie à bras-le-corps* (Paris: Editions sociales).

Hincker, F. (1981), *Le Parti Communiste au carrefour. Essai sur quinze ans de son histoire, 1965–1981* (Paris: Albin Michel).

Hobsbawm, E., with Napolitano, G. (1977), *The Italian Road to Socialism* (London: Journeyman Press).

Hook, S. (1984), Review of A. Zinoviev's *The Reality of Communism*, *Times Literary Supplement*, 6 April, pp. 365–6.

Horvat, B. (1982), *The Political Economy of Socialism: A Marxist Social Theory* (London: M. E. Sharpe).

Hough, J. (1977), *The Soviet Union and Social Science Theory* (Cambridge, Mass.: Harvard University Press).

Huntington, S. P. (1968), *Political Order in Changing Societies* (New Haven, Conn.: Yale University Press).

Huntington, S. P. (1983), *American Politics: The Promise of Disharmony* (Cambridge, Mass.: Harvard University Press).

Ingrao, P. (1977), *Masse e potere* (Rome: Editori Riuniti).

Ingrao, P. (1979), *La Politique en grand et en petit* (Paris: Maspéro); trans. of *Crisi e terza via* (Rome: Editori Riuniti, 1978).

Ingrao, P. et al. (1981), *Il partito politico e la crisi dello Stato sociale: ipotesi di ricerca* (Bari: De Donato).

Ingrao, P. (1982), *Tradizione e potere* (Bari: De Donato).

Jacobs, D. N. (ed.) (1979), *From Marx to Mao and Marchais: Documents on the Development of Communist Variations* (New York: Longman).

Jeambar, D. (1984), *Le PC dans la maison* (Paris: Calmann-Lévy).

Johnson, C. (ed.) (1970), *Change in Communist Systems* (Stanford, Calif.: Stanford University Press).

Johnson, R. (1981), *The Long March of the French Left* (New York: St. Martin's Press).

Jouary, J.-P. et al. (1980), *Giscard et les idées. Essai sur la guerre idéologique* (Paris: Editions sociales).

Juquin, P. (1983), *Produire français, le grand défi* (Paris: Editions sociales).

Kaiser, R. (1976), *Russia: The People and the Power* (New York: Pocket Books).

Kardelj, E. (1977), *The Directions of Development of the Political System of Socialist Self-Management* (Belgrade: Kommunist).

Kautsky, K. (1964), *The Dictatorship of the Proletariat* (Ann Arbor, Mich.: University of Michigan Press).

Kehayan, J., and Kehayan, N. (1978), *Rue du prolétaire rouge* (Paris: Seuil).

Kemp-Welch, A. (ed.) (1984), *The Birth of Solidarity: The Gdańsk Negotiations* (New York: St. Martin's Press).

Kende, P. (ed.) (1982), *Le Système communiste. Un monde en expansion* (Paris: EFRI).

Khrushchev, N. (1970, 1974), *Khrushchev Remembers*, 2 vols. (Boston: Little, Brown).

Kirchheimer, O. (1969), *Politics, Law and Social Change: Selected Essays of Otto Kirchheimer*, ed. F. S. Burin and K. L. Schell (New York: Columbia University Press).

Kissinger, H. A. (1978), "Communist parties in Western Europe: challenge to the West," in G. Sartori and A. Ranney (eds.), *Eurocommunism: The Italian Case* (Washington, D.C.: American Enterprise Institute), pp. 183–96.

Kissinger, H. A. (1979), *White House Years* (Boston, Mass.: Little, Brown).

Kissinger, H. A. (1982), "Reflections on a partnership: British and American Attitudes to Postwar Foreign Policy," *International Affairs*, vol. 58, no. 4 (Autumn), pp. 571–87.

Knei-Paz, B. (1978), *The Social and Political Thought of Leon Trotsky* (Oxford: Oxford University Press).

Koestler, A. (1966), *Darkness at Noon* (New York: Bantam Books).

Bibliography

Kriegel, A. (1972a), "La dimension internationale du PCF," *Politique Etrangère*, vol. 37, no. 5, pp. 639–70.

Kriegel, A. (1972b), *Les Grands Procès dans les systèmes communistes: la pédagogie infernale* (Paris: Gallimard).

Kriegel, A. (1974), *Les Communistes français. Essai d'ethnographie politique*, 3rd ed. (Paris; Seuil).

Kriegel, A. (1977), *Un Autre Communisme? Compromis historique, eurocommunisme, union de la gauche* (Paris: Hachette).

Kundera, M. (1984), Interview, *New York Times Review of Books*, 29 April 1984.

Lange, P. (1979a), "Il PCI e i possibili esiti della crisi italiana," in L. Graziano and S. Tarrow (eds.), *la crisi italiana* (Turin: Einaudi), Vol. 2, pp. 657–718.

Lange, P. (1979b), "Crisis and consent, change and compromise: dilemmas of Italian communism in the 1970s," in P. Lange and S. Tarrow (eds.), *Italy in Transition* (London: Frank Cass), pp. 110–32.

Lange, P., and Tarrow S. (eds.) (1979), *Italy in Transition* (London: Frank Cass); special issue of *West European Politics*, vol. 2, no. 3 (October).

Lange, P., and Vannicelli, M. (eds.) (1981), *The Communist Parties of Italy, France and Spain: Postwar Change and Continuity* (London: Allen & Unwin).

Lange, P., Ross, G., and Vannicelli, M. (1982), *Unions, Change and Crisis: French and Italian Union Strategy and the Political Economy, 1945–1980* (London: Allen & Unwin).

Lanucara, A. (1978), *Berlinguer segreto. Carriere e lotta interna nel PCI* (Rome; Telesio).

La Palombara, J., and Weiner, M. (eds.) (1966), *Political Parties and Political Development* (Princeton, N.J.: Princeton University Press).

Laqueur, W. (1982), "What Poland means," *Commentary*, vol. 73, no. 3, (March), pp. 25–30.

Laurent, P. (1977), "Oui, le centralisme démocratique," *France Nouvelle*, no. 1647 (6 June).

Laurent, P. (1978), *Le PCF comme il est* (Paris: Editions sociales).

Lavau, G. (1981), *A Quoi Sert le Parti Communiste français?* (Paris: Fayard).

Lazitch, B. (1978), *L'Echec permanent, l'alliance communiste-socialiste* (Paris: Robert Laffont).

Lefort, C. (1981), *L'Invention démocratique. Les limites de la domination totalitaire* (Paris: Fayard).

Leonhard, W. (1974), *Three Faces of Marxism* (New York: Holt, Rinehart & Winston).

Linden, Carl (1966), *Khrushchev and the Soviet Leadership, 1957–1964.* (Baltimore, Md.: Johns Hopkins University Press).

Lippmann, W. (1922), *Public Opinion* (New York: Harcourt Brace).

Lombardo, A. (1978), *Le trasformazioni del comunismo italiano* (Milan: Rizzoli).

Lowenthal, R. (1964), *World Communism: The Disintegration of a Secular Faith* (New York: Oxford University Press).

Lowenthal, R. (1970), "Development vs. utopia in communist policy," in C. Johnson (ed.), *Change in Communist Systems* (Stanford, Calif.: Stanford University Press), pp. 33–116.

Lowenthal, R. (1977), *Model or Ally? The Communist Powers and the Developing Countries* (New York: Oxford University Press).

Lowenthal, R. (1983), "The post-revolutionary phase in China and Russia," *Studies in Comparative Communism*, vol. XVI, no. 3. (Autumn), pp. 191–201.

McInnes, N. (1975a), *The Communist Parties of Western Europe* (London: Oxford University Press).

McInnes, N. (1975b), "World communism in fragments," *Problems of Communism*, vol. XXIV (November–December), pp. 43–6.

McInnes, N. (1976), "Euro-Communism," *Washington Papers*, vol. 4, no. 37 (Beverly Hills, Calif., and London: Sage).

Magri, L. (1970), "Problems of the Marxist theory of the revolutionary party," *New Left Review*, no. 60 (March–April), pp. 97–128.

Marchais, G. (1975), "Rapport de G. Marchais au Comité Central du PCF (juin 1972)," in E. Fajon (ed.), *L'Union est un combat* (Paris: Editions sociales), pp. 75–127.

Marcou, L. (1979), *L'Internationale après Staline* (Paris: Grasset).

Martinelli, A., and Pasquino, G. (1978), *La politica nell'Italia che cambia* (Milan: Feltrinelli).

Medvedev, R. (1983), *Khrushchev* (Garden City, N.Y.: Doubleday/Anchor).

Meisel, J. H., and Kozera, E. S. (1953), *Materials for the Study of the Soviet System*, 2nd ed. (Ann Arbor, Mich.: George Wahr).

Meyer, A. (1957), *Leninism* (New York: Praeger).

Meyer, A. (1965), *The Soviet Political System: An Interpretation* (New York: Random House).

Michels, R. (1962), *Political Parties: A Sociological Study of the Oligarchical Tendencies of Modern Democracy* (New York: The Free Press); originally published 1911.

Middlemas, K. (1980), *Power and the Party; Changing Faces of Communism in Western Europe* (London: Deutsch).

Mieli, P. (ed.) (1978), *Il socialismo diviso* (Rome: Laterza).

Mills, C. W. (1962), *The Marxists* (Harmondsworth: Penguin).

Molina, G., and Vargas, Y. (1978), *Dialogue à l'intérieur du Parti Communiste français* (Paris: Maspéro).

Molina, G., and Vargas, Y. (1979), *Ouverture d'une discussion? Dix interventions à la rencontre de 400 intellectuels à Vitry* (Paris: Maspéro).

Montaldo, J. (1977), *Les Finances du PCF* (Paris: Albin Michel).

Montaldo, J. (1978), *La France communiste* (Paris: Albin Michel).

Moore, B., Jr. (1950), *Soviet Politics – The Dilemma of Power* (Cambridge, Mass.: Harvard University Press).

Moore, B., Jr. (1954), *Terror and Progress, USSR: Some Sources of Change and Stability in the Soviet System* (Cambridge, Mass.: Harvard University Press).

Morin, E. (1983), *De la Nature de l'URSS. Complexe totalitaire et nouvel empire* (Paris: Fayard).

Mujal-Leon, E. (1983), *Communism and Political Change in Spain* (Bloomington, Ind.: Indiana University Press).

Napolitano, G., and Berlinguer, E. (1981), *Partito di massa negli anni ottanta* (Rome: Editori Riuniti).

Bibliography

Nicholson, N. K. (1972), "The factional model and the study of politics," *Comparative Political Studies* (October 1972), pp. 291–315.

Niebuhr, R. (1932), *Moral Man and Immoral Society* (New York: Charles Scribner's Sons).

Nilsson, K. R. (1981), "The EUR Accords and the historic compromise: Italian labor and Eurocommunism," *Polity*, vol. XIV, no. 1 (Fall), pp. 29–50.

Nugent, N., and Lowe D. (1982), *The Left in France* (New York: St. Martin's Press).

Pajetta, G. C. (1978), *La lunga marcia dell'internazionalismo* (Rome: Editori Riuniti).

Panebianco, A. (1982), *Modelli di partito. Organizzazione e potere nei partiti politici* (Bologna: Il Mulino).

Parisi, A., and Pasquino, G. (1979), "Changes in Italian electoral behaviour: the relationships between parties and voters," in P. Lange and S. Tarrow (eds.), *Italy in Transition*, (London: Frank Cass), pp. 6–30.

Pasquino, G. (1980a), *Crisi dei partiti e governabilità* (Bologna: Il Mulino).

Pasquino, G. (1980b), "From Togliatti to the *compromesso storico*: a Party with a governmental vocation," in S. Serfaty and L. Gray (eds.), *The Italian Communist Party: Yesterday, Today, and Tomorrow* (Westport, Conn.: Greenwood Press), pp. 75–106.

Pasquino, G. (1980c), *Organizational models of southern European communist parties: a preliminary approach*, Occasional Paper No. 29 (Bologna: Johns Hopkins University Bologna Center).

Pasquino, G. (1982a), *Degenerazioni dei partiti e riforme istituzionali* (Rome: Editori Laterza).

Pasquino, G. (1982b), "Il PCI nel sistema politico italiano degli anni settanta," *Il Mulino*, vol. 31, no. 6, pp. 859–97.

PCF (1971), *Changer de Cap. Programme pour un gouvernement démocratique d'union populaire* (Paris: Editions sociales).

PCF (1972), *Programme commun de gouvernement du Parti Communiste et du Parti Socialiste* (Paris: Editions sociales).

PCF (1978), *Programme commun de gouvernement actualisé* (Paris: Editions sociales).

PCF (1982), "24th PCF Congress," special issue, *Cahiers du Communisme* (February).

PCI (1978), *Proposta di progetto a medio termine* (Rome: Editori Riuniti).

PCI (1979a), "The 15th National Congress of the PCI," special issue, *Italian Communists* (Rome), no. 1–2 (January–June).

PCI (1979b), *La politica e l'organizzazione dei comunisti italiani. Le tesi e lo statuto approvati dal XV Congresso nazionale del PCI* (Rome: Editori Riuniti).

PCI (1979c), *Data sull'organizzazione del PCI* (Rome: PCI).

Pizzorno, A. (1978), "Political exchange and collective identity in industrial conflict," in C. Crouch and A. Pizzorno (eds.), *The Resurgence of Class Conflict in Western Europe since 1968* (London: Holmes & Meier), Vol. 2, pp. 277–98.

Pizzorno, A. (1980), *I soggetti del pluralismo. Classi, partiti, sindacati* (Bologna: Il Mulino).

Bibliography

Poggi, G. *et al.* (1968), *L'organizzazione partitica del PCI e della DC* (Bologna: Il Mulino).

Poperen, J. (1972), *La Gauche française*, 2 vols. (Paris: Fayard).

Pospelov, P. N. *et al.* (1971), *Development of Revolutionary Theory by the CPSU* (Moscow: Progress).

Prenant, M. (1980), *Toute une Vie à gauche* (Paris: Editions Encre).

Regalia, I., Regini, M., and Reyneri, E. (1978), "Labour conflicts and industrial relations in Italy," in C. Crouch and A. Pizzorno (eds.), *The Resurgence of Class Conflict in Western Europe since 1968* (London: Holmes & Meier), Vol. 1, pp. 101–58.

Regini, M. (1979), "Labour unions, industrial action, and politics," in P. Lange and S. Tarrow (eds.), *Italy in Transition* (London: Frank Cass), pp. 49–66.

Rejai, M. (ed.) (1971), *Decline of Ideology?* (New York: Atherton).

Reshetar, J. S., Jr. (1971), *The Soviet Polity: Government and Politics in the USSR* (New York: Dodd, Mead).

Revel, J-F. (1977), *The Totalitarian Temptation* (Harmondsworth: Penguin).

Rigby, T. H. (1968), *Communist Party Membership in the USSR: 1917–1967* (Princeton, N.J.: Princeton University Press).

Robrieux, P. (1975), *Maurice Thorez. Vie publique et vie secrète* (Paris: Fayard).

Robrieux, P. (1980–4), *Histoire intérieure du Parti Communiste. Vol. 1, 1920–1945* (Paris: Fayard, 1980); *Vol. 2, 1945–1972* (1981); *Vol. 3, 1972–1982* (1982); *Vol. 4, Documents* (1984).

Rocard, M. (1980), *Parler Vrai* (Paris: Seuil).

Ronchey, A. (1982), *Chi vincera in Italia? La democrazia bloccata, i comunisti e il "fattore K"* (Milan: Arnoldo Mondadori).

Ross, G. (1975), "Party and mass organization: the changing relationship of PCF and CGT," in D. L. M. Blackmer and S. Tarrow (eds.), *Communism in Italy and France* (Princeton, N.J.: Princeton University Press), pp. 504–40.

Ross, G. (1982), *Workers and Communism in France: From Popular Front to Eurocommunism* (Berkeley, Calif.: University of California Press).

Rubbi, A. (1978), *I partiti comunisti dell'Europa occidentale* (Milan: Teti Editore).

Sabine, G. (1963), *A History of Political Theory*, 3rd ed. (London: Harrap).

Salvadori, M. (1952), *The Rise of Modern Communism* (New York: Holt).

Salvadori, Massimo (1979), *Karl Kautsky and the Socialist Revolution, 1880–1938* (London: NLB).

Salvati, M. (1979), "Muddling through: economics and politics in Italy, 1969–1979," in P. Lange and S. Tarrow (eds.), *Italy in Transition* (London: Frank Cass), pp. 31–48.

Sani, G. (1979a), "Ricambio elettorale, mutamenti sociali e preferenze politiche," in L. Graziano and S. Tarrow (eds.), *La crisi italiana* (Turin: Einaudi), Vol. 2, pp. 303–28.

Sani, G. (1979b), "Italy: the changing role of the PCI," in D. E. Albright (ed.), *Communism and Political Systems in Western Europe*, (Westport, Conn.: Westview Press), pp. 43–94.

Sartori, G. (1966), "European political parties: the case of polarized pluralism," in J. La Palombara and M. Weiner (eds.), *Political Parties and Political Development* (Princeton, N.J.: Princeton University Press), pp. 137–76.

Sartori, G. (1976), *Parties and Party Systems: A Framework for Analysis* (New York: Cambridge University Press), Vol. 1.

Sartori, G., and Ranney, A. (eds.) (1978), *Eurocommunism: The Italian Case* (Washington, D.C.: American Enterprise Institute).

Sartre, J.-P. (1956–7), "Le fantôme de Staline," *Les Temps Modernes*, no. 129–31 (November 1956–January 1957); cited in J. Pontusson, thesis, Amherst College, Amherst, Mass.

Sassoon, D. (1977), "Vers l'eurocommunisme. La stratégie européenne du PCI," *Dialectique*, no. 18–19 (Spring), pp. 39–57.

Sassoon, D. (1981), *The Strategy of the Italian Communist Party: From the Resistance to the Historic Compromise* (New York: St. Martin's Press).

Schapiro, L. (1971), *The Communist Party of the Soviet Union* (New York: Vintage Books).

Schapiro, L. (ed.) (1972), *Political Opposition in One-Party States* (London: Macmillan).

Schapiro, L. (1983), Review of Roy Medvedev's *Khrushchev, New York Review of Books*, 28 April 1983.

Schorske, C. E. (1955), *German Social Democracy, 1905–1917: The Development of the Great Schism* (Cambridge, Mass.: Harvard University Press).

Sechi, S. (1979), "L'austero fascino del centralismo democratico," in M. Barbagli *et al.*, *Dentro il PCI* (Bologna: Il Mulino), pp. 61–111.

Sechi, S. (1980), "Il nuovo statuto del PCI: tra rinnovamento e continuità," *Il Mulino*, no. 273, pp. 585–613.

Segre, S. (1977), *A chi fa paura l'eurocomunismo?* (Florence: Guaraldi Editore).

Selznick, P. (1952), *The Organizational Weapon: A Study of Bolshevik Strategy and Tactics* (New York: McGraw-Hill).

Serfaty, S., and Gray, L. (eds.) (1980), *The Italian Communist Party: Yesterday, Today, and Tomorrow* (Westport, Conn.: Greenwood Press).

Shipler, D. (1983), *Russia: Broken Idols, Solemn Dreams* (New York: New York Times Books).

Simis, K. (1982), *USSR: The Corrupt Society* (New York: Simon & Schuster).

Sivini, G. (1974), "Le parti communiste: structure et fonctionnement," in J. Besson *et al.*, *Sociologie du communisme en Italie* (Paris: Armand Colin), pp. 55–141.

Sivini, G. *et al.* (1968), *La Presenza sociale del PCI e della DC* (Bologna: Il Mulino).

Skilling, H. G. (1972), "Background to the study of opposition in Communist Eastern Europe," in L. Schapiro (ed.), *Political Opposition in One-Party States* (London: Macmillan), pp. 72–103.

Skilling, H. G. (1983), "Interest groups and Communist politics revisited," *World Politics*, vol. XXXVI, no. 1 (October), pp. 1–27.

Skilling, H. G., and Griffiths, F. (eds.), (1971), *Interest Groups in Soviet Politics* (Princeton, N.J.: Princeton University Press).

Smith, H. (1976), *The Russians* (New York: Quadrangle/New York Times Books).

Bibliography

Solzhenitsyn, A. (1980), "Misconceptions about Russia are a threat to America," *Foreign Affairs*, vol. 58, no. 4 (Spring), pp. 797–834.

Spinelli, A. (1978), *PCI, che fare?* (Turin: Einaudi).

Spire, Arnaud (1977), "Centralisme démocratique et démocratie poussée jusqu'au bout," *Cahiers du Communisme* (October).

Spire, Antoine (1980), *Profession: permanent* (Paris: Seuil).

Spriano, P. (1983), *Gli comunisti europei e Staline* (Rome: Mondadori).

Stalin, J. (1932), *Foundations of Leninism* (New York: International); originally published 1924.

Sweeney, J. P. (1984), "The left in Europe's Parliament: the problematic effects of integration theory," *Comparative Politics*, vol. 16, no. 2 (January), pp. 171–90.

Tamburrano, G. (1978), *PCI e PSI nel sistema democristiano* (Rome: Laterza).

Tannahill, R. N. (1978), *The Communist Parties of Western Europe: A Comparative Study* (Westport, Conn.: Greenwood Press).

Tarrow, S. (1967), *Peasant Communism in Southern Italy* (New Haven, Conn.: Yale University Press).

Tarrow, S. (1969), "Economic development and the transformation of the Italian party system," *Comparative Politics*, vol. 1, no. 2 (January), pp. 161–83.

Tarrow, S. (1975), "Communism in Italy and France: adaptation and change," *Communism in Italy and France* (Princeton, N.J.: Princeton University Press), pp. 575–640.

Tarrow, S. (1977), *Between Center and Periphery* (New Haven, Conn.: Yale University Press).

Tartakowsky, D. (1982), *Une Histoire du PCF* (Paris: Presses universitaires de France).

Thorez, P. (1982), Interview in *L'Express*, 22–28 October 1982.

Tiersky, R. (1974), *French Communism 1920–1972* (New York: Columbia University Press).

Tiersky, R. (1976), "French communism in 1976," *Problems of Communism*, vol. XXV (January–February), pp. 20–47.

Tiersky, R. (1979a), "Das Problem des demokratischen Zentralismus," in H. Timmermann (ed.), *Die kommunistischen Parteien Südeuropas* (Baden-Baden: Nomos Verlagsgesellschaft), pp. 429–74.

Tiersky, R. (1979b), "French communism, Eurocommunism and Soviet power," in R. Tökés (ed.), *Eurocommunism and Detente* (New York: New York University Press), pp. 138–203.

Tiersky, R. (1979c), "Ambivalence yet again unresolved: the French left 1972–78," in W. E. Griffith (ed.), *The European Left: France, Italy, Spain* (Lexington, Mass.: Lexington Books), pp. 49–80.

Timmermann, H. (1974), *I comunisti italiani* (Bari: De Donato).

Timmermann, H. (1977), *Aspekte der innerparteilichen Struktur und Willensbildung bei den "Eurokommunisten"*, BOTS Occasional Paper (Cologne: BOTS, October).

Timmermann, H. (ed.) (1979), *Die kommunistischen Parteien Südeuropas* (Baden-Baden: Nomos Verlagsgesellschaft).

Titarenko, S. L. (1971), "Modern times and Lenin's teaching of the party," in CPSU, *Development of Revolutionary Theory by the CPSU* (Moscow: Progress), pp. 168–203.

Tobagi, W. (1980), *Che cosa contano i sindacati* (Milan: Rizzoli Editore).

Tökés, R. L. (ed.) (1978), *Eurocommunism and Detente* (New York: New York University Press).

Touraine, A. (1979), *Mort d'une gauche* (Paris: Editions Galilée).

Trotsky, L. (1941), *Stalin: An Appraisal of the Man and His Influence* (New York: Harper).

Trotsky, L. (1943), *The New Course* (New York: New International); first published 1924.

Ulam, A. (1965), *The Bolsheviks* (New York: The Macmillan Co.).

Valenza, P. (ed.) (1978), *I paesi socialisti nell'analisi dei comunisti italiani* (Rome: Newton Compton).

Vespa, B. (ed.) (1980), *Interviste sul socialismo in Europa* (Rome: Laterza).

Von Beyme, K. (1975), "A comparative view of democratic centralism," *Government and Opposition*, vol. 10, no. 3 (Summer) pp. 259–77.

Wall, I. (1983), *French Communism in the Era of Stalin* (Westport, Conn.: Greenwood Press).

Waller, M. (1981), *Democratic Centralism: An Historical Commentary* (New York: St. Martin's Press).

Weber, M. (1958), *From Max Weber: Essays in the Sociology of Politics*, ed., Hans Gerth and C. Wright Mills (London: Oxford University Press).

Weitz, P. (1975), "The CGIL and the PCI: from subordination to independent political force," in D. L. M. Blackmer and S. Tarrow (eds.), *Communism in Italy and France* (Princeton, N.J.: Princeton University Press), pp. 541–71.

Wesson, R. (1980), *The Aging of Communism* (New York: Praeger).

White, S. (1979), *Political Culture and Soviet Politics* (London: Macmillan).

Zinoviev, A. (1979), *The Yawning Heights* (New York: Random House).

Zinoviev, A. (1980), *The Radiant Future* (New York: Random House).

Zinoviev, A. (1981), *Le Communisme comme réalité* (Paris: L'Age d'Homme), English trans. (1984), The Reality of Communism (London: Gollanz).

Zinoviev, A. (1982), *Homo Sovieticus* (Paris: Julliard).

Zuckerman, A. S. (1979), *The Politics of Faction: Christian Democratic Rule in Italy* (New Haven, Conn.: Yale University Press).

Index